Christine de Pizan and Medieval French Lyric

∾ EDITED BY EARL JEFFREY RICHARDS

University Press of Florida
GAINESVILLE · TALLAHASSEE · TAMPA · BOCA RATON
PENSACOLA · ORLANDO · MIAMI · JACKSONVILLE

CHRISTINE DE PIZAN

and

Medieval

French

Lyric

Copyright 1998 by the Board of Regents of the State of Florida
Printed in the United States of America on acid-free paper
All rights reserved

03 02 01 00 99 98   6 5 4 3 2 1

Library of Congress Cataloging-in-Publication Data

Christine de Pizan and medieval French lyric / edited by Earl Jeffrey Richards
p. cm.
Earlier versions of the papers were delivered at two sessions of the Sept. 1993 conference of the Southeast Medieval Association held in New Orleans and at a Special Session held at the 29th Annual Congress of Medieval Studies in Kalamazoo, April 1994.
Includes bibliographical references and index.
ISBN 0-8130-1618-5 (cloth: alk. paper)
1. Christine de Pisan, ca. 1364–ca. 1431—Criticism and interpretation—Congresses.
2. French poetry—To 1500—History and criticism—Congresses. I. Richards, Earl Jeffrey.
PQ1575.Z5C468 1998   98-14268
841'.2—dc21

The University Press of Florida is the scholarly publishing agency for the State University System of Florida, comprising Florida A&M University, Florida Atlantic University, Florida International University, Florida State University, University of Central Florida, University of Florida, University of North Florida, University of South Florida, and University of West Florida.

University Press of Florida
15 Northwest 15th Street
Gainesville, FL 32611
http://nervm.nerdc.ufl.edu/~upf

In memoriam

Daniel Poirion

Contents

Acknowledgments ix

Christine de Pizan and the Freedom of Medieval French Lyric:
  Authority, Experience, and Women in the Republic of Letters 1
  Earl Jeffrey Richards

Part One. The Dynamics of Generic Innovation

  1. Christine de Pizan and the Transformation of Late Medieval
     Lyrical Genres 27
     William D. Paden

Part Two. The Marriage of Lyric and Narrative

  2. The *Cent balades:* The Marriage of Content and Form 53
     James C. Laidlaw

  3. Last Words: Reflections on a "Lay mortel" and the Poetics
     of Lyric Sequences 83
     Barbara K. Altmann

  4. *Tous parlent par une mesmes bouche*: Lyrical Outbursts,
     Prosaic Remedies, and Voice in Christine de Pizan's
     Livre du Duc des vrais amans 103
     Judith Laird and Earl Jeffrey Richards

Part Three. The Limits of Lyrical Self-Representation

5. Clerkliness and Courtliness in the Complaintes
   of Christine de Pizan   135
   Nadia Margolis

6. *Translatio Studii*: Christine de Pizan's Self-Portrayal in Two Lyric
   Poems and in the *Livre de la mutacion de Fortune*   155
   Lori Walters

7. Lyrical Conventions and the Creation of Female Subjectivity in
   Christine de Pizan's *Cent ballades d'Amant et de Dame*   168
   Christine McWebb

**Part Four. The Critique of Courtliness and Expanding
the Boundaries of Lyric**

8. Christine de Pizan's Phenomenology of Beauty in the Lyric and
   the Dream Vision   187
   Benjamin Semple

9. Poems of Water without Salt and Ballades without Feeling,
   or Reintroducing History into the Text: Prose and Verse
   in the Works of Christine de Pizan   206
   Earl Jeffrey Richards

Contributors   231
Index   233

Acknowledgments

It is a great pleasure to present the nine essays here on the lyrical works of Christine de Pizan. Earlier versions of the papers were delivered at two sessions of the September 1993 conference of the Southeast Medieval Association held in New Orleans and at a Special Session, sponsored by the Christine de Pizan Society, devoted to Christine's lyrics at the Twenty-ninth Annual Congress of Medieval Studies in Kalamazoo in April 1994. With the exception of Barbara K. Altmann's article, which was first published in *French Studies*, 1996, and which is reprinted here with the kind permission of that journal, all of the essays here appear for the first time. They represent the current state of scholarship on Christine's lyrics and offer a unique synthesis of critical opinion in this area of research.

On behalf of all the contributors, I wish to thank Christine Reno, Vassar College, for her invaluable and extensive comments and suggestions on earlier versions of the essays here. I also wish to acknowledge the help of James C. Laidlaw, University of Edinburgh, who provided answers to innumerable questions, large and small. My warmest thanks as well go to Nadia Margolis, whose selfless efforts in editing the *Christine de Pizan Newsletter* have helped promote scholarly exchange in a singular example of how the Republic of Letters is supposed to work. My thanks go as well to the readers of the manuscript for their helpful critiques.

Finally, it is a sad but also proud honor for me to dedicate this volume to the memory of Daniel Poirion, the great French scholar of medieval French lyric poetry. Without his pioneering works, much of the scholarship here would not have been possible.

Earl Jeffrey Richards

Christine de Pizan and the Freedom of Medieval French Lyric: Authority, Experience, and Women in the Republic of Letters

EARL JEFFREY RICHARDS

The appearance of the 1982 modern English translation of Christine de Pizan's *Book of the City of Ladies* marked a watershed in Christine studies, crowning the preceding half century of patient and sober research produced by Marie-Josèphe Pinet, P. G. C. Campbell, Suzanne Solente, Millard Meiss, Kenneth Varty, Daniel Poirion, Gianni Mombello, Angus Kennedy, and Charity Cannon Willard. Without their pioneering efforts, the publication of at least seven monographs, anthologies, and essay collections on Christine within the last five years alone would have been inconceivable and the wide-reaching reevaluation of all of Christine's works impossible. Christine's position as a feminist, as a political thinker, as an intermediary of Italian humanism to France, and as an innovative prose writer, well trained in medieval rhetoric, is now firmly established. In light of these hard-won gains in research, it is now opportune to return to what had earlier been the major focus of interest in Christine, her significance as a lyric poet.

The first substantial fact to remember is a simple, material one with far-reaching consequences: in the manuscripts of her collected works whose copying she herself supervised, Christine inserted several prose works among the larger body of lyrical compositions. In all, she supervised four transcriptions of her lyrics (which were transmitted only in these copies).[1] The later transcriptions contain considerably more prose than the first ones and include the *Livre du Duc des vrais amans* [Book of the Duke of True Lovers]. This work, which combines a wide range of lyrical genres and prose letters, mirrors the general mixed composition of the longer manuscripts themselves, that is, it occupies a paradigmatic position within the corpus of Christine's works in defining the limits and possibilities of both verse and prose. Finding prose and verse together in the same codex is not unusual in itself, but the remarkable fact is that Christine viewed her prose as a commentary on her lyric.

The next simple facts to consider are that Christine produced one of the largest bodies of lyric in all of medieval French literature and that her works are formally experimental and innovative. This formal freedom contrasts starkly with the reigning currents of her time: As Jean Frappier noted, after the thirteenth-century poet Rutebeuf, lyrical forms in medieval French evolved not toward more formal freedom, but toward more constraint, in effect toward the triumph of prescribed models of composition.[2] Thus the question immediately arises whether there is a correlation between Christine's formal freedom as a lyric poet and the way in which she addressed the questions of authority, experience, and women's place in "the field of Letters." Answering this question has been the challenge for the essays gathered in this volume.

Christine dated her debut as a poet to 1394, the fifth anniversary of her husband's death in 1389. Verse was her preferred form until 1401 when, in a series of prose letters, she initiated the Quarrel over the *Romance of the Rose*, for reasons that spring from what might be termed the late fourteenth-century "crisis" of medieval vernacular lyric, namely its formal perfection and its accompanying emptiness of meaning and neglect of intellectual and moral beauty. In Thomas Hibernicus's anthology of quotations from patristic authors that frequently served as Christine's source, there is an allusive quotation from Jerome's treatise against marriage, the *Adversus Jovinianum*, that might have caught her attention: "amor formæ, oblivio rationis" [the love of form (or beauty), (means) forgetting reason].[3] The quotation is found in Book I, chapter 49 of Jerome's work and bears closer scrutiny here. In Jerome's original context, the observation is part of a larger argument why wise men should not marry, since their wives' beauty distracts them from rational pursuits. In the context of Thomas's collection, the citation takes on a larger meaning: that beauty as an end in itself entails the abandonment of reason. Applied to lyric poetry, this quotation would mean that poets' exclusive concentration on formal beauty deprived their poetry of its moral and sapiential beauty, of its reason.

Prior to Christine, medieval French lyric had become so self-conscious and self-referential that for all intents and purposes it had achieved what, in speaking of the lyrics of Baudelaire, Fredric Jameson called "the dissolution of the referent."[4] Christine later explained that her earlier lyrics treated "lighter matters" than her subsequent works, a kind of *mene tekel* that found the preceding lyric tradition wanting. This judgment in no way diminishes the progress made by earlier specialists of medieval lyric who labored mightily to recuperate its formal beauty, perhaps in part in defense of the "joy of the text." Rather, this evaluation springs from the powerful insight that Horace formulated in his *Ars poetica* that "it is not enough for poems to be beautiful" [non satis poemata esse pulchra].[5]

If lyric aestheticizes the experiences it represents in the name of formal perfection or of self-referentiality, why is this not enough? Eugene Vance connected the conventionalized portrayal of women in trouvère lyric to the "joy of the text" and in so doing articulated clearly the position under scrutiny here: "if the sign expresses *more* than what is merely conventional, its discourse becomes threatened. Thus, in trouvère lyric, the female body remains rigorously stereotyped. The woman must be perceived through a repertory of conventional signs, lest her presence become so amplified as to disturb those mechanisms of language which give rise to the joy of the text."[6] Christine reacts specifically against this conventionalization in order to threaten and disturb the discourse of courtly poetry, in order to recuperate and to amplify her historical presence placed under erasure by convention. The very different joy of her text thus radically calls into question the self-absorbed narcissistic joy of the courtly tradition because its formal beauty is missing two important qualities identified by the great expert in medieval aesthetics Edgar De Bruyne as moral and sapiential beauty.[7]

Christine was sensitive to the fact that for her French contemporaries with their conventions about the representation of women, a woman author herself was an anomaly. Form, content, and author: here in a nutshell are the central issues raised by Christine's lyric. While these problems are certainly not unique to Christine's lyric, her solutions to them are. Indeed, gender and genre were inextricably linked in medieval French, as Simon Gaunt would have it, though not because of any inherent epistemological or aesthetic grounds, but instead for no other reason than that men wrote the lyrics in which women appeared.[8]

Christine's standard iconographic self-portrayal shows how she challenged the misogynistic appropriation of the literary republic. Her first three collectanea begin with the *Cent balades* and are introduced by Christine's trademark miniature, showing her writing in her book-lined "estude" [study, *L'Avision-Christine*] or "cele" [cell, *Cité des Dames*]. The iconography here, alluding to portrayals of the Annunciation in which the Virgin Mary is always portrayed with a book, suggests that Christine sets the key for her work in erudition and authority modeled after the Virgin herself. The last of these collectanea, the Queen's Manuscript, begins with a dedication to Isabeau de Bavière in which Christine reflects on the unity and diversity of the various works assembled. In her trademark subordinate style (that she used to mark her voice), she assures the queen first and foremost that "for the book that I insist on presenting to you there is nothing narrated or written that was not conceived in the pure thought or style that I derive from the single sentiment that I retain from the gifts of God and nature" [Pour ce livre cy que je tiens / Vous presenter, ou il n'a riens, / en histoire n'en escripture, / Que n'aye en ma pensee pure / Pris ou stile que je detiens / du seul sentiment que je retiens / Des dons de Dieu et de nature] (ed. Roy, vol. 1, p. xiv).

Christine then explains that the different styles adopted in the book correspond to her changing didactic strategies. Here she was following the observation of her older contemporary and friend Eustache Deschamps who had observed that "subject matters differ according to the intention and the sentiment of their maker" [les materes se different selon la volunté et le sentement du faiseur].[9] As this opening demonstrates, Christine views her authority as deriving from the purity of her intention and sentiment and from her understanding of the "pure gifts of God and nature." Deschamps's guidelines were perfectly consistent with the Thomist notion of the authorial intent or the *intentio auctoris*, a critical category that fell into disfavor with the New Critics in the 1950s. As Alastair Minnis noted, "St. Thomas rejected those received interpretations which do not pay sufficient attention to the *intentio auctoris* . . . but accepted those which keep close to the letter."[10] Christine's decision to adopt different styles also corresponds to the Thomist distinction between "appropriately speaking" or "speaking in one's own person" [*proprie dicta*] and speaking "in/by figures" or "figuratively" [*figurate*]. Her mastery of various discourses, figures, and genres thus proves and demonstrates her authority as a poet whose identity both includes and transcends her gender, just as for Christine and the medieval Church the mystery of the Incarnation announced in the Annunciation both includes and transcends the human condition.

The opening illustration of the Harley manuscript offers subtle proof of how the authority topos is incorporated in the material format of Christine's manuscript itself. It shows a group of female courtiers surrounding the queen in her private chambers in a conventional presentational scene. The walls of the queen's chambers are hung with panels of the French royal *fleur de lys* in burnished gold against a red background and with blue and (originally) white checkered banners of the kingdom of Bavaria, Isabeau's home. The "impaled arms" of France and Bavaria represent in heraldic terms the union of two of the most powerful and prosperous kingdoms of Europe (indeed, a powerful symbol of German-French reconciliation). The original artist used silver to depict the white in the Bavarian royal arms. The silver is now gray from tarnish, but when the manuscript was first presented to the queen around 1410, this opening scene must literally have dazzled the reader opening the manuscript. This presentation scene perfectly epitomizes Christine's situation: a woman from Venice presents a book in French to a woman from Ingolstadt in the private chambers of the most powerful national monarch in Europe of the time. An Italian and a German woman meet in another language that is the mother tongue of neither: the ramifications of this stylized encounter for our understanding of authority, women's experience, language, and rhetoric are perhaps more dazzling than the gold and silver of the illustration itself.

Hitherto the "personal" aspect of Christine's lyrical output, enormous both in volume and range, attracted the lion's share of critical scrutiny. Nigel Wilkins stressed the "deeply personal inspiration" of her work, just as Daniel Poirion argued that the unity of her verse flowed from the unity of her personality—which, though true enough, could be said of virtually any writer.[11] While Christine clearly incorporates herself into her verse in a self-conscious manner hardly seen before in French poetry (or, arguably, in other medieval literatures, even considering, or perhaps under the influence of, Dante and Petrarch), if one confuses the Christine of the poetry with the historical person, one is left with little more than commenting on the "pathos" of some poems or on the "delicacy" of others, always explaining the "special" subjectivity of her perspective. These approaches all reflect the worst kind of historicism, more typical of late nineteenth-century approaches to medieval literature, and they distort a more accurate historical contextualization. They also sometimes tend to be as formally superficial as they are psychologically condescending and successfully ignore more substantive, and ultimately more productive, questions: How original is Christine? What did she know about other medieval French and

Italian (or even Provençal) poets? Is she formally different from her predecessors? How does she incorporate "women's experience" into her work unlike her male predecessors? What is the nature of her "authority" as a poet? What is her proper place in literary history?

These specific questions regarding Christine in turn acquire a new urgency in light of post-structuralist literary critical approaches of the last fifteen years. Writing in *Feminist Theory, Women's Writing* (1992), Laurie A. Finke succinctly summarized the challenges raised by "social constructivism" present in the claim, advanced by Michel Foucault, that there is no author, and the argument, proposed by Teresa de Lauretis, that experience itself is "a simulacrum, a set of *discursive* practices." If these two contentions are true, a third problem arises, namely that "women's 'experience' is saturated with and not separate from the practices by which masculinist cultures reproduce their domination."[12]

In terms of Christine's lyric, "the practices of masculinist culture" are the very conventions of courtly poetry itself that deny the validity of women's experiences and indeed repress those experiences from literary consideration. Doubtless, the issues of authorship, authority, and experience are as old as literary criticism itself. The answers to such simple questions as who is speaking? to whom and where is it being spoken? and why should one believe what has been said? help reconstruct a historical community sharing a common language and system of social hierarchies and references. This common language reflects in turn the social hierarchy of the community itself so that language never exists in a historical or social vacuum. A careful philological approach can never neglect the fact that meaning cannot be separated from historical realities. When the speaker is a woman (rather than a man pretending to speak as a woman) and when that woman speaker chooses a forum hitherto reserved for men, the implicit assumptions governing linguistic and literary norms become suddenly transparent and are unmasked as conventions rather than eternal norms. Aesthetic formalism links this unmasking with the self-referential qualities of literary art, whereas Christine uses this unmasking to make literary art refer to the experiences of women. She takes particular pains to identify herself in concrete, historical terms, calling special attention to her marginalized position as foreigner, woman, and widow. While a consummate lyric poet, she insists she would rather be writing something more serious. Christine deploys this "self-referentiality" on three specific historical levels (foreigner, woman, and widow) against the very self-referentiality of the courtly tradition itself in order to subvert it and to recuperate women's experiences.

The studies here explore the aspects of this recuperation. Many arise from the mundane and growing sense of Christine's close connection to late medieval rhetorical and dictaminal arts. The most important immediate combined result of the works presented here is a heightened appreciation of the technical skill, at both macroscopic and microscopic levels, of Christine's lyrical production. The care with which Christine uses word plays, rhyme schemes, meter, and refrains corresponds to her ability to incorporate individual poems into larger narratives. This practice shows that her status as a lyrical artist rests on a highly rational understanding of poetry rather than on some timeless, ineffable "lyrical" subjectivity, more commonly associated with Romanticism. The issue in courtly lyric is that by Christine's time, the lyrical "I" had become so conventionalized that it had lost any touch with "reality." As Paul Zumthor noted, "Despite the 'I' who grammatically controls the [*grant chant courtois*], the writing appears to be divested completely of personal origin: only the text—neutral, composite, intransitive—seems to speak (or rather to sing)."[13] Christine's response to this situation was to reinvest the lyrical "I" with a new historical specificity, and she comes closest to Dante's equation of authenticity with authority.[14] Authenticity in Christine refers to purity of intent and action, without modern associations of archaism, of the rejection of urban, industrial society, of a craving for a lost purity, organicity and union as timeless norms, of a hunger for being bound to the land, of biological rootedness that made possible a cultural rootedness, or of a yearning for a simpler, more immediate life—elements that consistently underlie modern notions of authenticity and beliefs that fuel most modern forms of political reaction and fascism (*le culte des morts, Blut und Boden Romantik*). Like the Virgin, purity and erudition are the key elements of Christine's freedom, authority, and experience.

In the scholarly discussion of late medieval French lyric three names are invariably mentioned together: Guillaume de Machaut, Eustache Deschamps, and Christine de Pizan. Usually Christine's works are mentioned perfunctorily, with the not always implicit assumption that when compared to her predecessors, Christine was a diligent poetaster, but definitely the inferior and most derivative of the three. Recent research has gone a long way to reverse this fundamentally inaccurate evaluation of Christine. The period during which Christine wrote exhibited an enormous range of formal and thematic experimentation, and it is against this background of formal and thematic transformation that Christine's work must be judged.

Peter Dronke, writing in his classic study *The Medieval Lyric* (1968), suggested the term "transformation" as a critical criterion for evaluating medieval poetical works. Analyzing the "transformation" of medieval lyric situates discussion on a practical and technical—perhaps even mechanical—level and thus avoids the mystification that often results from ambiguous references to "artistic form." By narrowing the consideration of lyrical forms to technique, a transformational approach avoids the pitfalls of claims raised for lyric as a transhistorical form[15] or as a privileged epistemological mode (echoes of the standard Romantic belief in "poetic genius"). The difficulties present in much modern analysis of medieval lyric arise in the application of methods developed to explain nineteenth- and early twentieth-century European poetry (the works of Byron, Shelley, and Keats; of Vigny, Baudelaire, Mallarmé, Rimbaud, and Verlaine; of Foscolo; of Hölderlin, Rilke, and Stefan George immediately come to mind here). According to these methods, poetry is seen either as a function of the poet's personality or biography[16] or as the elusive expression of some organic form (a biological metaphor that veils the worst racist and nationalist assumptions) or some "inner form" (a notion first proposed by Goethe in 1776 in his criticism of prescriptive dramatic rules and the three unities [Jubiläum-Ausgabe, 36.115]). Such approaches to lyric lead to claims regarding "absolute" poetry that substitute metaphysical speculation for careful textual interpretation and, following characteristic Romantic beliefs, confuse questions of ontology with those of epistemology.

The essays here follow a different, alternative approach, concentrating more productively and more soberly on the concrete techniques of lyrical composition. The issues that connect Christine's transformation of medieval French lyric to modern European lyric are nevertheless central to the entire discussion of lyric: What and how does language in poetry "mean"? How does the "meaning" of poetry change because of the techniques it employs? Did the formal codification of medieval lyric also promote or hinder its transformation? How are form and content interwoven in lyric? Did Christine's own dissatisfaction with the interrelationship between form and content in lyric lead to her cultivation of prose?

Literary transformation probably bears some affinity to group theory in mathematics: in a particular genre a certain form paired with a certain content offers a specific range of permutations and combinations, and once these possibilities have been completely exploited, the genre in its original form is exhausted as such. The question then arises whether courtly lyric, especially with the "rhetorical" twist given to it by Guillaume de Machaut, amounts ultimately to a cult of sheer virtuosity, reminiscent of the schoolboy exercises in formal composition recommended by Matthew of Vendôme to his pupils. According to the current consensus regarding late fourteenth-century lyric, Guillaume de Machaut and Eustache Deschamps are seens as the masters of a supremely "rhetorical" kind of poetry, more precisely of technical virtuosity, that is, as craftsmen who had virtually exhausted the possibilities of medieval lyric before Christine began to write. Here the ambiguity of the term "rhetoric" becomes evident, for Christine is also a highly "rhetorical" poet not only in the sense that her rhetoric evidences formal sophistication but also, and more importantly, in the sense that the rhetorical principles behind her poetry, while hardly ignoring French poetic arts such as Deschamps's *L'Art de dictier*, reveal a profound debt to the Italian humanist revision of earlier medieval models. This new component in Christine's lyric produced its innovative quality and defined its new freedom. Here is the starting point of the present collection.

The contributions in this volume demonstrate how Christine transforms the literary traditions that she inherited. The first section, on the dynamics of generic innovation, features William D. Paden's study "Christine de Pizan and the Transformation of Late Medieval Lyrical Genres," which affords a systematic and synoptic introduction to the generic issues raised by Christine's lyrics. Paden's analysis represents a methodological breakthrough because he demonstrates that generic transformation follows an internal dynamics of its own, not entirely divorced from social historical reality to be sure, but hardly a mirror of changing social conditions. Paden's essay lays the groundwork for understanding the dynamics of generic innovation. In so doing, Paden offers a new answer to the challenge raised by Erich Köhler. The great German scholar wrote in 1977 that any theory of medieval genre must show its consciousness of historical change because genre cannot be either a normative system of historical or realistic universals before the fact or *ante rem* (*universalien-realistisch normativ ante rem*) or a nominal classification after the fact or *post rem* (*nominalistisch-klassifikatorisch post rem*) but rather a dynamic description of immanent literary processes (*in re*). Köhler's own solution was to postulate structural relationships between literature and society as mirrored in generic transformations and in the reception of various genres (as though genre projected social ideologies).[17] Paden shows that genre works as part of a larger literary system that—like the vowels in any language at any given time—are subject to change resulting from influences both within and outside of the system of genres. The transformation of generic systems bears comparison to changes in the vowel system: dynamic, interdependent, based on distinctions which evolve. Paden begins with a quantitative analysis of the wide range of lyrical genres, carefully delimiting the kinds of formal parameters behind lyrical composition. Although in terms of traditional source studies the direct influence of Provençal lyric on Christine seems minimal, Paden correctly situates Christine's poetic works within the larger context of lyric in both *langue d'oïl* and *langue d'oc*, since medieval French genres cannot be separated from Provençal models. (Earlier, it might be recalled, Dante had stressed the preeminence of Provençal for lyric in his *De vulgari eloquentia*: the difference is that Provençal lyric remained linked to music whereas beginning with Deschamps, French lyric did not.)[18] Paden finds that while Christine wrote in sheer quantity significantly more lyric than the troubadours, she compresses their work into far tighter formal constraints. Moreover, Christine's combination of carefully defined lyrical forms with new and unusual themes such as bereavement and widowhood confer on her poems a more distinctively and more intensively "subjective" tone than is present in earlier, more conventional forms of lyric celebrating love or the loneliness of the lover. Subjectivity in Christine results from a break with convention.

How does this new subjectivity relate to Christine's other seemingly "personal" works and to the "voice" heard there? In the opening passages of *The Book of the City of Ladies*, Christine repeatedly stresses how her experience and the experience of other women directly contradict the testimony of the authors regarding the character and conduct of women. This argument pitting women's experience against received tradition—an absolute first for a woman writer that would find its echoes in the 1980s when feminist critics sought to recover and to reconstruct women's historical experiences—represents a new twist on the questioning of the *auctoritas* of received writers that began with the rise of science in the twelfth century. It also points to the critical, experimental spirit, what Christine called the *pioche d'inquisition*, that is always present beneath the seemingly so conventional and staid surface of Christine's work. When one moreover recalls that Christine later cites the personal experiences of the very women most likely represented in this scene, one begins to realize how Christine exploited convention to new ends.

The question of Christine's subjectivity in turn leads to the question how Christine combined lyric and narrative in her works to create something innovative. The second section of this volume concerns the marriage of lyric and narrative in Christine's works and includes three contributions: James C. Laidlaw on "The *Cent balades*: The Marriage of Content and Form," Barbara K. Altmann on "Last Words: Reflections on a 'Lay mortel' and the Poetics of Lyric Sequences," and Judith Laird and Earl Jeffrey Richards on "*Tous parlent par une mesmes bouche*: Lyrical Outbursts, Prosaic Remedies, and Voice in Christine de Pizan's *Livre du Duc des vrais amans*." The question of the relationship between lyric and narrative has been a recurrent focus of critical scrutiny. The essays here address this question in a close textual manner that has important theoretical ramifications for the general question.

Laidlaw demonstrates how Christine uses symmetrically arranged lyrical poems in the *Cent balades*, the work that begins all of her collected works, and the *Cent ballades d'Amant et de Dame*, which ends the last copied manuscript of her collected works, to create a narrative from lyrical components. Christine's technique amounts to one of the most important formal and generic breakthroughs in late medieval French literature. Laidlaw shows how Christine's questioning, critical spirit recast the received form of a ballade sequence in her *Cent balades*. The *Cent balades* were copied as the first work in the four collectanea whose copying Christine supervised, and thus, in musical terms, give to these collections their *Auftakt* and define the roles of author and readers. Christine's practice combines both literary production and literary reception. Laidlaw reconstructs in detail what Christine's original public would have expected from a series of poems bearing the title *Cent balades*, and he demonstrates both Christine's compositional indebtedness to Machaut and her formal innovations in stanzaic structure. Laidlaw contrasts in detail the structure of the 207 ballades in Machaut's late fourteenth-century work *La louange des dames* with the symmetrical scheme followed in the *Livre des cent balades* (composed by four poets around 1389–90) and the tighter, more self-conscious structure of Christine's *Cent balades* (originally written between 1399 and 1402, but twice slightly revised for inclusion in the Duke's Manuscipt and the Queen's Manuscript). The *Livre des cent balades* is a symmetrically organized narrative of the dilemmas between loyalty and falsehood faced by a young unmarried knight. Christine's *Cent balades*, on first view, appears more heterogeneous, but as Laidlaw shows, Christine incorporates new and sorrowful topics presented by several speakers in which the conflict between loyalty and falsehood takes on far wider ramifications. As this single case shows, Christine went beyond the simple formal givens of a narrative ballade sequence, such as symmetry, in order to create a work more challenging both formally and thematically.

Complementing Laidlaw's analysis are Barbara K. Altmann's insights into the dynamics of lyrical narratives, how Christine went beyond the givens of discrete poems in order to create a new form of narrative, stemming from her discovery, as Altmann puts it, of "the potential of poems to signify beyond their own textual boundaries." Here Christine simultaneously recognizes and transcends the limits of preexisting lyrical models. Altmann initiates a new analysis of the poetics of lyrical sequences, focusing on the *Lay de Dame* [Lay of the Lady] as the last composition in Christine's corpus of lyrical poetry (with the notable exception of her much later tale of Joan of Arc). The crucial position occupied by the *Lay de Dame* with respect to the rest of Christine's entire body of lyrical production cannot be underestimated, as Altmann carefully shows.

The works studied by Laidlaw and Altmann frame Christine's lyrical collections. By contrast, the *Livre du Duc des vrais amans* occupies a middle position within these collections. Judith Laird and Earl Jeffrey Richards explore how Christine creates different and conflicting voices (combining the Thomist notions of *proprie dicta* and *figurate*) within this work by relying on the medieval rhetorical practice of the *figura personarum* or *prosopopoeia*—the technique according to which an author assumes the personality of a fictional or even historical character, a process in which narrative self-referentiality is modified by different patterns of rhetorical displacement. For example, by using elaborate syntactical subordination to mark her own voice at the opening of the work and then letting only one of the characters within the work, Sebille de Monthault, adopt a similar style, Christine sets Sebille's opinions in tandem with her own. Even in the verse sections, in which the verse narrative is interrupted by changing speakers and lyrical monologues, Christine creates not a variant of courtly romance but a new kind of lyrical drama. Thus Christine speaks, as it were, "through" Sebille de Monthault in a way different from the more conventional courtly discourse of the Duke and Lady. Since, significantly, the *Livre du Duc des vrais amans* combines verse and prose, this construction of voice becomes doubly interesting for the light it sheds on Christine as a writer of both forms and as a master of formal heterogeneity. The various prose letters in the work are written in different styles, revealing a conflict between courtly and dictaminal prose. Laird and Richards present a thorough analysis of the various rhetorical devices that Christine exploited in order to identify herself with Sebille. They also point out that Christine's commitment to rhetoric sprung from deeply ethical concerns; thus Sebille (and through her, Christine) instructs and moralizes in order to condemn the courtly world which her public too easily and too superficially inhabit. Their analysis is a salutary reminder that not all witnesses to late medieval courtly spectacles, and least of all Christine, were overwhelmed by the pomp and circumstance, that there was space for critical thought and reflection, and that Christine to her credit opened up and resided in just such a space, the metaphorical extension of her book-lined study. This ethical concern explains why Christine's first lyrical collection, the *Cent balades*, places *belles meurs* (fair deeds) at its geometrical center in Ballade 50. Courtly form is preserved but infused with a new content.

The third section of the essays here examines the limits of lyrical self-representation, a topic that follows naturally from the preceding discussion of voice because it raises the question of what modifications a woman poet brings to courtly poetry, which had been a domain traditionally dominated by men for the celebration of unobtainable female beauty. Christine mastered the language and conventions of courtly poetry, and she ended up subverting it in the name of a higher truth. Here one must think of Caliban's anguished and bitter statement in *The Tempest* that the entire utility of having learned Prospero's language was that he learned to curse: "You taught me language; and my profit on 't Is, I know how to curse: the red plague rid you, / For learning me your language!" (I.2.363–65). Christine does not learn to curse, as it were, that is, she does not learn to master courtly poetry only to curse it. Instead, she makes courtly poetry say things it had never said before.

The section here includes three essays: Nadia Margolis, "Clerkliness and Courtliness in the Complaintes of Christine de Pizan," Lori Walters, "*Translatio Studii*: Christine de Pizan's Self-Portrayal in Two Lyric Poems and in the *Livre de la mutacion de Fortune*," and Christine McWebb, "Lyrical Conventions and the Creation of Female Subjectivity in Christine de Pizan's *Cent ballades d'Amant et de Dame*." Christine's complex relationship to the *Roman de la Rose* raises the question of her overall attitude toward *clergé*, the male preserve of clerkliness that she consistently challenges, toward the "courtly" conventions of lyric, and toward the claims that France had emerged as the cultural successor to Rome (the topos of *translatio studii*).[19] This last point might seem unrelated at first glimpse to the social and aesthetic aspects of the first two questions, but it flows from them logically: male poets and writers, especially modern ones, have often begun their careers celebrating their subjectivity and individuality, only to end their careers by embracing their respective nations as a kind of transcendent ego. The cult of the ego often, but not always, leads to the cult of the nation. Thus it comes as no surprise that Jean de Meun simultaneously saw himself as a lyric love poet in the best tradition of classical antiquity and that he used his identity as a poet to demonstrate that France had emerged as the successor to Rome. Christine's allegiances lie elsewhere, and her break with courtly values goes hand in hand with her universalism. Her career seems marked by an increasingly more apparent discontent with the courtly values celebrated in her male predecessors and by an increasingly more humanistic emphasis on the universal rather than the national.

Lori Walters examines this pattern of thematic and formal innovation in her essay "*Translatio Studii*: Christine de Pizan's Self-Portrayal in Two Lyric Poems and in the *Livre de la mutacion de Fortune.*" Walters shows how Christine incorporates themes associated with the topos of *translatio studii* (the transfer of literary culture from Greece to Rome to France) into her larger strategies of self-portrayal, demonstrating carefully how Christine took her cue from Petrarch. This finding must necessarily revolutionize the study of late medieval French lyric since it opens the possibility that late medieval French poets were influenced not only by Provençal lyric but also by Italian humanism. Christine presents herself as a literal incarnation of the *translatio studii* in order to lend greater credibility and intensity to the solutions that she proposes for France's problems. The results of Laidlaw and Walters complement each other: Christine expanded the concerns of the lyrical audience to include contemporary political problems, surely a gesture far removed from Guillaume IX's famous line, "farei un vers de dreyt nien" [I will compose a verse about/from absolutely nothing], in which the ambiguity of *de* is central to the self-absorption, not introspection, of much medieval lyric.

Nadia Margolis extends scholarly scrutiny on this difficult topic of Christine's relationship to "male" erudition in her essay "Clerkliness and Courtliness in the Complaintes of Christine de Pizan." Margolis argues that Christine's three complaintes represent experiments in writing in the male voice and form a crucial stage in her development both as a lyric poet and as a polemicist. The backdrop to Christine's complaintes was her final rejection of the *locus amoenus*, the *biau lieu* of the *Chemin de long estude*. Margolis shows how Christine subtly and innovatively incorporated didactic elements and exempla into these complaintes, following what should now appear to be a pattern and demonstrating more openly her fundamental dissatisfaction with the conventional depreciation of content in earlier lyric. The care that Christine took in incorporating didactic elements into her complaintes also points to the fact that Christine's techniques must be viewed within the context of medieval rhetorical teachings.

Not surprisingly, the "construction" of a male or a female voice is deeply rooted in medieval rhetoric and its theory of the attributes of persons. The teachings of medieval rhetoricians such as Matthew of Vendôme and John of Garland regarding the "eleven attributes of persons" [*xi.*

personæ attributa] show how old the contemporary interest in recuperating the "female voice" in medieval literature actually is. Matthew of Vendôme, for example, explains in his twelfth-century *Ars versificatoria* that the diction employed by speakers must conform to their countenance and intrinsic or internal character: "verborum proprietas vultibus personarum loquentium et fortunæ instrinsecæ debet conformari" [the diction (literally, "the quality of words") must conform to the countenance of the speaking persons and to their intrinsic fortune].[20] Matthew explains the various attributes that appropriate diction must observe: "debet enim observari proprietas conditionis, ætatis, proprietas officialis, sexus naturalis, locus naturalis, et ceteræ proprietates quæ a Tullio personæ attributa vocantur" [for it is necessary to take into account the social condition, age, official standing, natural gender, natural place and other properties that are called by Cicero attributes of person].[21] Interestingly, these rhetorical prescriptions find their closest modern equivalent in the linguistic theories of Émile Benveniste and Roman Jakobson. When Paul Zumthor, for example, distinguishes between personal and impersonal subjects in lyric, he refers to Benveniste. Zumthor's remarks are worth repeating: "les formes de discours à prédominance idéationnelle comportent, à quelques exceptions près, un sujet-chose, distinct à la fois de l'auteur et de l'auditeur; les autres, le sujet personnel, *je*" [forms of discourse that are predominantly cognitive tend, with few exceptions, to have an impersonal subject, distinct from the author and audience; other forms of discourse tend to have a personal subject, *I*].[22] Because Christine's lyrics are so heavily weighted with a cognitive or ideational content, the issue is more complicated: on the one hand, an impersonal subject seems to hide behind even her most personal lyrics, a subject enunciating careful critiques of the ruling courtly ideology via a rhetorical strategy incorporating formal heterogeneity (different genres combined innovatively) with many different speakers or voices. On the other hand, Christine follows another strategy that Zumthor finds characteristic of the personal subject, namely the reference to a "here and now": "le discours personnel intègre, au moins fictivement, au texte, la présence de son énonciateur, et se réfère à un *hic et nunc*" [personal discourse integrates, at least fictionally, the presence of its speaker into the text and refers to a here and now] (p. 172). Christine's reliance on the *hic et nunc*, the here and now, in her lyrics is what frees them from earlier conventional restraints and simultaneously recuperates the experience of women. No other lyric poet in medieval French literature undertook to do so much, and it is little wonder that we are only now beginning to appreciate the depth and complexity of Christine's lyrics.

Whereas in the complaintes Christine experiments in writing in a male voice or voices, the *Cent ballades d'Amant et de Dame* challenge her to write in female voices, a topic that has generated considerable scholarly interest in recent years. Christine McWebb examines this phenomenon in her contribution here. It takes its cue in part from the insights of linguists on how speakers communicate their identity. Given the debate between representationalism and essentialism in current feminist scholarship, it is important to stress how Christine constructed a female voice, or better, female voices, without trying to rely on some ineffable female subjectivity: the language of women, in terms of linguistic appropriateness, or to use the rhetorical formula, in terms of *verborum proprietas*, can be reproduced in literary terms if "women's speech" recuperates its historical specificity. The key here is to demonstrate the linguistic techniques with which Christine created her "female" voices. This analysis situates Christine's poetry, as it should, in the area of communicative competence, to borrow the term coined by Jürgen Habermas,[23] that is, in the real social world in which language is used, in which language is not "only words," to recall Catharine MacKinnon's study of pornography.[24]

Borrowing from the model originally developed by Benveniste regarding enunciation and the enunciating subject, McWebb demonstrates the homosocial system of reference behind courtly lyric which created an androcentric framework for the reception of lyrical poetry. McWebb shows how Christine recast courtly conventions, by comparing specifically Christine's practice with that of Froissart. Her conclusions, based on a synchronic linguistic approach, afford correlative substantiation for earlier claims raised by scholars that the humanist critique of courtliness, which called among other things for enhancing the status of women in marriage, partially inspired Christine's critique of courtliness.

The issue of courtliness runs through many of the essays in this volume, and here we approach one of the thorniest questions in Christine studies: Christine's attitude toward courtliness itself. This subject organizes the last section of the volume, on the critique of courtliness and expanding the boundaries of lyric.

In order to understand Christine's critique of courtliness, one needs to return to the question of generic transformation. As Paden's synopsis makes clear, generic change occurred dynamically, in part because of internal reasons (particularly the separation of lyric from a musical setting), in part because of external reasons (such as changing public expectations). It is apparent in Christine's lyrics that internal reasons (her dissatisfaction with the conventions of courtly poetry as such) and external reasons (her composing poetry in the first place) combined to create an entirely new kind of poetry. It should be clear now that Christine's poetry hardly served courtly ideals but instead called them profoundly into question, in part because Christine probably viewed courtly ideals as outmoded from a humanistic perspective.

As Aldo Scaglione has demonstrated, "courtliness" existed as a pan-European ideology of the noble classes from 950 to 1620 in societies as different in their political structures and gender hierarchies as Ottonian Germany from Renaissance Italian city states.[25] The historical continuity or prevalence of such a courtly ideology, independent of changing social structures, illustrates the simple fact that ideologies survive and indeed thrive independently of social reality, although they undeniably interact with it. By the same token, vernacular narratives, in verse and prose, were written for and appreciated by all of these societies as well, though the particular complexity of various authors and audiences can hardly be underestimated, ranging from church-trained clerics (especially in France) to barely literate knights (as in Germany, where a knight such as Hartmann von Aue excuses himself for being able to read and write), from assembled townspeople in public markets (as in northern Italy) to queens and their attendants in private royal chambers (such as Eleanor of Aquitaine or Isabeau of Bavaria). Against the background of such heterogeneous historical and social conditions, it is simplistic to assume that a genre such as courtly romance by virtue of its formal qualities "dramatizes the tensions of the class and gender system," as Roberta Krueger postulated regarding Christine de Pizan's *Livre du Duc des vrais amans*.[26] The formal heterogeneity of this work, as analyzed by Laird and Richards, does not stem directly from the tensions of the class and gender system but from a combination of external and internal factors that demonstrate that Christine criticizes this system, rather than reaffirming it, as Krueger would see it. She posits furthermore that the gender hierarchy of male patron and female poet in the commissioning of the *Livre du Duc des vrais amans* created a dilemma for Christine because "in a romance of male desire for an unattainable married lady, the female poet cannot inhabit the role of the knight and serve her patron in the same way that the male clerk can to serve his patroness" (p. 228). The only patron whom Christine in effect served was the truth; her courtly patrons, from Charles VI to Isabeau de Bavière, to Louis d'Orléans and Jean de Berry, were always secondary.

Christine's representation of aristocratic life was in fact unrealistic: the revelry depicted in the work, as Thelma Fenster has noted, "would have been too costly, even for the very rich, to be an everyday event" and the setting for the tournament is not so much an actual historical place as "a *locus amoenus* with a view of a six-turreted castle and a pond."[27] Fenster's concrete analysis avoids the pitfalls of Krueger's claims: the dramatic setting of the *Livre du Duc des vrais amans* is tied to the specific circumstances of the work's commissioning, combined with inherited courtly commonplaces, and not to a generalized statement about estatist tensions in early fifteenth-century France as these tensions find their expression in the generically innovative *Livre du Duc des vrais amans*. This point is important because it is becoming increasingly clearer that Christine rejected the notion of inherited nobility in favor of the nobility of virtue, whence her opening her "City of Ladies" to women from all classes. These two insights cast doubt on Christine's adherence to an "asymmetrical class and gender hierarchy."[28]

Scholarly inquiry like Krueger's relies in part on an unspoken attempt to revive a recurrent claim of Marxian and sociological criticism that literature mirrors social conditions, specifically class struggles. As important and as valuable as Marxian criticism is, especially for discussing the nineteenth-century European novel, the Marxian *Widerspiegelungstheorie* affords little purchase when applied in such a blunt way to Christine. Christine's deep concern for social issues is reflected in her belief that feudal estatist structures founded on an hereditary nobility need to be replaced by a nobility of virtue. This nobility of virtue means that one must examine more closely how Christine calls courtly aesthetics into question as part of a larger ethical project. The two essays in the fourth section of this volume, on Christine's critique of courtliness and her expanding the boundaries of lyric, make a good start in this direction.

Benjamin Semple, in his essay "Christine de Pizan's Phenomenology of Beauty in the Lyric and the Dream Vision," shows the interdependence of aesthetic pleasure and ethical teaching in Christine's lyrics and in the *Chemin de long estude*. He notes that Christine made a superficial concession to "pleasure" in her lyrics, but that this aesthetic pleasure was an inducement to practice "fair acts" or *belles meurs*, a term that occurs in the central ballade, number 50, of the *Cent balades*. Semple shows how Christine sought an authenticity of feeling as the true source of poetic inspiration, that Christine's *intentio auctoris* lay in the recuperation of true feeling, feeling that refers, in terms of the larger themes of this volume, to women's ignored experience. Christine deploys the tradition of moral and sapiential beauty squarely against the aesthetic pleasures of courtly literature. Semple then demonstrates that Christine appeals to readers of the *Rose* to be aware of the sensual temptations in the text that cloud the faculties of discernment and volition, that lead to "humanity's limp," an allegory in both Dante and Christine for the debility of the will. Christine presents these ethical arguments with a veneer of courtliness that signals, as Semple cogently argues, "not a transformation or alteration of Christine's courtly aesthetic but rather the creation of an entirely new conceptual framework in which reader response and the aesthetic impact of texts could be understood." This ethical appeal leads to a new aesthetic that is presented in the pleasance or *biau lieu* of the *Chemin de long estude*. The contrast between the allegorical techniques followed by Guillaume de Lorris and Jean de Meun in the *Rose* with those adopted by Christine in her *Chemin de long estude* could not be greater. The *locus amoenus* as conventional lyrical stage, far removed from the impingements of day-to-day concerns, receives two radically different meanings in the two works. Part of Christine's transformation of the *biau lieu* stems from her very sincere and very openly declared didacticism. Both Guillaume and Jean claim, tongue firmly in cheek, that their work presents a summary of the entire art of love but naturally never fulfills this proclaimed didactic mission. (Any late medieval Christian reader sincerely interested in love, as opposed to erotic casuistry, could consult Bernard of Clairvaux's still provocative and deeply moving *De diligendo Deo*, but secular love poetry, for all its wit, lightness, and sparkle, inhabits a different planet from Bernard's theology and necessarily pales when compared with Bernard's still penetrating analysis.)[29] Striking, however, is Christine's emphasis not on physical or sensual beauty, so stereotypically present in lyric, but on intellectual beauty instead. Here again Christine radically recasts lyrical convention to new ends.

Earl Jeffrey Richards shows in his "Poems of Water without Salt and Ballades without Feeling, or Reintroducing History into the Text: Prose and Verse in the Works of Christine de Pizan" the affinities linking these two compositional modes in Christine. The previous temptation in scholarship of late medieval prose has been to separate carefully prose and verse in order to emphasize their opposition. Just as there is no single verse style in Christine, there is no single prose style, and this stylistic diversity corresponds to the overall variety of Christine's work. Christine produced an enormous corpus of writings in both verse and prose, but the aesthetic and moral values to which she adhered did not shift according to the compositional mode adopted. While she worked under the pressure of deadlines—she finished *The Book of the City of Ladies* in less than six months while working on other projects, a workload that only sharpened her vision—Christine was hardly a *polyscribator* cranking out her work as fast as she could. Richards examines the shortcomings of contemporary scholarly analysis of the rise of prose, especially the alleged antithesis between prose and verse and the mistaken attempt to link prose to written language and verse to oral speech (one should not forget how Molière has M. Jourdain remark that his conversation was in fact prose, "*et c'est de la prose!*").

The question is complicated because Christine's use of prose has little in common with earlier fourteenth-century *mises en prose* which have been the principal object and focus of scholarly analysis hitherto. For Christine the choice of verse or prose was a practical one. The issue here is the use of prose narrative to do things that courtly lyric did not do. By erasing the artificial boundaries drawn between prose and verse by some scholars, one gains a deeper sense of the profound continuity underlying Christine's career.

The studies here thus demonstrate Christine's knowledge and manipulation of the generic givens of her day, her creative recasting of lyrical ballades to form larger narrative units, her techniques of forging identities for herself and for the characters in her works, the complementarity of her verse and prose works and the redefinition of aesthetic and ethical values in literature. Taken together, the studies gathered here point to the enormous freedom that Christine enjoyed as a verse writer. "Freedom" as such is rarely a quality associated with the narrow formal constraints of medieval lyric. Here is where Christine's greatest significance as a lyric poet lies. Inspired by humanism, dissatisfied with the artificiality and the hypocrisy of courtly lyric as practiced by her predecessors, troubled (not to say enraged) by the misogyny lurking below the surface of most courtly verse, Christine sought to transform French lyric into a more nuanced, less artificial, and more sensitive mode of composition. We are just beginning to discover and appreciate her success here.

Notes

1. The first two of these four collectanea—Chantilly, Musée Condé 492–93, and Paris, Bibliothèque Nationale, Fonds français 12779—are referred to as *Le Livre de Christine* [The Book of Christine]. The third, the so-called Manuscript of the Duke because it was acquired by the Duke de Berry in 1408 or 1409, was originally composed of five manuscripts in Paris, Bibliothèque Nationale, Fonds français: 835, 606, 836, 605, and 607. The final transcription is found in the Manuscript of the Queen (British Library, Harley 4431), presented to Isabeau de Bavière in 1410 or 1411.

2. Jean Frappier, *La poésie lyrique française aux XIIe et XIIIe siècles: Les*

auteurs et les genres (Paris: Centre de Documentation Universitaire, 1954), p. 232: "Quant aux formes lyriques, elles évolueront après lui [Rutebeuf] non pas vers plus de liberté, mais au contraire vers plus de contrainte et vers le triomphe des genres fixes, ballade, chant royal, rondeau et virelai" [As for lyric forms, they will evolve after him [Rutebeuf] not toward more freedom, but on the contrary toward more constraint and toward the triumph of fixed genres, ballade, chant royal, rondeau and virelai].

3. *Flores omnium pene doctorum qui tum in Theologia, tum in Philosophia hactenus claruerunt, per Thomam Hibernicum olim summa cum diligentia collecti ac ordine alphabetico in unum congesti* [Flowers of almost all learned men who have shown forth until now in theology and philosophy, collected by Thomas Hibernicus with the greatest diligence and brought together in alphabetical order] (Lugduni [=Lyons]: apud Theobaldum Paganum, 1567): amor formæ, rationis oblivio.

4. The phrase is from Fredrick Jameson's essay "Baudelaire as Modernist and Postmodernist: The Dissolution of the Referent and the Artificial Sublime," in *Lyric Poetry, Beyond New Criticism*, ed. Chaviva Hošek and Patricia Parker (Ithaca: Cornell University Press, 1985), pp. 247–63.

5. See my essay, "Christine de Pizan, the Conventions of Courtly Lyric and Italian Humanism," *Reinterpreting Christine de Pizan*, ed. Earl Jeffrey Richards with Joan Williamson, Christine Reno, and Nadia Margolis (Athens: University of Georgia Press, 1992), pp. 250–71.

6. Eugene Vance, "Greimas, Freud, and the Story of Trouvère Lyric," p. 105.

7. Edgar De Bruyne, *The Esthetics of the Middle Ages*.

8. Simon Gaunt, *Gender and Genre in Medieval French Literature*, p. 1: "in medieval French and Occitan literature gender and genre are inextricably linked." For unexplained reasons, Gaunt nowhere mentions Christine's lyrics.

9. Eustache Deschamps, *L'Art de dictier*, p. 94.

10. Alastair J. Minnis, *Medieval Theory of Authorship*, p. 73.

11. Daniel Poirion, *Littérature française: Le Moyen Age*, II: *1300–1480*, p. 206: "Il y a une unité, derrière cette diversité, et une qualité, sous cette quantité. Cette unité est celle de sa personalité" [There is a unity behind this diversity, and a quality behind this quantity. This unity is that of her personality].

12. Laurie Fink, *Feminist Theory, Women's Writing* (Ithaca: Cornell University Press, 1992), p. 3.

13. Paul Zumthor, "Style and Expressive Register in Medieval Poetry," p. 267.

14. In *Convivio* IV.vi.5, Dante notes, "L'altro principio, onde 'autore' descende ... è uno vocabulo greco che dice 'autentin' che tanto vale in latino quanto 'degno di fede e d'obedienza'" [The other principle from which the word "author" derives is the Greek word *authentin*, which means in Latin "worthy of belief and obedience"]. Two other medieval writers, Uguccione da Pisa and Évrard de Béthune, conflated the etymologies of *auctor* (from *augere,* to increase, promote, originate, as in "augment") and *authenticum*. They claimed that the medieval form of *auctor*, without the *c*, derived directly from the Greek word *autentin* (*recte, authentes*),

"doer, perpetrator, master," but also "murderer, and self-murderer." In fact, it first derives from the term *authentikos*, "principal, genuine," itself derived from *authentia*, "original authority." The Graecism *authenticum* was used in the Middle Ages to designate the original manuscript of a work as opposed to other copies.

15. André Jolles's *Einfache Formen* (which, translated into French, experienced a revival in the 1970s under the influence of the journal *Poétique*) pointedly illustrates this kind of methodological confusion. The survival, indeed the flourishing of such critical mystification, is all too clear in the collection of essays assembled by Reinhold Grimm in *Zur Lyrik-Diskussion*.

16. Sainte-Beuve's dictum that the "lion is but digested lambs" represents the excesses of this overly simplistic and quite correctly pilloried form of positivistic biographical criticism.

17. Erich Köhler, "Gattungssystem und Gesellschaftssystem," *Romanische Zeitschrift für Literaturgeschichte/Cahiers d'Histoire des littératures romanes* 1 (1977): 7–21.

18. Deborah Sinnreich-Levi speaks clearly of "Deschamps' tacit acceptance of the vernacular as opposed to Dante's need to establish the vernacular's primacy, and Deschamps' disassociation of the musical setting from the lyric as opposed to Dante's adherence to their traditional linkage," p. 21.

19. For an exhaustive treatment of *translatio studii*, see Ulrike Krämer, *Translatio imperii et studii, Zum Geschichts- und Kulturverständnis in der französischen Literatur des Mittelalters und der frühen Neuzeit*.

20. Matthieu de Vendôme, *Ars versificatoria*, in Faral, *Les Arts poétiques du XIIe et du XIIIe siècle: Recherches et documents sur la technique littéraire du moyen âge*, p. 120.

21. Ibid., p. 119.

22. Zumthor, *Essai de poétique médiévale*, p. 171. Zumthor here refers to Benveniste, *Problèmes de linguistique générale* (Paris: Gallimard, 1966), pp. 255–57.

23. Jürgen Habermas, "Vorbereitende Bemerkungen zu einer Theorie der kommunikativen Kompetenz."

24. See Catharine A. MacKinnon, *Only Words*, a work comparable to Christine's critique of the *Romance of the Rose*.

25. Aldo Scaglione, *Knights at Court: Courtliness, Chivalry, and Courtesy from Ottonian Germany to the Italian Renaissance* (Berkeley: University of California Press, 1991).

26. Roberta Krueger, *Women Readers and the Ideology of Gender in Old French Verse Romance* (Cambridge: Cambridge University Press, 1993), p. 246.

27. Fenster, Introduction to Christine de Pizan, *The Book of the Duke of True Lovers*, p. 30.

28. One traditional school of thought, with roots dating back to Voltaire, has always held that Christine was essentially politically conservative, especially because as the biographer of Charles V she did not call medieval class structure into question. Yet as early as 1947, the German Romance specialist Franz Walter Müller

argued that Christine's concept of the French nation was progressive because Christine held that the nation included all estates and not just the nobles. Müller was a student of Werner Krauss, the most important German Romanist to have been imprisoned by the Gestapo for plotting against Hitler and the most influential scholar of Romance languages and literatures in the German Democratic Republic. Krauss's allegiance to the Communist party has made him, his works, and those of his students, like Müller, unknown in the United States.

29. Bernard isolates four steps in loving God: love of self for self, love of God for self, love of God for God, and love of self for God. The kind of self-absorption common in medieval love lyric fails to transcend this first step. The kind of torment entailed in searching for and loving God is hardly the same as the torment of unrequited erotic desire, since, as the *Pervergilium Veneris* puts it, *cras amet qui numquam amavit / qui numquam amavit cras amet* (Tomorrow he will love who has never loved / who has never loved, tomorrow will love).

Works Cited

De Bruyne, Edgar. *The Esthetics of the Middle Ages.* Trans. Eileen B. Hennessy. New York: Frederick Ungar, 1969.

Deschamps, Eustache. *L'Art de dictier.* Ed. and trans. Deborah M. Sinnreich-Levi. East Lansing, Mich.: Colleagues Press, 1994.

Dronke, Peter. *Poetic Individuality in the Middle Ages: New Departures in Poetry, 1000–1150.* Oxford: Clarendon, 1970.

Faral, Edmond. *Les arts poétiques du XIIe et du XIIIe siècle: Recherches et documents sur la technique littéraire du moyen âge.* Paris: Champion, 1924, 1971.

Fenster, Thelma. Introduction to Christine to Pizan, *The Book of the Duke of True Lovers.* Trans. Thelma Fenster with lyric poetry trans. Nadia Margolis. New York: Persea, 1991.

Gaunt, Simon. *Gender and Genre in Medieval French Literature.* Cambridge: Cambridge University Press, 1995.

Grimm, Reinhold, ed. *Zur Lyrik-Diskussion.* Darmstadt: Wissenschaftliche Buchgesellschaft, 1974.

Habermas, Jürgen. "Vorbereitende Bemerkungen zu einer Theorie der kommunikativen Kompetenz." In J. Habermas and N. Luhmann, *Theorie der Gesellschaft oder Sozialtechnologie.* Frankfurt: Suhrkamp, 1971.

Jolles, André. *Einfache Formen.* Tübingen: Max Niemeyer, 1930, 1972.

Krämer, Ulrike. *Translatio imperii et studii, Zum Geschichts- und Kulturverständnis in der französischen Literatur des Mittelalters und der frühen Neuzeit.* Bonn: Romanistischer Verlag, 1996.

MacKinnon, Catharine A. *Only Words.* Cambridge: Harvard University Press, 1993.

Minnis, Alastair J. *Medieval Theory of Authorship: Scholastic Literary Attitudes in the Later Middle Ages.* London: Scolar Press, 1984.

Paden, William D. "Old Occitan as a Lyric Language: The Insertions from Occitan in Three Thirteenth-Century French Romances." *Speculum* 68 (1993): 36–53.

Poirion, Daniel. *Littérature française: Le Moyen age.* Vol. II: *1300–1480.* Paris: Arthaud, 1969.

Vance, Eugene. "Greimas, Freud, and the Story of Trouvère Lyric." In *Lyric Poetry: Beyond New Criticism*, ed. Chaviva Ho_ek and Patricia Parker, pp. 93–105. Ithaca: Cornell University Press, 1985.

Zumthor, Paul. *Essai de poétique médiévale.* Paris: Seuil, 1972.

———. "Style and Expressive Register in Medieval Poetry." In *Literary Style, A Symposium*, ed. Seymour Chatman, pp. 263–81. London: Oxford University Press, 1971.

∽ *The Dynamics of Generic Innovation*

∾ CHAPTER I

Christine de Pizan and
the Transformation of Late
Medieval Lyrical Genres

WILLIAM D. PADEN

I am interested in investigating the practice of Christine de Pizan, in her lyric verse, in relation to the array of genres that was available to her. This array may be thought of as the system of Middle French genres. As we have all heard, this system was characterized by so-called fixed forms or *formes fixes*, genres such as the ballade, the rondeau, and the virelai. I shall argue that the term *formes fixes* is a misnomer and that Christine exploited flexibility of form for expressive purposes. Far from being static, the system of genres within which she worked continually grew, changed, and developed, offering both resistance and fluidity for poetic use.

I.

To begin with the broad picture, we may compare the system of genres in Middle French with the systems in Old French and the Renaissance. One convenient way to get an initial, general impression is to turn to Pierre Bec for a listing of the genres in Old French, and to Warner Patterson for genres in practice in the latter two periods. The following table shows the genres they list, excluding some that are manifestly not lyric, such as Patterson's "epic verse," and vaguely defined terms such as Bec's "registre pieux."

Lyric Genres in Old French, Middle French,
and Renaissance French Verse[1]

	Old French	Middle French	Renaissance
1.	Aube	Amoureuse	Baiser
2.	Ballette	Ballade (no envoi)	Blason
3.	Chanson d'ami	Ballade double	Cantique
4.	Chanson de croisade	Ballade layée	Chanson
5.	Chanson de toile	Ballade with envoi	Chanson lamentable
6.	Estampie	Chanson	Chanson spirituelle
7.	Fatrasie	Chant royal	Chansonette
8.	Lai "arthurien"	Eclogue	Chapitre in terza rima
9.	Lai lyrique	Epître	Coq-à-l'asne
10.	Malmariée	Fatras double	Dizain
11.	Motet	Pastourelle	Eclogue
12.	Pastourelle	Rondeau	Elégie
13.	Resverie	Rondeau double	Elégie-épître
14.	Reverdie	Rondeau redoublé	Epigramme
15.	Rondet de carole	Serventois	Epitaphe
16.	Rotrouenge	Triolet	Epître
17.	Sotte chanson	Villanelle	Fable
18.	Virelai et virelai	Virelai double	Hymne
19.		Virelai simple	Idillie
20.		Virelai triple	Noël
21.			Ode (various types)
22.			Pindaric ode
23.			Psaume
24.			Satire
25.			Sextine
26.			Sonnet
27.			Stance
28.			Villanesque, villanelle

A first glance suggests that the numbers of genres grew in the Renaissance, implying, perhaps, a greater enthusiasm for taxonomic distinctions. A second glance suggests something more meaningful: the discontinuity from period to period. Of the eighteen genres listed for Old French, only three continued, according to these lists, into Middle French; the percentage (three of eighteen) is 17 percent. The *fatrasie* became the *fatras double*, the *pastourelle* remained, and the virelai became the virelai simple, each of them with some adjustments. The rest of the Old French genres, 83 percent of the total number, did not continue to function as alternatives in the system. It is true, however, that some of the discrepancies between Old French and Middle French appear to be arbitrary: why, for example, does Patterson not list the lai and the motet for Middle French? If he had, the rate of continuity from Old to Middle French would have risen to five of eighteen, or 28 percent, reducing the discontinuity from the first to the second period and highlighting the break from the second to the third. From Middle French to the Renaissance, three genres continued out of a total of twenty, the *éclogue*, the *épître*, and the *villanelle*: that is, 15 percent continued, 85 percent did not. Any apparent continuity from the *chanson d'ami* in Old French to the chanson in Middle French and the Renaissance is deceptive, since in the chanson d'ami a young woman sings about her lover, whereas the later chanson is simply a "free lyric" (Patterson, p. 155, n. 1). Therefore not one genre appears to continue through the three periods. We gain an initial impression that these are three very different systems.[2]

A third glance suggests the obvious characterization of each one. In Old French the name of a genre tends to indicate what it is about: thus the *aube, chanson d'ami, chanson de croisade, chanson de toile, chanson de malmariée, pastourelle,* and *reverdie*. In Middle French, the names tend to suggest variations on a small number of basic forms: we see four types of ballade, three types of rondeau, and three types of virelai. In the Renaissance they tend to evoke a prestigious cultural sphere, either classical antiquity with the eclogue, elegy, epigram, epitaph, idyll, and ode—Horatian, Anacreontic, Sapphic, or Pindaric—or the Church with the canticle, hymn, noël, and psalm. The three systems seem to focus, respectively, on subject matter, form, and humanist poetics.

All of this is to suggest the historical contingency of genres and the genre system, which means, for any given poet, the newness of the genres available, the dynamism of the system. In the last decades of the fourteenth century, Christine de Pizan confronted an array of poetic possibilities which, if our first impression is sound, was less than a century old.

The shift from the Old French to the Middle French system had been marked by several stages. About 1300, in his *Dit de la panthère* [Story of the Panther], Nicole de Margival narrated a dream experienced by the protagonist, a first-person lover.[3] Upon waking, the lover reports, he composed a series of poems illustrating six types, the *chanson, chansonette, ballade, balladelle, chant royal,* and *rondel*. Guillaume de Machaut, in his *Remède de Fortune* [Remedy of Fortune], which he wrote perhaps around

1340, says that he expressed his love in chansons, lais, ballades, rondeaux, virelais, and chans.[4] Without pausing to wonder about the relation between chansons and chans, we may note that Nicole de Margival and Machaut both refer to chansons, ballades, and rondeaux, while Nicole adds the chansonette, balladelle, and chant royal, and Machaut adds chants, virelais, and lais. Continuity has risen to 50 percent. Later in the *Remède de Fortune*, Machaut provides a set of models of lyric forms, including the lai, chanson royale, ballade, virelai, rondeau, complainte, and balladelle—seven genres, including all those named by Nicole (if we may assume that Nicole's chansons are Machaut's chanson royale, and except for the puzzling chans) and adding the complainte.

First Nicole de Margival, then Machaut proposed an implicit art of poetry. Machaut's student Eustache Deschamps offered an explicit one, the *Art de dictier*, dated 25 November 1392, in which he defined the *ballade, serventois, virelai, rondeau, sotte chanson, pastourelle,* and *lai*, seven genres in all but not the same seven illustrated by Machaut in the *Remède de Fortune*.[5] Deschamps drops the *chanson royale, complainte,* and *balladelle*, while adding the *serventois, sotte chanson,* and *pastourelle*. Continuity now reaches 57 percent. Four genres constitute the core of elements common to Machaut's and Deschamps's lists: the *lai, ballade, virelai,* and *rondeau*.

II.

Today these four genres are commonly referred to as *formes fixes*, a term as widely employed as it has been little discussed. The expression does not seem to occur in the sources. It is not in the implicit poetic of the *Dit de la panthère* or the *Remède de Fortune*; not in Deschamps's *Art de dictier*, which offers to teach the manner of ballades, *chançons,* and rondeaux "en pluseurs et diverses manieres" [in several and various ways] (p. 272); not in the *Règles de la seconde rhétorique*, written between 1411 and 1432, which credit Machaut with beginning "toutes tailles nouvelles," "all the new cuts" or "sizes" [*taille* from *taillier*, "to cut"; compare English "tailor"].[6] This remark implies a consciousness of a new set of genres, but not necessarily, or exactly, of *formes fixes*. In 1549 Du Bellay did not use the phrase *formes fixes* when he begged the aspiring poet to abandon "toutes ces vieilles poësies françoyses . . . comme rondeaux, ballades, vyrelaiz, chantz royaulx, chansons et autres telles episseries, qui corrumpent le goust de nostre langue, et ne servent si non à porter temoingnaige de notre ignorance" [all of these old French poems . . . like *rondeaux, ballades, virelais, chants royaux, chansons* and other such spices, which corrupt the taste of our language, and serve only to testify to our ignorance].[7]

The term *formes fixes* was perhaps invented in the late nineteenth century by Théodore de Banville, the Parnassian poet and man of letters; at least Banville says he invented it. In the *Petit traité de poésie française* which he published in 1872, he wrote:

> J'ai nommé *poëmes traditionnels à forme fixe* ceux pour lesquels la tradition a irrévocablement fixé le nombre de vers qu'ils doivent contenir et l'ordre dans lequel ces vers doivent être disposés. Ce groupe de poëmes est l'un de nos plus précieux trésors, car chacun d'eux forme un tout rhythmique, complet et parfait, et en même temps ils ont la grâce naïve et comme inconsciente des créations qu'ont faites les époques primitives.[8]

> [I have called traditional poems with a fixed form those for which tradition has irrevocably fixed the number of verses that they must contain and the order in which these verses must be arranged. This group of poems is one of our most precious treasures, for each of them forms a rhythmical whole, complete and perfect, and at the same time they have the naive grace, virtually unconscious, of the creations that primitive ages have made.]

Banville shows a sensitivity to Romantic aesthetics with his enthusiasm for the naive grace of the fixed forms as an expression of primitive eras, but his appreciation of these forms as offering "un tout rhythmique, complet et parfait" echoes the more recent advent of the Parnassian school. The aesthetic of this school had been formulated by Théophile Gautier in his poem "L'art," published in 1857, which was a response to an earlier poem by Banville, published in 1856. Banville had called his poem "A Th. Gautier":

> Quand la chasse est finie
> Le poète oiseleur
>   Manie
> L'outil du ciseleur.
>
> Car il faut qu'il meutrisse,
> Pour y graver son pur
>   Caprice,
> Un métal au coeur dur . . .[9]

[When the hunt is over / the bird-hunter of a poet / wields / the engraver's tool. // For he must beat, / in order to engrave his pure / caprice, / a hard-hearted metal.]

And Gautier, originally titling his poem "A Monsieur Théodore de Banville: Réponse à son Odelette," answered in identical metrical form—might we say, in a *forme fixe*?

> Oui, l'oeuvre sort plus belle
> D'une forme au travail
>   Rebelle,
> Vers, marbre, onyx, émail.
>
> Point de contraintes fausses!
> Mais que pour marcher droit
>   Tu chausses,
> Muse, un cothurne étroit. . . .[10]

[Yes, the work comes out more fair / from a form that rebels against / handling, / verse, marble, onyx, enamel. // No false constraints! / But in order to walk straight / you must put on / Muse, a tight-fitting buskin.]

In comparison with flowing Romantic verse, the ballade or the rondeau, like marble, onyx, or enamel, qualifies as "une forme au travail rebelle," and so promises to yield the jewel-like effect that the Parnassians admired.[11] Banville elaborated upon this aesthetic ideal in the *Petit traité*:

> La Poésie doit toujours être noble, c'est-à-dire intense, exquise et achevée dans la forme. . . . Elle est à la fois Musique, Statuaire, Peinture, Eloquence; elle doit charmer l'oreille, enchanter l'espirit, représenter les sons, imiter les couleurs, rendre les objets visibles . . . ; aussi est-elle le seul art complet, nécessaire, et qui contienne tous les autres. (p. 9)

[Poetry must always be noble, that is, intense, exquisite, and accomplished in its form. . . . It is at once music, statuary, painting, eloquence; it must charm the ear, enchant the mind, represent sounds, imitate colors, make objects visible . . . ; thus it is the only perfect and necessary art which contains all the others.]

For Banville, then, his phrase "poëmes traditionnels à forme fixe" [traditional poems with a fixed form] echoed Gautier's "forme . . . rebelle": the words "forme fixe" resonate with Parnassian aesthetics. Note that Banville did not exactly speak of genres, although he came very close with "ce groupe de poëmes." He explained that he meant poems "pour lesquels la tradition a irrévocablement fixé le nombre de vers qu'ils doivent contenir et l'ordre dans lequel ces vers doivent être disposés" [for which tradition has irrevocably fixed the number of verses that they must contain and the order in which these verses must be arranged]. This definition poses several problems. The ballade had no envoi at first but gradually acquired one; furthermore the number of verses in each of the ballade's three stanzas ranged from six to sixteen lines,[12] so the total number of verses can scarcely be said to have been irrevocably fixed. The rondeau may grow from eight lines (or seven) to as long as thirty-two.[13] As for the virelai, one scholar has described its structural principle as one of "ordered fantasy."[14] The order in which the verses of the three genres must be arranged proceeds, of course, from the first to the last. Banville must have been thinking vaguely of the refrain, which occurs at the end of each stanza of the ballade and at the beginning, middle, and end of the rondeau and virelai; as Michel Zink has put it, the "poèmes à formes fixes" are "lovés autour de leur refrain" [coiled around their refrain].[15] Banville's use of "tradition" raises a third difficulty, since he left ambiguous whether he meant that by 1872 a tradition five hundred years long had finally determined what, in his judgment, the exact form of the *formes fixes* should be, or that it had already done so by the fourteenth century; if he meant the latter, he was demonstrably wrong. Finally, Banville's admiration for "la forme rebelle," by leading him to exaggerate the fixity of the *formes fixes*, produced an unintended effect of devaluing the poems when their forms are seen to be less fixed than the term implies. On the other hand, if readers reject the ideal of "la forme rebelle" they may be deterred by the term *formes fixes* from appreciating the poems to which it applies, however loosely.[16] Either way, the reader is the loser.

Variations in the pattern of the so-called fixed forms have led Elwert to the surprising claim that the troubadour *canso* was a fixed form too, on the grounds that the design of its stanza was required to correspond to the two *pedes* [feet] and *cauda* [tail] defined by Dante in the *De vulgari eloquentia*, or to the *ouvert* [opening], *clos* [closure], and *queue* [tail] of French theorists.[17] Elwert is right that the troubadour stanza was not altogether freely constructed. He has simplified Dante's language, however, which does not require such a prescriptive form, but explicitly allows the alternative of a through-composed tune; indeed the tripartite structure of the stanza, while common throughout medieval lyric, nowhere became obligatory.[18] Nevertheless Elwert's claim regarding troubadour lyric is useful because it allows us to understand how the earlier system of Provençal verse, which applied the pattern of *pedes* and *cauda* to various genres distinguished by subject, yielded to the later one, which distinguished genres by constraints on formal structure without regard for subject. The principle of generic distinction has shifted from subject to form by promoting formal considerations from their subordinate role in the earlier system to a dominant role in the later one. The margin has become canonical and the canon has been marginalized.[19] Elwert's insight provides us with an understanding of the evolution from one system to the other. The two systems were not, of course, totally dissimilar or unrelated.

A more extreme version of this view has been taken by the musicologist Nigel Wilkins, who asserts that the *formes fixes* were indeed fixed clearly and simply in terms of musical form.[20] Wilkins, following the tradition of speaking of Provençal and Old French genres together, defines the musical form of the ballade, for example, as I I II, which, as he observes, is "the most common underlying pattern of the troubadour and trouvère *chanson*" (p. 339), that is, Dante's *pedes* and *cauda*. Such a pattern is, as Wilkins rightly says, "one of great simplicity but one which offers endless possibilities for variation" (p. 338). It is not, however, the kind of "forme fixe" or "forme rebelle" that Banville meant; indeed, it is fixed on a level of a certain abstraction from the text, an abstraction which remains palpable as long as we conceive the poetry in musical terms. Even in musical terms the pattern was never obligatory, as we have seen. When the poets ceased to be musicians, as happened after Machaut with Deschamps, Christine de Pizan, and others, the hard shape of that former musical pattern became increasingly difficult to grasp. Wilkins justifies the term and concept of the *formes fixes*, which he accepts axiomatically and without discussion, by assuming musical form in cases where it may have been only remembered, or perhaps had been quite forgotten. Furthermore he justifies it in a way which overrides any fundamental distinction between the genres of the troubadours and the trouvères in Old French, on the one hand, and the Middle French poets on the other.[21]

Georges Lote takes the more reasonable view, in my opinion, when he writes of Machaut's array of genres in the *Remède de Fortune*:

> Son but a été, en effet, de donner à ses contemporains un tableau complet des formes lyriques alors en usage.... Il renonçait ainsi à l'art des troubadours, qui ne connaissaient que des chansons librement construites, dont chacune avait sa facture propre...; désormais

ne régneraient plus que les poèmes à forme fixe, seules dignes d'être admirés et cultivés.[22]

[His goal was, in effect, to give his contemporaries a complete survey of lyrical forms then in use.... He therefore moved beyond the art of the troubadours, who were familiar with freely constructed songs, each with its own composition ... ; from then on only poems with fixed form would dominate—the only ones (judged) worthy to be admired and cultivated.]

The *formes fixes* are relatively fixed, varying within parameters more narrowly restrictive than the troubadour canso or the trouvère chanson.

III.

When Christine began writing poetry in the 1390s, she confronted a dynamic situation. To judge by the definitions soon to be propounded by her friend Deschamps or by Christine's own practice, the genres allowed a wide range of experimentation.[23] Christine finds her position after the implicit poetics (the *Dit de la panthère* and the *Remède de Fortune*), simultaneous with the first codification by Deschamps, and before the *Arts de seconde rhétorique*, during the process of actual production by Machaut, Deschamps, and others of the forms that would later be called the *tailles nouvelles* or "new cuts." Douglas Kelly has formulated major factors in the emergence of the vernacular arts of poetry, all of which were vigorously in play in the very years when Christine, the young widow, set herself to study: the example of earlier poets to stimulate imitation, in Christine's case most conspicuously Machaut, but many others as well; a conscious reflection on poetic technique, as in the *Dit de la panthère* and the *Remède de Fortune*; formal education such as she personally set out to acquire; and "a desire to distinguish the new literary language."[24] Analogous factors had produced the first Occitan poetic treatise almost two centuries earlier, the *Razos de trobar* of Raimon Vidal de Besalu; by comparison, within the stream of lyric in Old French, Christine found herself in a position like that of a troubadour around 1200.[25]

Kenneth Varty has outlined the variations in Christine's ballades: "The ballade was Christine's favourite fixed form and analysis shows that she was always experimenting with line length, stanza length, and rhyme scheme. She rarely wrote two ballades on exactly the same pattern. In fact, if one takes into account line length, stanza length, rhyme scheme, and the use of masculine and feminine rhymes, not one of the sixty-nine ballades contained in this anthology is exactly the same as another."[26] Suzanne Bagoly has analyzed Christine's total production of ballades, numbering 290, and found 68 distinct structures ("Christine de Pizan et l'art de 'dictier' ballades," p. 43). As for the virelais, Varty observes that the three in his anthology "are all different in line length, one having seven, one eight, and one ten syllables per line, and they all differ in the arrangement of masculine and feminine rhymes" (p. xxxi). These forms do not seem to be fixed, if fixed means "regulated in advance, in a precise manner and once and for all" [réglé d'avance, de façon précise et une fois pour toutes], as it does for the *Grand Larousse de la langue française* ([1973], 3:1965).

In his edition of Christine's poetry, Maurice Roy included 427 examples of lyric genres. This means that Christine single-handedly wrote almost one-fifth as many lyric poems as all the trouvères put together, or all the troubadours; if we added her even more prolific colleague Deschamps, with his 1,500-odd ballades, the two of them would about balance the lyric production in the *langue d'oïl* during the thirteenth century. On a quantitative basis, a distinction between major and minor genres in Christine's work comes easily to mind. There are 263 ballades, or 62 percent of her lyric output; 74 rondeaux, or 17 percent; and 70 *jeux à vendre*, or 16 percent. These three genres account for 95 percent of her total. The other three are the virelais, 16 in number, or 4 percent; the two lais, less than 1 percent; and the two complaintes amoureuses, also less than 1 percent. The overall pattern recalls, once again, that of the troubadours, who concentrated about 80 percent of their work in three genres, the canso with 40 percent, the *sirventes* with 20 percent, and the *cobla* with 20 percent. The six genres practiced by Christine differ from the seven defined by Deschamps in the *Art de dictier* because she omits the *serventois, sotte chanson,* and *pastourelle,* and adds the *jeux à vendre* and the *complaintes.*[27]

If we survey Christine's lyric output while attempting to suppress the term *formes fixes* in our minds, we observe a certain variety in gross exterior size. Her ballades range in length from twenty-one lines to forty-three; the rondeaux, from seven to twenty-two; the *jeux à vendre*, from four to ten. (For the whole array see the appendix.) I submit that no one considering these observations would be likely to propose the term *formes fixes* to describe them, particularly not with the exact meaning that Banville intended, as poems "for which tradition has irrevocably fixed the number of verses that they must contain and the order in which these verses must be arranged" [pour lesquels la tradition a irrévocablement fixé le nombre de vers qu'ils doivent contenir et l'ordre dans lequel ces vers doivent être disposés]. A more reasonable suggestion would observe the characteristic use of the refrain, implicit in the last part of Banville's definition. A refrain occurs at the end of each of the three stanzas of the ballade (and again at the end of the envoi, when there is one); in the rondeau, at the beginning of the first stanza, the end of the second, and the end of the third and last; and in Christine's virelais, at the beginning of the first stanza, the end of the third, and the end of the fifth and last. The *jeux à vendre* do not repeat a refrain within a single composition, but they begin with a refrain-like element, "Je vous vends . . . " [I offer to sell you] whatever item is selected to set the rhyme for the individual poem, with occasional variations in word order.[28] The two *lais*, of 266 and 246 lines, proceed in pairs of metrically matched stanzas, including the first and last, the second and third, the fourth and fifth, and so on. The two complaintes amoureuses are written in identical stanzas of sixteen lines, one running to twelve stanzas, the other to fifteen.

Clearly *formes fixes* is too strong a term to describe Christine's practice. Suzanne Bagoly made the same observation on the basis of Christine's ballades:

> La diversité des dispositions de rimes et de rythmes, évidente même pour qui en ignore le chiffre exact, justifierait quelque réticence envers l'expression de "forme fixe" qui qualifie la ballade. Sans nier sa pertinence progressive au cours du XVe siècle, on lui préférerait ici un synonyme moins exclusif comme "forme limitée" ou "arrêtée": appliquée aux rondeaux, ballades, virelais . . . , il les discrimine toujours des poèmes extensibles à souhait. . . . ("Christine de Pizan et l'art de 'dictier' ballades," p. 43)

> [The diversity of (Christine's) patterns of rhymes and rhythms, which is obvious even for someone who does not know the exact number, would justify reservations regarding the expression "fixed form" which describes the ballade. Without denying its increasing appropriateness later in the fifteenth century, here we would prefer a less exclusive synonym such as "limited" or "arrested" form; applied to the rondeaux, ballades, and virelais, such a synonym distinguishes them from poems which may be freely extended. . . .]

But the terms Bagoly proposes, "limited" or "arrested" forms, say little about the mechanism which prevents their being freely extended. The key term "refrain" is encumbered by its usage in the Old French *chansons à refrain*, which, though they may be considered the source of Middle French practice, do not employ refrains in the same manner as do the ballade, the rondeau, and the virelai.[29] I suggest that Zink's expression cited above, "poèmes à formes fixes, lovés autour de leur refrain" [poems with fixed forms, coiled around their refrain], might be condensed into a useful term such as *poèmes lovés* (*poèmes à formes lovées*) or, to avoid the connotation of technical maritime language, *poèmes enroulés* (*poèmes à formes enroulées*), meaning poems coiled or wound around their refrains or themselves.

Some such term may help us to see in a new light the formal constraints to which Christine willingly subjected herself. We should appreciate that her variation in form can be palpably functional. The *jeux à vendre*, for example, range from four to ten lines, but always in an even number because they are composed in rhymed couplets, and the inspiration of the moment provides more or less to say, in these very occasional pieces, about a particular item offered for sale. As for the ballade, why should we not suppose that its variable form was adapted to suit the inspiration of a particular refrain? This is obviously the case when, exceptionally, the refrain itself expands to two lines instead of one.[30] It is true in another way when, at the end of her collection of rondeaux, Christine winds down from a group of twelve-liners to a final series in seven lines apiece, with the line-length decreasing from five syllables to four, then to three, then to two, and finally to one syllable.[31] Far from fixed, such form is wittily playful.

By freeing ourselves from an obsession with supposedly fixed forms, we may also learn to appreciate more fully the structures which Christine develops in other dimensions of the poetic artifact. Every reader of the *Cent ballades d'Amant et de Dame* has felt the subtlety with which she creates the implicit narrative running from beginning to end of this love story, which is a proto-epistolary novel in lyric form. Earlier, in the *Cent balades* she had experimented with sequences of poems that project over shorter arcs, beginning or breaking off in ways difficult to predict and sometimes difficult to be sure about, like snatches of passionate conversation overheard in a crowded room.[32] Another sort of overarching structure recurs coherently in the *Cent balades*, the virelais, and the rondeaux, all of which take the widow's grief [*deuil*] as their point of departure; they then move on to poems of love, their principal subject, interspersed with occasional reflections on fortune, ethics, or politics; and they conclude on a note of religion. Unlike Varty, I do not find the subject matter of Christine's rondeaux any less serious than that of her ballades or virelais—or indeed very different from theirs—although the treatment of a given subject may vary in tone.[33]

I have chosen *Cent balades*, no. 6 to illustrate the nonformalistic achievement of Christine's *tailles nouvelles*. It is one of the opening sequence of poems on her grief, "deuil," which provides the poem's first word. The little we know about the personal experience motivating the poem sets Christine apart from legions of other medieval poets, and I think it perverse to neglect that personal element. I also think it odd to patronize her as a conventional, technically accomplished versifier while observing that her most characteristic theme is that of her bereavement in a lyric tradition which very rarely wrote of marriage at all.

> Deuil engoisseux, rage desmesurée,
> Grief desespoir, plein de forsennement,
> Langour sanz fin, vie maleüree
> Pleine de plour, d'engoisse et de tourment,   4
> Cuer doloreux qui vit obscurement,
> Tenebreux corps sus le point de perir,
> Ay, sanz cesser, continuellement;
> Et si ne puis ne garir ne morir.   8
>
> Fierté, durté de joye separée,
> Triste penser, parfont gemissement,
> Engoisse grant en las cuer enserrée,
> Courroux amer porté covertement,   12
> Morne maintien sanz resjoïssement,
> Espoir dolent qui tous biens fait tarir,
> Si sont en moy, sanz partir nullement;
> Et si ne puis ne garir ne morir.   16
>
> Soussi, anuy qui tous jours a durée,
> Aspre veillier, tressaillir en dormant,
> Labour en vain, a chiere alangourée
> En grief travail infortunéement,   20
> Et tout le mal, qu'on puet entierement
> Dire et penser sanz espoir de garir,
> Me tourmentent desmesuréement;
> Et si ne puis ne garir ne morir.   24
>
> Princes, priez a Dieu que bien briefment
> Me doint la mort, s'autrement secourir

Ne veult le mal ou languis durement;
Et si ne puis ne garir ne morir.   28

[Grief full of anguish, rage without measure,
Heavy despair, full of insanity,
Langour without end, an unhappy life
Full of tears, anguish and torment,   4
A grief-stricken heart that lives in darkness,
A shadowy body on the verge of perishing,
I have, ceaselessly, continually;
And yet I can neither recover nor die.   8

Pride, harshness divided from joy,
Sad thought, profound moaning,
Great anguish compressed in a weary heart,
Bitter anger borne in secret,   12
Mournful behavior without rejoicing,
Grieving hope that withers all good things,
Are indeed in me, without any relief;
And yet I can neither recover nor die.   16

Care, worry that lasts forever,
Bitter wakefulness, trembling in sleep,
Toil in vain, with a grief-stricken face
In heavy travail under adverse fate,   20
And all the pain that can ever be said
And thought, with no hope of cure,
Torment me without measure;
And yet I can neither recover nor die.   24

Princes, pray God to give me death
Very soon, unless He intends to assuage
The pain in which I languish severely;
And yet I can neither recover nor die.]   28

The poem lists the effects of Christine's bereavement, filling the first six lines of each stanza with a series of nouns or noun phrases. The seventh line provides the verb: "Ay" [I have] in the first stanza, then "sont" [are] in the second, then "tourmentent" [torment] in the third, marking gradual loss of agency and progressive victimization. The refrain situates the widow insistently between recovery and death, and the envoi begs for death if she cannot recover. Bereavement, depicted as a pitiless disease, is a "mal" in which she languishes.

The immobility of the refrain contrasts with the diversity of Christine's torments, which range to include repeated contradiction. The first stanza begins with emotions: anguished grief, intemperate anger, heavy despair driving her out of her mind. These emotions vary from the compression of anguish to release of feeling in anger, back again to heavy despair, and out again to madness. Alternately crushed and exploding, Christine suffers exhaustion. She turns to physical symptoms: tears, a grieving heart "that lives in darkness" [qui vit obscurement] and her "tenebreux corps" [shadowy body]. The words "obscurement" and "tenebreux" cloak her grief in mystery. The second stanza begins astonishingly with "fierté"—pride in the husband she has lost? in her survival skills? in her studies?[34] Then it reverts to the harshness of joy remembered, to sadness, sighs, anguish, bitter anger, mournful behavior, and ends, surprisingly again, on "espoir dolent"—hope that contradicts the despair of the first stanza, but hope so mournful that it withers all good things. The third stanza becomes yet more physical: cares and worries, bitter wakefulness, trembling in sleep (but how does she know? another mystery), pointless labor, a grief-stricken face, and hopelessness—contradicting, again, the hope of the stanza before.

The poem enacts an experience of living grief which finds no rest. It does so stretched tight between the "garir ne morir" of the refrain and molded strictly within its three stanzas of identical form. It is anything but a fixed form as an end in itself—rather it expresses emotional dynamics constrained. Just as Christine's bereavement launched her literary career, so in this poem it propels her into form.

It is tragedy in this poem that wears the tight-fitting buskin, Gautier's "cothurne étroit." Form here contains more than the poet's "pur caprice," as Banville would have had it. Perhaps Gautier's "cothurne" and his warning against "contraintes fausses" were a response and a warning to the capricious Banville. Undoubtedly Gautier was the greater poet, but it was Banville who launched the *formes fixes*, term and concept. Although his successors in the study of versification, struggling with the shortcomings of his notion, have redefined it in various ways, it implies, simply because it isolates form, that form precedes thought and is somehow more fundamental to the system. Such an intuition strikes me as Parnassian and gratuitous; even in Christine's *jeux à vendre*, the function of a witty, flirtatious, even capricious social game is coextensive and coeval with form. The *formes fixes* are a misnomer and a misreading from which we should distance ourselves.

To return to the broad picture, we may attempt to contrast Christine's genre system, as a synecdoche for that of Middle French, with the genre system of her predecessors, particularly the troubadours. Christine and her contemporaries wrote vastly more lyric poems than the troubadours did, to the best of our knowledge, while compressing their work into tighter constraints. One change in evolving lyric practice was the move from musical composition in the troubadours, the trouvères, and Machaut to the nonmusical composition that Deschamps called "musique naturele," and that we call lyric poetry.[35] If it is true that a prolific troubadour might have turned out two or three songs a year,[36] no doubt Christine's freedom from musical exertion was one factor in her dazzling facility. But another factor in the specialization of lyric form must have been its contrast with other forms that were not employed by the trouvères or troubadours, forms such as narrative verse and prose. Christine's ballades of bereavement contrast with *L'Avision* and other retellings of her grief. The lyric impulse has become not only more tightly constrained but also more distinctively, hence more intensely, lyrical.

Appendix

Number of Lines (N) in Christine's Lyric Poems

Ballades

N	Cent b.s	Bal. d'e. f.	Aut. b.	Encore a. b.	A. & d.	Total
21	43					43
23					24	24
24	36					36
25	4	2	6		16	28
26					10	10
27	1					1
28	13	1	27	1	31	73
29					2	2
30					1	1
31	1		11	1	11	24
32					2	2
33			1			1

N	Cent b.s	Bal. d'e. f.	Aut. b.	Encore a. b.	A. & d.	Total
34		1	4	3	3	11
35			2			2
36	1		1		1	3
37			1			1
40	1					1
43			1			1
	100	4	54	5	101	264

Rondeaux

N	Rondeaux	Autres b.	Encore a. b.	Total
7	13			13
10	19			19
12	32	1	4	37
17	2			2
18	1			1
22	2			2
	69	1	4	74

Jeux à vendre

N	Total
4	19
6	44
8	6
10	1
	70

Virelays

N	Total
22	8
25	3
28	1
29	1
35	3
	16

Lays

N	Total
246	1
266	1
	2

Complaintes amoureuses

N	Total
192	1
240	1
	2

Notes

1. The list of Old French genres follows Pierre Bec, *La lyrique française au moyen-âge (XIIe-XIIIe siècles)*, vol. 1, but excludes the "registre pieux." The list of Middle French genres follows Warner Forrest Patterson, *Three Centuries of French Poetic Theory*, p. 60, but excludes "dramatic verse," "longer poems in couplets," "longer poems in lyrical strophes," "pastoral verse (neither pastourelle nor eclogue)," and "poetic prose." The list of Renaissance lyric genres follows Patterson (pp. 204–5) but excludes "discours," "dramatic verse," and "epic verse."

2. This is not to deny the antecedents of later genres in earlier practice. For example, the prehistory of the Middle French ballade can be traced to the Old French *ballette* and the troubadour *balada*. On this last form see Pierre Bec, "Pour une typologie de la balada occitane." Nevertheless the ballade became a major option—a significant element in the system of genres—only in Middle French. Similarly the rondeau evolved from the *rondet de carole*.

3. Nicole de Margival, *Le dit de la panthère d'amours*, ed. Henry A. Todd. See also, on the title of the *dit* and on the songs it contains, Ernest Hoepffner, "Les poésies lyriques du *Dit de la panthère* de Nicole de Margival."

4. Guillaume de Machaut, "*Remede de Fortune*," vv. 401–6.

5. Eustache Deschamps, *Oeuvres complètes*, vol. 7, pp. 266–92.

6. Ernest Langlois, ed., *Receuil d'arts de seconde rhétorique*, p. 12: "Taille: Ce mot, jusqu'au commencement du XVIe siècle, signifie: Disposition générale de la strophe. Il implique tous les détails de la construction de celle-ci"; Gaëtan Hecq and Louis Paris, *La poétique française au moyen âge et à la Renaissance*, p. 212. For Hecq and Paris, *taille* does not seem to mean "genre."

7. Joachim Du Bellay, *La deffence et illustration de la langue françoyse*, Livre II, chapitre iv, pp. 201–3. For the absence of the adjective *fixe*, see Suzanne Hanon, ed., *Joachim Du Bellay; taille* does not occur either, although "genre de poëme" does (II.iv, p. 210.5; II.vii, p. 262.2).

8. Thédore de Banville, *Petit traité de poésie française*. I use the edition published by G. Charpentier, 1883, p. 185; Banville's italics. For discussion of the *Petit traité*, see Alvin Harms, *Théodore de Banville*, pp. 149–63; Italo Siciliano, *Dal romanticismo al simbolismo*, pp. 297–310.

9. Théophile Gautier, *Poésies complètes*, 1:cxxviii.

10. Gautier, 3:128. The key word *forme* in vol. 2 was a revision. Cf. the "Variante inédite": "Oui, je veux qu'à l'artiste / Courbé sur son travail / Résiste / Vers, marbre, onyx, émail." Charles de Louvenjoul, *Histoire des oeuvres de Théophile Gautier*, 2:137.

11. Banville's coinage found an early, unacknowledged echo in E. O. Lubarsch, *Französische Verslehre:* "Die in der französischen Verskunst überlieferten Gedichte fester Form (*poèmes traditionnels à forme fixe*) sind Gedichte, deren Form und Umgang genau vorgeschrieben sind" [The poems of fixed form transmitted in French poetic art ("traditional poems with a fixed form") are poems whose form

and disposition are strictly prescribed] (p. 375). In 1896 Hecq and Paris used the term in their *Poétique française au moyen âge et à la Renaissance*, but not exactly as Banville had: they wrote of the *conte*, or short story, that "ce genre n'a pas de forme fixe" [this genre has no fixed form] (p. 66). In 1903 L. E. Kastner included a chapter "Of Certain Fixed Forms of French Poetry" in his *History of French Versification*, pp. 233–94, and listed Banville's *Petit traité* in his bibliography. According to Clive Scott, *French Verse-Art*, during "the period between 1850 and 1900 . . . fixed forms underwent a dramatic revival, thanks to the promotional energy of Théodore de Banville" (p. 155).

12. Georges Lote, *Histoire du vers français*, 2:274. For a table of various stanza lengths in ballades by eleven poets including Christine, see Daniel Poirion, *Le poète et le prince*, pp. 374–75.

13. Lote, *Histoire du vers français*, 2:292. A table of rhyme patterns in rondeaux by six poets including Christine is in Poirion, *Le poète et le prince*, pp. 333–34.

14. "'Ordered fantasy' might well be a term used to describe the virelai form," according to Robert L. Gieber, "Poetic Elements of Rhythm in the Ballades, Rondeaux and Virelais of Guillaume de Machaut," p. 9. Poirion offers a table of rhyme schemes in the virelai and observes: "Ce tableau fait d'abord apparaître l'intention des poètes de varier, surtout dans le détail, leurs combinaisons de rimes, pour ne pas faire exactement la même chose que les autres" [This table shows, first, the poets' intention to vary, especially in detail, their combination of rhymes, to avoid doing exactly the same thing as the others] (*Le poète et le prince*, pp. 344–45).

15. Michel Zink, "Lyrique (poésie)," p. 974.

16. Thus Lote, reviewing the variety of the rondeau, complains of "une infraction aux règles" (*Histoire du vers français*, 2:292). Hoepffner writes of "des règles de plus en plus étroites et mesquines," and of a "réglementation pédante et sévère" in his study, "Les poésies lyriques du *Dit de la panthère* de Nichole de Margival," p. 228. Suzanne Bagoly defends Christine against criticisms that she indulged in excessive diversity of form; see "Christine de Pizan et l'art de 'dictier' ballades."

17. W. Theodor Elwert, *Traité de versification française des origines à nos jours*, paragraphs 194, 209.

18. "Dante discusses this tripartite system as opposed to the through-composed tune or *oda continua* in *De vulgari eloquentia* II, x–xi; far from making the former a prerequisite of the canso, he expressly states that the *oda continua* was equally acceptable, and that Arnaut Daniel set most of his cansos to through-composed melodies, a style that Dante himself followed in *Al poco giorno*" (Frank M. Chambers, *An Introduction to Old Provençal Versification*, 127 n). Roger Dragonetti observed among thirteenth-century *trouvères* a large number of stanzas comprising *pedes* and *cauda*, or *pedes* and *versus* (that is, "feet" and "verses," showing repetition in the *cauda* as well); see his *La technique poétique des trouvères dans la chanson courtoise*, p. 384. "The actual stanza shapes we encounter in the monophonic repertories often belie the terminology [i.e., Dante's terminology] in one or another of their aspects. . . . So while very often the stanza divisions encountered in

both text and music can be described by the judicious use of Dante's terminology, the terminology itself, just like the myriad other technical terms that can characterize different types of stanzas, should not replace our direct appreciation of the variety of formal inventions typical of medieval song-stanzas. These frequently defy any categorization whatsoever, and our task becomes, as always, to move beyond categories to assess rhetorical purpose or expressive intent": Margaret Switten, "Remarks on Versification with Some Definitions of Poetic Styles and Forms," pp. 68–69. On the *ouvert* and *clos*, see Lote, *Histoire du vers français*, 2:213–14.

19. The formula is Elzbieta Sklodowska's, in "Ardiente paciencia y *La casa de los espíritus*: traición y tradición en el discurso del post-boom," p. 33, with reference to Jurij Tynjanov, "On Literary Evolution" (1929), translated into English in *Readings in Russian Poetics*.

20. Nigel Wilkins, "The Structure of Ballades, Rondeaux and Virelais in Froissart and in Christine de Pisan."

21. I have examined the inseparability of Old French romance narrative from Provençal lyric in my "Old Occitan as a Lyric Language."

22. Lote, *Histoire du vers français*, 2:243. See also Jean Frappier, *La poésie lyrique française aux XIIe et XIIIe siècles*, p. 232: "Quant aux formes lyriques, elles évolueront après lui [Rutebeuf] non pas vers plus de liberté, mais au contraire vers plus de contrainte et vers le triomphe des genres fixes, ballade, chant royal, rondeau et virelai" [As for the lyric forms, they would evolve after Rutebeuf not toward greater liberty, but to the contrary toward greater constraint and toward the triumph of the fixed genres, ballade, chant royal, rondeau, and virelai].

23. She calls him "chier maistre et amis" in her *Epistre a Eustace Mourel* (1403), *Œuvres poétiques de Christine de Pisan,* ed. Maurice Roy, II, pp. 295–301. Deschamps responded with a ballade; see *Œuvres complètes de Eustache Deschamps*, vol. 6, p. 251.

24. Douglas Kelly, *The Arts of Poetry and Prose*, pp. 172–73.

25. On the development of the *arts poétiques*, see Lote, *Histoire du vers français*, 2:239–52.

26. Kenneth Varty, ed., *Christine de Pisan's Ballades, Rondeaux and Virelais: An Anthology*, p. xxviii.

27. On the relatively rare *jeux à vendre*, see Roy, *Oeuvres poétiques de Christine de Pisan*, I:xxxiv–xxxv, and Rejean Bergeron, "Examen d'une oeuvre vouée à l'oubli."

28. Two examples (ed. Roy, I:187, 189):

1 (She)	9 (He)
Je vous vens la passerose.	Du pré d'Amours vous vens l'usage.
—Belle, dire ne vous ose	—Pas n'apert a vostre visage
Comment Amours vers vous me tire,	Que vous soiez d'amours malade;
Si l'apercevez tout sanz dire.	Car la maladie est moult sade
	Dont le visage en riens n'empire;
	Mais tel n'a nul mal qui souspire.

29. Zink, "Refrain," p. 1248.
30. *Cent balades* (ed. Roy, I), nos. 7, 17, 19, 55, 61, 92; *Autres balades*, nos. 25, 34; *Encore aultres balades*, no. 4; *Cent ballades d'Amant et de Dame*, ed. Jacqueline Cerquiglini, nos. 4, 16, 18, 22, 24, 47, 60, 62, 63, 87.
31. Texts of the four final rondeaux in the collection:

66	67	68	69
Amoureux oeil,	Ma dame,	Je vois	Dieux
Plaisant archier;	Secours!	Jouer.	Est.
De toy me dueil,	Par m'ame,	Au bois	Quieux?
Amoureux oeil,	Ma dame.	Je vois.	Dieux.
Car ton accueil	J'enflame	Pour nois	Cieulx
Me vens trop chier,	D'amours,	Trouver	Plaist
Amoureux oeil.	Ma dame.	Je vois.	Dieux.

32. See James C. Laidlaw, "L'unité des *Cent Balades*."
33. Bereavement: *Cent balades*, nos. 1, 5, 6, 9, 11, 14, 15 (on the death of her mother), 17–20; *Virelays*, nos. 1, 15; *Rondeaux*, nos. 1–7, 11, 55. Fortune: *Cent balades*, nos. 7, 10, 12, 97; *Virelays*, nos. 4, 14; *Rondeau*, no. 62. Ethics: *Cent balades*, nos. 2, 4, 92, 94, 96, 98; *Virelay*, no. 12; *Rondeau*, no. 63. Politics: *Cent balades*, no. 95 (the illness of Charles VI). Religion: *Cent balades*, no. 99; *Virelay*, no. 16; *Rondeau*, no. 69. For Varty, the ballade was "an adequate vehicle for almost every kind of subject" and the virelai was "used for all kinds of subjects," while the rondeau "was rarely used as a vehicle for serious subject-matter" (pp. xxviii–xxxi).
34. Poirion, *Le poète et le prince*, p. 254: "Son comportement devant le malheur, son laborieux apprentissage philosophique, cette conquête méthodique de la société masculine entreprise par une pauvre veuve, ne s'expliquent que par l'ambition et la volonté de ne pas s'abandonner à la mauvaise fortune. . . . En tout cas on comprend mal son ambition littéraire, son projet poétique, sa création lyrique, si l'on ne reconnaît pas dans son travail et ses œuvres un effort constant pour se maîtriser, s'élever, s'améliorer" [Her behavior when faced by unhappiness, her laborious apprenticeship in philosophy, this methodical conquest of masculine society by a poor widow, cannot be explained except by ambition and the determination not to abandon herself to misfortune. . . . In any case, we fail to understand her literary ambition, her poetic project, her lyric creation, unless we recognize in her effort and her poetic accomplishment a constant effort to control herself, to raise herself, to better herself].
35. Kenneth Varty, "Deschamps's *Art de dictier*."
36. Bertran de Born seems to have composed forty-seven songs over seventeen years, Guiraut Riquier one hundred and one songs over thirty-eight years. Both troubadours averaged less than three songs a year. Cf. Martín de Riquer, *Los trovadores: historia literaria y textos*, 1:71.

Works Cited

Bagoly, Suzanne. "Christine de Pizan et l'art de 'dictier' ballades." *Moyen Age* 92 (1986): 41–67.

Banville, Théodore de. *Petit traité de poésie française.* Paris: Lemerre, 1872.

Bec, Pierre. *La lyrique française au moyen-âge (XIIe–XIIIe siècles: contribution à une typologie des genres poétiques médiévaux.* 2 vols. Paris: Picard, 1977–78.

———. "Pour une typologie de la balada occitane: A propos de la pièce 'Quant lo gilos er foras'." In *Hommage à Jean-Charles Payen,* pp. 53–65. Caen: Université de Caen, 1989.

Bergeron, Rejean. "Examen d'une œuvre vouée à l'oubli: Les *jeux à vendre* de Christine de Pizan." In *Préludes à la Renaissance: Aspects de la vie intellectuelle en France au XVe siècle,* ed. Carla Bozzolo and Ezio Ornato, pp. 163–89. Paris: Editions du CNRS, 1992.

Christine de Pisan. *Cent ballades d'amant et de dame.* Ed. Jacqueline Cerquiglini. Paris: Union Générale d'Édition, 1982.

———. *Œuvres poétiques.* Ed. Maurice Roy. SATF. 3 vols. Paris: Firmin-Didot, 1886–96.

Chambers, Frank M. *An Introduction to Old Provençal Versification.* Philadelphia: American Philosophical Society, 1985.

Deschamps, Eustache. *Œuvres complètes de Eustache Deschamps.* Ed. Marquis de Queux de Saint-Hilaire and Gaston Raynaud. Société des Anciens Textes Français. 11 vols. Paris: Firmin Didot, 1878–1903.

Dragonetti, Roger. *La technique poétique des trouvères dans la chanson courtoise.* Brugge: De Tempel, 1960.

Du Bellay, Joachim. *La deffence et illustration de la langue françoyse.* Ed. Henri Chamard. Paris: Albert Fontemoing, 1904.

Elwert, W. Theodor. *Traité de versification française des origines à nos jours.* Paris: Klincksieck, 1965.

Frappier, Jean. *La poésie lyrique française aux XIIe et XIIIe siècles: Les auteurs et les genres.* Paris: Centre de Documentation Universitaire, 1954.

Gautier, Théophile. *Poésies complètes de Théophile Gautier.* Ed. René Jasinski. Paris: Nizet, 1970.

Gieber, Robert L. "Poetic Elements of Rhythm in the Ballades, Rondeaux and Virelais of Guillaume de Machaut." *Romanic Review* 73 (1982): 1–12.

Hanon, Suzanne. *Joachim Du Bellay: La deffence et illustration de la langue françoyse, Concordance.* Odense: Odense University Press, 1974.

Harms, Alvin. *Théodore Banville.* Boston: Twayne, 1983.

Hecq, Gaëtan, and Louis Paris. *La poétique française au moyen âge et à la Renaissance.* Paris: Emile Bouillon, 1896; reprint, Geneva: Slatkine, 1978.

Hoepffner, Ernest. "Les poésies lyriques du *Dit de la panthère* de Nichole de Margival." *Romania* 46 (1920): 204–30.

Kastner, L. E. *History of French Versification.* Oxford: Clarendon, 1903.

Kelly, Douglas. *The Arts of Poetry and Prose.* Typologie des Sources du Moyen Age Occidental. Turnhout: Brepols, 1991.

Laidlaw, James Cameron. "L'unité des *Cent balades.*" In *The City of Scholars: New Approaches to Christine de Pizan*, ed. Margarete Zimmermann and Dina De Rentiis, pp. 97–106. Berlin: De Gruyter, 1994.
Langlois, Ernest. *Recueil d'arts de seconde rhétorique.* Paris: Imprimerie Nationale, 1902.
Lote, Georges. *Histoire du vers français.* 2 vols. Paris: Boivin, 1949–55.
Louvenjoul, Charles de. *Histoire des œuvres de Théophile Gautier.* Paris: G. Charpentier, 1887.
Lubarsch, E. O. *Französische Verslehre.* Berlin: Weidmann, 1879.
Machaut, Guillaume de. *"Le Jugement du roy de Behaigne" and "Remede de fortune."* Ed. James I. Wimsatt and William W. Kibler. Athens: University of Georgia Press, 1988.
Nicole de Margival. *Le dit de la panthère d'amours par Nicole de Margival.* Ed. Henry A. Todd. Société des Anciens Textes Français. Paris: Firmin Didot, 1883.
Paden, William D. "Old Occitan as a Lyric Language: The Insertions from Occitan in Three Thirteenth-Century French Romances." *Speculum* 68 (1993): 36–53.
Patterson, Warner Forrest. *Three Centuries of French Poetic Theory.* University of Michigan Publications: Language and Literature, 15. Ann Arbor: University of Michigan Press, 1935.
Poirion, Daniel. *Le poète et le prince: L'évolution du lyrisme courtois de Guillaume de Machaut à Charles d'Orléans.* Paris: Presses Universitaires de France, 1965.
Riquier, Martín de. *Los trovadores: Historia literaria y textos.* 3 vols. Barcelona: Planeta, 1975.
Scott, Clive. *French Verse-Art: A Study.* Cambridge: Cambridge University Press, 1980.
Siciliano, Italo. *Dal romanticismo al simbolismo: Théodore de Banville, poeta, commediografo, prosatore (1823–1891).* Turin: Fratelli Bocca, 1927.
Sklodowska, Elzbieta. "Ardiente paciencia y *La casa de los espíritus*: Traición y tradición en el discurso del post-boom." *Discurso literario* 9.1 (1991): 33–40.
Switten, Margaret. "Remarks on Versification with Some Definitions of Poetic Styles and Forms." In *The Medieval Lyric: Commentary Volume*, ed. Howell Chickering and Margaret Switten, pp. 59–75. South Hadley, Mass.: Mount Holyoke College, 1988.
Tynjanov, Jurij. "On Literary Evolution." In *Readings in Russian Poetics: Formalist and Structuralist Views*, pp. 66–78. Cambridge, Mass.: MIT Press, 1971.
Varty, Kenneth. "Deschamps's *Art de dictier.*" *French Studies* 19 (1965): 164–68.
———. ed. *Christine de Pisan's Ballades, Rondeaux and Virelais: An Anthology.* Leicester: Leicester University Press, 1965.
Wilkins, Nigel. "The Structure of Ballades, Rondeaux and Virelais in Froissart and in Christine de Pisan." *French Studies* 3 (1969): 337–48.
Zink, Michel. "Lyrique (poésie)." In *Dictionnaire des lettres françaises: Le moyen âge*, ed. G. Hasenohr and M. Zink, pp. 966–76. Rev. 2d ed. Paris: Fayard, 1992.
———. "Refrain." In *Dictionnaire des lettres françaises: Le moyen âge*, ed. G. Hasenohr and M. Zink, p. 1248. Rev. 2d ed. Paris: Fayard, 1992.

∾ *The Marriage of Lyric and Narrative*

ART TWO

∽ CHAPTER 2

The *Cent balades*: The Marriage of Content and Form

JAMES C. LAIDLAW

The Manuscripts of the *Cent balades*

In the *Livre de Christine* [Book of Christine], the collection of Christine de Pizan's works that was begun in 1399 and completed in June 1402, pride of place is given to the *Cent balades*, which are copied first and introduced by the earliest known version of the miniature which shows Christine writing in her study. Two copies of the *Livre de Christine* survive, Chantilly, Musée Condé, 492-93, ff. 2a-22d, and Paris, Bibliothèque Nationale, fonds fr. 12779, ff. 1a-21d. The texts of the poems were revised before being copied in the Duke's Manuscript, acquired by the Duke of Berry in 1408 or 1409, and some further changes were made when they were prepared for inclusion in the Queen's Manuscript, completed in 1410 or 1411.[1] Christine must have been generally well satisfied with her first version, however, for the alterations are few in number: some lines are recast; exceptionally, the Queen's Manuscript gives an entirely new version of the third stanza of Ballade 80. The most striking changes affect the envois. The *Livre de Christine* had included only fifteen ballades ending with an envoi, but in the Duke's Manuscript the total increases to seventeen. Although the Queen's Manuscript adds a further envoi, the total remains seventeen, since one envoi was either deleted by Christine or omitted by the scribe. The critical edition of the *Cent balades*, published by Maurice Roy in 1886, contains all eighteen envois.[2]

The *Cent balades* marked Christine's first appearance in print, to adopt today's idiom. She singles them out for special mention when she reviews her literary career in *L'Avision-Christine* of 1405 (old style): "Les musetes des pouetes ... me faisoient rimer complaintes plourables regraittant mon ami mort et le bon temps passé, sicomme il appert au commencement de mes premiers dittiez ou principe de mes *Cent balades*; et meismement, pour passer temps et pour aucune gayeté attraire a mon cuer douloureux, faire ditz amoureux et gais d'autrui sentement, comme je dis en un mien virelay" [The poets' pipes ... made me rhyme tearful complaints, lamenting my dead lover and the good times that are past, as can be seen at the beginning of my first poems at the start of my *Cent balades*; and above all, to pass the time and to bring some joy to my sad heart, they made me compose joyful love poems inspired by the sentiments of other people, as I stated in one of my virelays].[3] For Christine the *Cent balades* constituted a landmark, as that quotation makes clear. A detailed study of the collection will cast light on the beginning of her career and will give answers to important questions: what problems did Christine face as she began to write, what models was she influenced by, and what issues concerned her?

The Ballade before Christine de Pizan

When Christine began to write, the ballade had been common poetic currency for more than two generations. Like her contemporaries, Christine looked back with reverence to Guillaume de Machaut: "Machaut le noble rethorique" [Machaut the noble rhetorician], as Eustache Deschamps described him in the refrains of two ballades lamenting his death; "Guillaume de Machault, le grant retthorique de nouvelle fourme, qui commencha toutes tailles nouvelles" [Guillaume de Machault, the great rhetorician of the new style, who began all the new forms], to quote a later rhetorical manual.[4] That quotation emphasizes Machaut's role as an innovator, crediting him with the development of the new lyric genres—ballade, *chanson royal*, rondeau, and virelay, to name only four. It has become traditional to refer to them as *formes fixes* [fixed forms], a description which is more misleading than helpful, as William Paden's discussion in this volume shows. In a recent discussion of Christine's ballades, Suzanne Bagoly proposes *forme limitée ou arrêtée* [restricted or set form] as an alternative, rightly arguing that the limits of the ballade were fixed but that within those limits variation was permitted, even encouraged.[5]

What were those limits and how did the ballade develop in the years that separate the *Louange des dames*, Machaut's principal collection of lyric poetry, from the *Cent balades*? In considering those changes, it must be remembered that Machaut was as accomplished a musician as he was a poet. He was the foremost practitioner in France of the *ars nova* [new art], the new style of polyphonic music;[6] in Deschamps's estimation he was not only a noble rhetorician but also the "fleur des fleurs de toute melodie" [flower of flowers of all melody] (*Œuvres complètes*, I, p. 245). For Machaut the ballade and the other *formes* were different types of song, whose words should be set to a tune characteristic of the particular genre; music and words shared a common pattern.[7] In its classic form, the ballade consisted of three stanzas of seven or eight lines, ending in a refrain; normally a single line, the refrain could exceptionally be extended to one and a half or two lines. The ballade tune was made up of two musical phrases. The first, shorter phrase was sung twice, accompanying the first two parts of the stanza, the *ouvert* [opening] and the *clos* [closure], which were thus metrically identical; each generally consisted of two lines, rhyming *abab*. The *oultrepassé* [continuation] and the refrain, which together formed the third part of the stanza, were sung to the second, longer musical phrase. The beginning of the oultrepassé was an important junction, therefore, and was often marked by the introduction of a new rhyme. The oultrepassé was followed by the refrain, which gave a focus to each of the stanzas and to the poem as a whole.

Neither Machaut nor Deschamps discusses the refrain, no doubt because its importance seemed self-evident. However, the *Archiloge Sophie* of Jacques Legrand, which was completed about 1400, just after the *Cent balades*, contains some pertinent comments on the subject: "Et finablement on doit faire un refrain, le quel doit estre appartenant et declarié par les vers devant dis; et semblablement on doit tousjours aprés proceder en tendant tousjours a une fin, c'est assavoir a prouver et demonstrer son refrain, et a parler pertinanment a lui, autrement la balade n'est pas bien composee" [And lastly one must compose a refrain which must be appropriate and be elucidated by the lines which are recited before it; and likewise one must always move forward thereafter, always working towards one aim, that is to prove and to demonstrate the refrain and to speak in terms which are pertinent to it; otherwise it is not a well composed ballade].[8] Legrand provides useful criteria for assessing the quality of the refrain and the complete poem. The refrain must be appropriate and to the point [*appartenant*], it must be elucidated [*declarié*] by the lines which precede; the purpose of the stanza must be to prove and to demonstrate [*prouver et demonstrer*] the refrain.

After Machaut's death, poetry and music followed divergent paths. The complexities of the *ars nova* were such that it became rare for poets to write the music for their songs; increasingly, that responsibility passed to professional musicians. Now that poets were less subject to music's restraining influence, the ballade stanza had greater freedom to evolve. The traditional tripartite structure was retained, even though the need for it had become less compelling. However, changes began to be seen in the length and the proportions of the ballade stanza. The shape of the ouvert and the clos did not alter; they continued to be made up of two lines, generally rhyming *abab*. By contrast, the oultrepassé increased in length, often substantially. With Machaut the oultrepassé was generally two or three lines long: with Deschamps, its length ranged from two to ten lines, the average being just over four lines. Instead of counterbalancing the ouvert and the clos, as in earlier ballades, the oultrepassé came to dominate the stanza.

Now that the *formes fixes* no longer combined language and music but relied for their effect on language alone, was their character altered, was their quality impaired? Questions of that nature became matters of contemporary debate, to judge by the defense of poetry unaccompanied by music, which Deschamps presents in his *Art de dictier* of 1392. The treatise contains a provocative definition of music, or rather *musics*, since a sharp distinction is drawn between *musique artificiele* [artificial music] and *musique naturele* [natural music]. The composition of artificial music, that is music as it is understood today, is dismissed as a mechanical exercise which can be learned by the most untutored of men. Natural music is an altogether different matter:

> L'autre musique est appellée *naturele* pour ce qu'elle ne puet estre aprinse a nul, se son propre couraige naturelment ne s'i applique, et est une musique de bouche en proferant paroules metrifiées, aucunesfoiz en *laiz*, autrefoiz en *balades*. . . . Et ja soit ce que . . . les faiseurs de [ceste musique naturele] ne saichent pas communement la musique artificiele ne donner chant par art de notes a ce qu'ilz font, toutesvoies est appellée musique ceste science naturele, pour ce que les diz et chançons . . . ou les livres metrifiez se lisent de bouche, et proferent par voix non pas chantable, tant que les douces paroles ainsi faictes et recordées par voix plaisent aux escoutans qui les oyent. (*Œuvres complètes*, VII [1891], pp. 270–71)

[The other music is termed natural because it cannot be taught to anyone unless his own heart is naturally inclined thereto, and it is a music of the mouth, made by reciting words in meter, sometimes in lays, at other times in ballades. . . . And although . . . the composers of (this natural music) commonly do not know artificial music and do not know how to fit a melody to what they compose, using skill with notes, nevertheless this natural accomplishment is called music because the poems and songs . . . or the books in meter are read aloud, and are presented by a non-singing voice in such a way that the sweet words which have been composed in this manner and are given vocal expression, are enjoyed by the audience which hears them.]

Because the composition of poetry requires both natural ability and inspiration, poetry can properly be called natural music. Poetry, it is emphasized, is directed to an audience; it must be read aloud and performed, for only in that way can this natural music be fully enjoyed. Deschamps states that inspiration will lead the poet to sing of love and to write *a la louenge des dames* [in praise of ladies], a conscious echo of the title of Machaut's collection. However, it is also appropriate for the poet to choose other themes, if the spirit moves him to do so. Here, Deschamps is justifying his own practice, for he wrote ballades on the widest variety of subjects.[9]

One of the ballades cited in the *Art de dictier* has an envoi, a fact to which Deschamps draws particular attention: "Item en ladicte balade a *envoy. Et ne les souloit on point faire anciennement fors es chançons royaulx*" [Also in the said ballade there is an envoi. And in former times it was the custom not to compose an envoi except in the *chansons royales* (lit. the royal songs)] (*Œuvres complètes*, VII, p. 278). The extension of the ballade to include an envoi was a recent development, unknown to Machaut. The envoi took the form of a shortened stanza, which generally began with the vocative *Prince(s)*, for convention demanded that it be addressed to the prince of the *puy d'amours* or poetic academy (*Œuvres complètes*, VII, p. 271). The prince in question may also be a real prince or patron, as reference to Deschamps's works makes clear. Taken together, the introduction of the envoi and the extension of the oultrepassé make the ballades of Deschamps and his contemporaries considerably longer than those of Machaut.[10] Twenty-one or twenty-four lines had been the earlier norm: now ballades of thirty or more lines are quite usual, and poems of more than forty lines are not uncommon.

La Louange des dames

Machaut's poetic practice can be gauged by reference to the *Louange des dames*, his principal collection of lyric poetry. The most recent edition of the work, published in 1972 by Nigel Wilkins, is based on a comparison of all the available manuscripts and comprises 282 poems of which 207 are ballades. In his introduction Wilkins draws attention to the "great diversity of length, form and metre" which the poems exhibit, setting out his findings in tabular form. The table below is based on that of Wilkins but presents the information in a rather different way.[11] It gives more prominence to the refrain and distinguishes more sharply between the isometric ballade, in which all the lines are of the same length, and the heterometric ballade, in which different meters are combined and contrasted.

La Louange des Dames: Structure of the 207 Ballades

Stanza Construction
(a) *Three Isometric Stanzas*   124 poems
7 syllable lines   10 poems
8 syllable lines   14 poems
10 syllable lines   100 poems
(b) *Six Isometric Stanzas (Balade double)*   1 poem
7 syllable lines   1 poem
(c) *Three Heterometric Stanzas*   82 poems
Ballade layée: 10 & 7 syllables (line 5) 51 poems
Other forms   31 poems

Stanza Length
7 lines   120 poems
8 lines   77 poems
9 lines   9 poems
12 lines   1 poem

Refrain
One line   198 poems
1.5 lines   2 poems
2 lines   7 poems

Stanza Forms[12]   45 forms
Used once   36 forms
Used 2 times   4 forms
Used 3 times   1 form
Used 5 times   1 form
    7 lines; 7 syllables; *ababbcC*

Used 11 times   1 form
    7 lines; 8 syllables; *ababbcC*
Used 51 times   1 form
    8 lines; 10 & 7 syllables (line 5);
    ababccdD
Used 93 times   1 form
    7 lines; 10 syllables; *ababbcC*
Envoi   no examples

The collection includes thirty-five ballades that are formally unique. Five other stanza forms are almost as uncommon, being employed on only two or three occasions. Many of these unique or unusual forms are heterometric, combining lines of different lengths in intricate patterns; taken together they account for forty-six poems, just over one fifth of the ballades in the *Louange des dames*.

The effect of these rarer stanza forms is enhanced by being contrasted with the four plainer forms in which the remaining ballades are cast. Machaut employs these four forms so insistently that they become familiar, even standard; they are his *ballades bonnes à tout faire* [general purpose ballade forms]. Three of the four have in common stanzas of seven isometric lines rhyming *ababbcC* and differ only in meter: seven-syllable lines are used in five poems, octosyllables in eleven poems, and decasyllables in ninety-three poems. In the one standard form that remains to be considered, the stanzas are heterometric, but minimally so—seven decasyllables combine with a fifth line of seven syllables, rhyming *ababccdD*. The shorter fifth line is emphatic, for it marks the beginning of the oultrepassé and introduces a new rhyme. Later poets imitated this form so often that it became part of the conventional repertory. In the rhetorical manuals it is generally called a *ballade layée*, a term which embraces both the variety favored by Machaut and other forms which include a single shorter line.[13] The *Louange des dames* contains three other types of ballade layée, but only one example of each of them.[14]

Le Livre des cent balades

Hearing that Christine de Pizan's work was entitled *Cent balades*, a contemporary audience would have made an immediate connection between her collection and another, identical in name, which had appeared in 1389 or 1390, just ten years earlier. The *Livre des cent balades*, as it will be called here to distinguish it from Christine's work, was composed by four poets: Jean le Seneschal, who took the largest part, Boucicaut le Jeune, Jean de Cresecque, and the Count of Eu.[15]

Their hundred poems constitute a narrative which presents the dilemma of a young knight bachelor, faced by the competing claims of *Fausseté* [Fickleness, Flirtation] and *Loyauté* [Loyalty]. In the first fifty ballades the young bachelor is instructed in the rules of chivalry and love by an older, experienced knight who urges him to shun Fickleness and cultivate Loyalty. The second half of the collection is dramatic rather than didactic. Having accepted the knight's advice, the bachelor—Jean le Seneschal himself, as it becomes clear—is tested and teased. The lady he meets is a temptress who proclaims the pleasures of Flirtation and mocks the bachelor for his priggish adherence to old-fashioned standards. Her derision leaves the young knight in turmoil, and he turns to Boucicaut, Cresecque, and the Count of Eu, who pronounce in favor of Loyalty. In the closing poem they invite other lovers to contribute to the debate.

The *Livre des cent balades* uses eleven stanza forms—seven, if minor variations are discounted. They are arranged in a set pattern, each form being used four times before it is relieved and rested, ready for its reappearance twenty-four poems later; to give an example, Ballades 9–12, 37–40, 65–68, and 93–96 are metrically identical. The four knightly authors have arranged their hundred ballades with military precision.

Ballade Structures in the *Livre des cent balades*

Stanza Construction

(a) *Three Isometric Stanzas*	84 poems
8 syllable lines	84 poems
(b) *Three Heterometric Stanzas*	16 poems
12 lines; 7 & 3 syllables (lines 2, 5, 8, 11); aabaabbbabbA	15 poems
12 lines; 7 & 4 syllables (lines 2, 5, 8, 11); aabaabbbabbA	1 poem

Stanza Length

8 lines	16 poems
9 lines	12 poems
10 lines	16 poems
11 lines	12 poems
12 lines	32 poems
13 lines	12 poems

Refrain
One line   100 poems
Stanza Forms   11 forms
Used once   4 forms
Used 11 times   2 forms
   (a) 11 lines; 8 syllables; *ababbccddeE*
   (b) 13 lines; 8 syllables; *ababbccddefeF*
Used 12 times   1 form
   9 lines; 8 syllables; *ababccdcD*
Used 15 times   2 forms
   (a) 8 lines; 8 syllables; *ababbcbC*
   (b) see below
Used 16 times   2 forms
   (a) 10 lines; 8 syllables; *ababbccdcD*
   (b) 12 lines; 8 syllables; *ababbccddedE*
Envoi   No examples

The frequency with which stanzas of ten, eleven, twelve, or thirteen lines are used contrasts sharply with the *Louange des dames* where a length of seven or eight lines is the norm, and stanzas of nine lines are rare. Machaut wrote only one ballade with stanzas of twelve lines, devising for it a very demanding stanza form which combines lines of seven and three syllables and is built on only two rhymes (Poem 14, *La Louange des dames*, pp. 53–54). That form is adopted enthusiastically by the authors of the *Livre des cent balades,* which includes fifteen examples (or sixteen, if a minor variation is included). Its changing rhythms provide some relief from the monotony of the other stanza forms, which are uniformly octosyllabic and isometric.

Having invited other lovers to contribute to the debate, the authors of the *Livre des cent balades* receive thirteen *responces* [responses], eleven ballades, and two *chançons royaux*. The respondents are all aristocrats, prominent at court. They include the Duke of Berry and the Duke of Touraine, who in 1392 became Duke of Orléans; both royal dukes were later to become patrons of Christine, the role of the Duke of Orléans being especially important at the beginning of her literary career. The replies are well turned and show that their authors had more than passing skills in writing poetry. As a compliment to Jean le Seneschal and his friends, eleven of the thirteen replies adopt one of the stanza forms used in the *Livre des cent balades*.

Les Cent balades

As this discussion shows, the audience to which Christine de Pizan's *Cent balades* were addressed understood the ballade form and appreciated the subtleties of which it was capable. Experience had attuned their ears; to coin a phrase, they were well versed. Their knowledge of poetic practice would enable them to distinguish—more readily than a modern reader can—those poems that conformed to standard patterns and those that showed some degree of innovation or virtuosity. They were, moreover, aware of the recent changes in poetic practice and fashion. Examination of the *Livre des cent balades* confirmed the growing taste for longer ballades. The earlier discussion of the *Art de dictier* highlighted the near complete divergence of poetry and music and the increasing use of the envoi as a conclusion to the ballade. The fourth development that should be emphasized is the practice of linking ballades to create a poetic narrative. Daniel Poirion has drawn attention to the sequences which are to be found in Machaut, and similar runs of linked poems occur in Deschamps (*Le poète et le prince*, pp. 204, 218). But the authors of the *Livre des cent balades* seem to have been the first to apply that technique to a complete collection of poems.

Hearing the title of Christine's work, a contemporary audience would sense that she was issuing a challenge to her knightly predecessors. They must have waited expectantly to see what form the challenge would take and wondered what attitude the new poet would take to the recent changes in poetic fashion. The modern reader cannot, alas, join the late fourteenth-century audience which heard the work for the first time. However hard we try, we remain twentieth-century readers; we cannot recreate the immediacy and the excitement generated by a performance, far less a premiere. In our endeavor to understand Christine's work, we rely on our own inward reading, which we can supplement by reference to the very few commentaries which the *Cent balades* have inspired.[16]

Modern scholars have concentrated on two aspects of the *Cent balades*. They have highlighted the poems in which Christine introduces herself, explains why she has chosen to write poetry, and justifies her choice of themes. Ballades 1, 50, and 100 are most frequently quoted in that connection.[17] In the first poem Christine introduces herself, explaining that she has been urged to put the collection together by others, and seeking the audience's indulgence for her lack of poetic skills and for her inclination to sing in a doleful, melancholy vein. In Ballade 50 she selects the ballade layée form to defend herself against possible criticism, conscious that the love poems immediately preceding may appear to have been inspired by personal experience. She stresses that this is not the case, quoting precedent to justify her choice of subject matter: "Je m'en raport a tous sages ditteurs" [I refer the question to all wise poets] is the refrain of Ballade 50. Following the example set by her predecessors, she must sing of love, the lightest of poetic themes and a subject universally pleasing (vv. 11–12); the only alternative theme, *belles meurs* [morality] (v. 15), is by implication less popular and more difficult. In her final poem Christine stresses that the *Cent balades* are all her own work. Her pride in her collection is evident from the fact that the refrain of Ballade 100 incorporates an anagram of her name: "En escrit y ay mis mon nom" [I have put my name there in writing], *en escrit* [in writing] being a near anagram for "Cristine." She asks her audience to regard her collection as entertainment: "Qu'on le tiengne a esbatement, / Sanz y gloser mauvaisement, / Car je n'y pense se bien non" [Let it be regarded as entertainment, with no evil gloss being put on it, for my purpose is entirely good] (vv. 12–14). As the last line indicates, however, entertainment does not exclude a moral purpose.

Earlier critics have also noted that the *Cent balades* contain a number of sequences, in which poems are linked to form a narrative. In Ballades 5–11, for example, Christine describes her own situation, evoking the grief and the loneliness that have been her lot since the death of her beloved; she rails against Fortune and calls on Death to release her from her pains. Ballade 21 introduces the first of several sequences that describe the progress of a love affair, as seen from a woman's point of view. "A Woman's Story," as Kenneth Varty calls it in his anthology of Christine's lyric poetry.[18] "Women's Stories" would be more accurate, for themes recur and situations are repeated, suggesting that there is more than one narrative. And yet it is impossible to tell exactly where these narratives end, and then begin anew.[19] That is deliberate, for Christine's purpose is to show that the progress of a love affair is all too predictable. However grand the initial passion, however sincere the lovers' commitment to each other, strains and tensions will surely follow, whether they be the strains caused by the *mesdisans* [gossips, slandermongers] or the tensions caused by separation. The joy of mutual love is short-lived; all too soon it will give place to doubt and suspicion, before subsiding in recrimination and disillusionment. It is not just the women of the *Cent balades* who suffer in this way: the second half of the collection includes a series of "Men's Stories," which follow an equally inexorable course.

Earlier critics have also been aware that the *Cent balades* include poems on subjects other than love but have looked at them in much less detail. The best known is Ballade 95, on the mental illness of Charles VI. That poem is often quoted because of its historical interest but is not usually set in its context. And yet it is surely significant that the poem on the king is part of a concluding sequence, Ballades 91–99, which highlight the faults and shortcomings of contemporary society and urge repentance and amendment of life.

Content and Form in the *Cent balades*

The implicit view of earlier critics was that the *Cent balades* form a heterogeneous collection. And yet the *captationes benevolentiæ* or pleas for indulgence, the ballades in which Christine seeks the understanding of her audience as she justifies her choice of themes, occupy strategic positions. As has just been indicated, the final ballades convey a clear moral message, which had moreover been adumbrated in earlier poems. Does the collection not have a greater unity and coherence than has been supposed hitherto? An examination of Christine's choice of ballade forms will give insight into how the collection is constructed.

Ballade Structures in the *Cent balades*

Stanza Construction
(a) *Three Isometric Stanzas*	82 poems
7 syllable lines	16 poems
8 syllable lines	17 poems
10 syllable lines	49 poems
(b) *Four Isometric Stanzas*	1 poem
8 syllable lines	1 poem
Ballade 61.	
(c) *Three Heterometric Stanzas*	17 poems
Ballades layées	14 poems
8 lines; 10 & 7 syllables (line 5);	9 poems
ababccdD. Ballades 24, 40, 50, 71, 73, 87, 96, 97, 99.	
8 lines; 10 & 8 syllables (line 5);	3 poems
ababccdD. Ballades 28, 32, 34.	
8 lines; 10 & 8 syllables (line 5);	1 poem
ababcdcD. Ballade 66.	
9 lines; 10 & 7 syllables (line 6);	1 poem
ababbcdcD. Ballade 65.	
Other forms	3 poems
Ballades 29, 37, 56.	

Stanza Length

7 lines	47 poems
8 lines	49 poems
9 lines	2 poems
Ballades 54, 65.	
10 lines	1 poem
Ballade 61.	
12 lines	1 poem
Ballade 92.	

Refrain

One line	94 poems
One line (shorter meter)	2 poems
Ballades 29, 56.	
Two lines	4 poems
Ballades 7, 17, 19, 61.	

Stanza Forms — 24 forms

Used once	15 forms
Used 2 times	1 form
Used 3 times	2 forms
Used 6 times	1 form
7 lines; 7 syllables; *ababbcC*	
Used 7 times	1 form
8 lines; 7 syllables; *ababcdcD*	
Used 9 times	1 form
see above (*ballades layées*)	
Used 11 times	1 form
7 lines; 8 syllables; *ababbcC*	
Used 19 times	1 form
8 lines; 10 syllables; *ababbcbC*	
Used 25 times	1 form
7 lines; 10 syllables; *ababbcC*	

Envois — 18 poems

Ballades 1, 2, 3, 4, 5, 6, 7, 9, 11, 22, 43, 45, 52, 54, 58, 64, 72, 86 (see comments above, pp. 53–54.

Christine's collection contains forty-seven poems with stanzas of seven lines, and forty-nine with stanzas of eight lines. In choosing short stanzas for ninety-six of her hundred poems, Christine follows Machaut, preferring his example to the longer stanzas which predominate in Deschamps and above all in the *Livre des cent balades*. Machaut's influence is also apparent in Christine's choice of meter: the decasyllabic line is her favorite, being used here in two poems out of three, but she also makes regular use of seven- and eight-syllable lines. The varied cadences of the *Louange des dames* are preferred to the sustained octosyllabic rhythms of the *Livre des cent balades*.

Christine's indebtedness to Machaut is also apparent in the structure of her ballades. She too has her *ballades bonnes à tout faire*. The most popular is the isometric seven-line stanza with the rhyme scheme *ababbcC*, for which Machaut had shown such a predilection. Christine uses the same three varieties, with lines of seven, eight, or ten syllables, and employs them in a total of forty-two ballades. The type of ballade layée favored by Machaut is also popular with Christine, who employs it in nine poems; three other ballade layée forms are found less frequently. Although she follows the tradition set by her master, Christine does not do so slavishly: she adopts the recently introduced envoi, albeit to a limited extent, for it is found in less than a fifth of the *Cent balades*. How creatively Christine employs these varied ballade structures will become clear when her use of different formal components is examined in more detail.

Envois, Refrains, and Changes of Voice

The opening ballades are all isometric and are all made up of stanzas of seven or eight lines. The audience has to wait until Ballade 24 before hearing the first heterometric poem, a ballade layée. Two stanza forms predominate, being employed in seventeen of the first twenty-three ballades; they are assuming the role of *ballades bonnes à tout faire*. The initial rhythms are preponderantly decasyllabic, the only variety being provided by Ballades 7 and 10, both in octosyllables. It is only later that the rhythm begins to change: Ballades 17 and 21 are octosyllabic, and the heptasyllabic line appears for the first time in Ballades 19 and 20. This analysis indicates that, so far as stanza construction is concerned, the opening of the *Cent balades* is deliberately restrained. It will be important to see what use Christine makes of other formal elements, such as the envoi, the longer refrain, and the choice of rhymes, to focus and sustain the audience's attention.

Taken together, the manuscripts of the *Cent balades* contain eighteen envois, which are distributed unevenly through the collection. Half of them cluster at the beginning, and form the conclusion to Ballades 1–7, 9, and 11. None of the poems immediately following has an envoi; Ballade 22 provides the next example, and the remaining envois are scattered through the rest of the collection. The way in which the envois are addressed is equally distinctive. Only eight of the envois begin with the traditional vocative, *Princes* [Prince or Princes], and they all form part of that initial group: Ballades 1–2, 4–7, 9, and 11. Seven envois have no addressee (Ballades 3, 45, 52, 58, 64, 72, and 86), while the other envois are directed as follows: *Mon doulz ami* [My sweet love—Ballade 22], *Medecins* [Physician—Ballade 43], and *Gentiz amans* [Gentle lovers—Ballade 54]. Christine's practice contrasts with that of Deschamps, whose envois are almost always addressed, most commonly to a prince.

In the first eleven poems Christine presents herself and the world in which she lives. Ballade 1, as was seen earlier, is a classic *captatio benevolentiæ* or plea for understanding, in which an apparently inexperienced poet seeks the audience's indulgence. The moral sickness of contemporary France is described in Ballades 2 and 4, which are separated by a poem which retells the myth of Hero and Leander. Christine's own situation is the subject of Ballades 5–11. She has suffered harshly at the hands of Death and Fortune. Even though some years have passed since her beloved died, grief continues to overwhelm her. When the eight envois which begin with the vocative *Princes* are taken together, it is clear that they are addressed not to the traditional *prince du puy* [prince of the poetic academy] but to a royal prince or, more probably, princes. Those envois combine to form a second *captatio benevolentiæ*, but of a different sort; they constitute an eloquent plea for moral and material support.

That plea has two focal points. In Ballade 7 Christine contrasts her past happiness with her present woe, attributing her plight to Fortune who bears the blame, "... de moy oster le soulas, / Qui ma vie tenoit joyeuse" [for taking away from me that pleasure which filled my life with joy]. Her pain is underlined by that refrain of two lines, one of only four examples in the collection. The envoi seeks the Prince's sympathy, and the appeal is made the more persuasive by beginning not *Princes*, as elsewhere, but *Tres doulz Princes* [Most sweet prince]. The refrain and the mode of address are not the only elements that attract the listeners' attention: the lines are octosyllabic, a contrast with the preceding ballades, and the poem is built on only two rhymes, rather than the more usual three or four. The sequence ends with Ballade 11, a further display of virtuosity, but of a different kind. In this celebrated evocation of loneliness, *Seulete suy* ... [Alone am I] makes up the first hemistich of every line but one. The rhymes are in *-estre* (*-aistre*), *-ciée* (*-siée*), and *rée*, a total of three rhymes which becomes two, if the two rich rhymes are taken as one.[20]

Ballade 3, on Hero and Leander, stands apart. It is a poem on the perils of love, as the story and the alliterative refrain emphasize: "Voyez comment Amours amans ordonne!" [See the state in which lovers find themselves at Love's command]. After retelling the myth in lines 1–21, Christine directs her conclusions at all lovers afflicted by the madness of love. The third stanza concludes: "Mirez vous cy, sanz que je plus sermone, / Tous amoureux pris d'amoureuse rage. / Voyez comment Amours amans ordonne!" [Recognize yourselves here and learn, all lovers infected by the madness of love, without further sermonizing from me. See the state in which lovers find themselves at Love's command] (vv. 22–24). Lovers should see an image of themselves in Hero and Leander, these two noble and tragic figures, and should draw appropriate lessons; *se mirer* has both those senses. The choice of *sermone* as rhyme word, and the repetition of *amoureux*, anticipating the references to love in the refrain, make the audience think that Christine has brought her poem to an emphatic close. However, the poem does not end there, for making a bold use of enjambement, Christine adds a further conclusion in an envoi which has no clear addressee. The tone changes as she reflects that her admonitions will almost certainly have no effect, for love makes a fool of even the wisest man: "Mais je me doubt que perdu soit l'usage / D'ainsi amer a trestoute personne; / Mais grant amour fait un fol du plus sage. / Voyez comment Amours amans ordonne!" [But I doubt whether everyone will quit the habit of loving in this way; but great love makes a fool of the wisest of men. See the state in which lovers find themselves at Love's command] (vv. 25–28).

Christine has used the envoi to give Ballade 3 a double ending. In an ideal world the fate of Hero and Leander would provide a moral and salutary lesson, but in reality it will have small effect. The nature of that reality is described in Ballades 2 and 4, which frame the myth. In contemporary France envy, wealth, and self-seeking hold sway, while goodness, honor, and vassalage are held in small esteem.

A contemporary audience, having heard that opening sequence of eleven poems, must have thought that Christine had decided to follow the example of Deschamps and make regular use of the envoi. At the junction between Ballades 11 and 12, however, the *Cent balades* make an abrupt change of direction. One element in that change is the disappearance of the envoi, which is not used again until Ballade 22. While it would take time for the audience to realize that the envoi had been temporarily banished, they could not fail to notice other unambiguous signals. In the Paris copy of the *Livre de Christine* the change in direction is marked by the rubric *Balades de personnages*, that is "Ballades in character" or "Dramatic ballades."[21] Ballade 11, *Seulete suy* . . . , the most feminine poem in the collection, is followed by a ballade on the outrages wrought by Fortune, which is sung not by Christine, but by a man. The audience is made aware of that unexpected change of voice only in line 17.

Ballade 12 is the first example of a series of changes of voice which punctuate the *Cent balades*; the change of voice is sometimes emphasized by a change of gender, but not always. Ballade 14 is feminine and Ballade 15 is masculine, but Ballades 13 and 16 are of indeterminate gender. The impression that Ballade 17 is feminine is confirmed by the poems immediately following.

As they listened to the opening ballades, the audience would naturally have come to identify the first person pronouns, so often repeated, with Christine de Pizan. The *Balades de personnages* which follow are intended to surprise, even disconcert her listeners, to make it clear that from that point on they should not automatically identify all subsequent examples of *je* and *moy* [I and me] with Christine. The rubric in the *Livre de Christine* shows where these dramatic ballades begin but does not indicate where they end, or begin again. It is for the audience to work that out; in that way Christine ensures their continued interest and attention.

Christine's own voice does not disappear. The opening lines of Ballade 14—"Seulete m'a laissié en grant martyre, / En ce desert monde plein de tristece, / Mon doulz ami" [Alone has my sweet love left me in great torment in this desert world full of sadness]—explicitly recall the start of Ballade 11: "Seulete suy et seulete vueil estre, / Seulete m'a mon doulz ami laissiée" [Alone am I and alone would I be, alone has my sweet love left me]. In Ballade 15, however, a young man laments the loss of his mother, which has left him an orphan in a hostile world. Christine's voice seems to resume in Ballade 17, on poetic inspiration, but confirmation must be awaited since the poem is of indeterminate gender. That reassurance comes in the next three ballades, which are all feminine and recall earlier themes associated with Christine. Attention is focused on Ballades 17–20 by changes of rhythm: Ballade 17 is in octosyllables, a meter last employed in Ballade 10, while Ballades 19 and 20 use the seven-syllable line for the first time. Christine's songs cannot but be sad for she continues to be beset by grief and loneliness, as is emphasized in the two-line refrain of Ballade 17: "Si est fort que joye recueille / Cuer qui en tel tristour demeure" [And so it is difficult for a heart which dwells in such sadness to welcome joy]. Following the death of her beloved, she has lost all pleasure and joy in life; she must henceforth be a stranger to Love. The point is underlined in Ballade

19, again in a refrain of two lines: "N'oncques puis je n'oz vouloir / De faire ami, ne d'amer" [And never since then have I wished to accept a lover or to love]. Wishing to leave her audience in no doubt that her grief continues to be so intense that neither joy nor love have any place in her heart, Christine finds an effective way of driving the point home in these two-line refrains. The *Cent balades* contain only four poems, Ballades 7, 17, 19, and 61, in which the refrain is extended to two lines. Three of the four are directly associated with Christine and are used in proximity at the start of the collection. The fourth example is set at some distance from the others; Ballade 61 is discussed in more detail below.

Having been persuaded by the first twenty poems that the leitmotiv of the *Cent balades* will be grief, the audience is confronted by another disconcerting change of direction. Christine had once more justified her choice of doleful themes in Ballade 20: "Si ay bien droit se je dis / Mes plains malencolieux; / Car en tristour est tousdis / Mon dolent cuer, ce scet Dieux" [And I am right indeed to voice my melancholy complaints, for my grieving heart is ever sorrowful, God knows that] (vv. 15–18). Her words have scarcely left the listeners' ears when, in Ballade 21, they meet a lady whose feelings surge as she pictures her suitor and savors his recent declarations of love; the effect is underscored by breathless octosyllables. That poem, as was seen earlier, marks the beginning of the "Women's Stories," which conclude in Ballade 49. Is there any possibility that the lady might be Christine de Pizan herself? Or are these *Balades de personnages*?

There is no immediate answer. Gradually, as they listen to these love poems, the audience realize that they are encountering not one lady, but several. That none of them can be identified with Christine de Pizan is confirmed by Ballade 50, discussed earlier, in which her voice resumes to explain why she has composed these love songs and to defend her choice of subject matter. Ballades 17–20 and 50 are strategically positioned; their combined effect is to indicate that the intervening poems are all *Balades de personnages*.[22]

Only three of these love poems, Ballades 22, 43, and 45, conclude with an envoi. In the first example, a lady accepts her suitor whose faithful service and reputation have shown him to be worthy of her; the envoi, addressed *Mon doulz ami*, provides an emphatic conclusion to this solemn grant of her love. The lady of Ballade 43 is sick; she describes her symptoms, her listlessness, and her weakness in three stanzas, before addressing the envoi to her *Medecins* and imploring him to restore her to health. The poem contains no reference to love; only the wider context in which the ballade is set suggests that the lady is lovesick and that her beloved is the only physician who can cure her. In Ballade 47, Pegasus, the messenger of *Renommée* [Fame, Reputation], has brought the lady news of her lover, who is said to have fallen in love with someone else. Can these rumors be true, the lady asks herself? Alas, her past experience indicates that they may well be. The envoi focuses on the lady's pain, which seems to stretch before her, unending.

Having pressed the envoi into intensive service in the opening section of the *Cent balades*, Christine has rested it for a space. The interval before the envoi reappears is long enough for it to have shed its close association with Christine's own voice. It is used sparingly thereafter, being reserved for ballades singled out for special emphasis. The envois to Ballades 54, 58, 64, and 72 are discussed below.

The Longer Ballades

The *Cent balades* contain only four poems with stanzas of more than eight lines: Ballades 54, 61, 65, and 92. It is no coincidence that they are all positioned in the second half of the collection, by which time Christine has attuned the ears of her audience to short stanzas. Once she has done so, she can deviate from that norm to create a particular effect. The theme of Ballade 54 is significant: it is a *Breviaire des nobles* [Breviary for Nobles] in miniature, which gives advice on behavior to those who aspire to be true lovers, and those counsels are summarized in the envoi addressed to *Gentiz amans* [lovers of gentle birth] in general. When she discussed poetic themes in Ballade 50, Christine had referred both to love and to *belles meurs*, which she described as a more difficult and less popular subject. This, the first poem on that theme, gains in emphasis by the use of stanzas of nine lines and by the presence of an envoi.

Poem 61 is extremely unusual, having not three but four stanzas, each of ten lines.[23] The fourth stanza cannot be considered an envoi, for convention decreed that the envoi was shorter than the stanzas that preceded it. And so Ballade 61 breaks the mold deliberately; it is, moreover, the last of the four poems in the collection that have a refrain of two lines. The poem retells the myth of Jupiter and Io, his mistress, whom he turned into a cow to save them both from the wrath of Juno, his wife. Juno entrusted the cow to Argus the watchman, but to no avail because Argus was lulled to sleep by Mercury, who stole the cow. Three stanzas are required to tell the tale and illustrate the refrain; its message is that there is no trouble that cannot be turned to good account. The fourth stanza draws the moral that love will out, no matter how strong the restraints put on a young man and a young woman in love; the obstacles set in their way will only be turned to their advantage.[24] At this point in the *Cent balades* Christine is concerned to underline her message that love is a consuming passion. If it can overwhelm the gods and heroes of old as easily as the myth indicates, what hope is there for common humanity? Ballade 61 echoes Ballade 3, on Hero and Leander, which is addressed to *Tous amoureux pris d'amoureuse rage* [all lovers infected by the madness of love]. Both poems look forward to another mythological poem, Ballade 90, described in the Duke's Manuscript as a *Balade pouetique* [poetic ballade]. Ballade 65 is emphatic in its context: a lovelorn suitor, who has been silent for six years and more, nerves himself to make an eloquent declaration of his love. It is appropriate that he should be expansive, and so he takes more than usual space and uses a distinctive stanza form; his ballade layée has stanzas of nine lines, rather than eight, and is the only example in the collection where the shorter line comes not fifth, but sixth in the stanza.[25] Eloquence and devotion have their reward, for in Ballade 66 the lady grants him her love. She responds in a second, shorter ballade layée, its rhyme scheme modeled on that chosen by her lover; the form of Ballade 66 is also unique in the context of the *Cent balades*.

Ballade 92, in stanzas of twelve lines, is substantially longer than any other poem in the collection. It celebrates the qualities of a good and valiant knight, whose prowess fits him to be ranked with the Nine Worthies. He is so outstanding a knight that, were Semiramis living at this hour, she would be honored by his love. The *gravitas* of the subject is matched by a poem of appropriate weight and substance.

Ballades layées

As they listened to the beginning of the *Cent balades*, a contemporary audience must have wondered if Christine had decided to make no use of the ballade layée. There are no examples of that stanza form in the opening section or in the first series of *Balades de personnages*. The ballade layée is merely held back, however, reserved for an appropriate occasion which will allow Christine scope to display her virtuosity.

Ballade 24 is addressed by a lady to her lover. Her love for him, inspired by his great virtues, has cured her of the ills and the sorrow that previously afflicted her. Christine takes great care with the rhythm of the poem, anxious to demonstrate that she has mastered the form made popular by

Machaut. Each stanza has its own distinctive movement, the ouvert, clos, and oultrepassé being linked or separated in different ways. Enjambement is used skillfully in the first stanza; it creates an effect of spontaneity, of breathlessness almost, as the lady thinks of further details to be added to her catalogue of praise.

> Ma doulce amour, ma plaisance cherie,
> Mon doulz ami, quanque je puis amer,
> Vostre doulceur m'a de tous maulz garie,
> Et vrayement je vous puis bien clamer   4
> Fontaine dont tout bien vient,
> Et qui en paix et joye me soustient,
> Et dont plaisirs me vienent a largece,
> Car vous tout seul me tenez en leece.   8
>
> Et la doulour qui en mon cuer norrie
> S'est longuement, qui tant m'a fait d'amer,
> Le bien de vous a de tous poins tarie.
> Or ne me puis complaindre ne blasmer   12
> De Fortune qui devient
> Bonne pour moy, se en ce point se tient;
> Mis m'en avez en la voye et adrece,
> Car vous tout seul me tenez en leece.   16
>
> Si lo Amours qui, par sa seigneurie,
> A tel plaisir m'a voulu reclamer,
> Car dire puis de vray sanz flaterie
> Qu'il n'a meilleur de la ne de ça mer   20
> De vous, m'amour. Ainsi le tient
> Mon cuer pour vray, qui tout a vous se tient
> N'a aultre rien sa pensée ne drece,
> Car vous tout seul me tenez en leece   24

[My sweet love, the pleasure I adore, my sweet beloved, all that I can love, your sweetness has cured me of all ills and truly indeed can I describe you as the fountain from which all good comes, which sustains me in peace and joy, and from which pleasures come to me in abundance, for you alone keep me in bliss. And the pain which has been nourished in my heart for so long, which has caused me such bitterness, has been stopped entirely by your goodness. Now I cannot complain about Fortune or cast blame on her who is becoming kind to me, if she remains of that mind; you have set me on that path, in that direction, for you alone keep me in bliss. And so I praise Love who by his power has been pleased to call me to such pleasure, for I can truly say without flattery that neither here nor beyond the seas is there one better than you, my love. Such is the true belief of my heart which cleaves to you entirely and directs its thoughts on none other, for you alone keep me in bliss.] (*Œuvres poétiques*, I, p. 25 [text repunctuated])

The shorter fifth line serves as a focal point. In stanza one it highlights the image of the fountain, which represents the lover as the source of all goodness. The lady's astonishment at her change of fortune is emphasized in like manner in stanza two. The short line is put to more dramatic use in stanza three, where it is broken by an unexpected caesura. It divides the stanza into two parts to match the sense; praise is followed by renewed commitment.

Elsewhere in the *Cent balades*, Christine reserves the ballade layée for poems of particular importance. The next three examples are set close together. In Ballade 28 a lady writes to her lover, explaining why she has been prevented from speaking to him, though she yearns to do so: the fault lies with the *mesdisans* who watch her every move. Ballade 32 centers on a journey abroad and the sorrow caused by the lover's departure, while Ballade 34 is a classic May poem in which the lady contrasts the joy of the natural world around her with the pain she feels at her lover's continued absence. The thematic links between these poems are underlined by the choice of stanza form, a variant on the standard ballade layée, in which the fifth line is of eight, not seven, syllables; the form is utilized only in these three poems. Elsewhere the standard form resumes and is used at intervals to treat a range of subjects: a lady's complaint to the God of Love who, having ensnared her, has brought her much more pain than joy (Ballade 40); Christine's defense of her choice of poetic themes (Ballade 50); a declaration of love addressed to a lady (Ballade 71); a lover's sorrow at his departure on a journey abroad (Ballade 73); a solemn adieu directed at a *belle dame sans mercy* [fair lady who has no mercy] (Ballade 87). To these ballades layées in standard mode there must be added the reciprocal declarations of love discussed earlier (Ballades 65 and 66), for which Christine reserves special stanza forms. The majority of these poems are, like Ballade 24, *Balades de personnages*.

The last three ballades layées, Poems 96, 97, and 99, are set close together and are also in standard mode. The subject of Ballade 96 is *Bonté*

[Goodness], which is presented as an integral part of Nobility. In Ballade 97 Christine emphasizes the impermanence of Fortune's gifts, recalling the opening poems where Fortune had been a leitmotiv.[26] Fortune can be salutary if her slings and arrows cause the sinner to repent, to have faith in God, and to prepare for the Last Judgment; Ballade 99 develops themes treated earlier in Ballade 16.

Conclusion

These last three ballades layées are set off by the poems that surround them, and together they make up the conclusion to the *Cent balades*. Ballades 91–99 form a sequence in which vice and virtue are contrasted by turns. The *mesdisans* are attacked in Ballade 91, the last in a series of poems directed against them.[27] Ballade 93, which inveighs against the covetousness and materialism that afflict contemporary society, echoes Ballades 2 and 4. As has just been seen, the audience is reminded in Ballade 97 of the danger of reposing trust in Fortune. The prevalence of sin, implicit in all the admonitory ballades, is brought into sharpest focus in Ballade 95: the sickness of Charles VI is the penance suffered by the king for the sins of his people. That note of actuality is the only new theme; the other ballades in the sequence contain echoes of earlier poems, and that is deliberate.

The audience is urged to prefer virtue to vice. Ballade 92, on prowess, noteworthy for its *gravitas*, recalls earlier poems: the qualities of the good knight had been celebrated in Ballade 64 and contrasted with the deft portrait of a *salon* knight and gossip in Ballade 58. *Loialté* [Loyalty] is commended in Ballade 94, and *Bonté* [Goodness] in Ballade 96. Ballade 98 extols *Sagece* [Wisdom] which, though often derided in contemporary society, is a treasure beyond price. That poem is complemented by Ballade 99, on faith in God: *initium sapientiæ timor Domini* [the fear of the Lord is the beginning of wisdom].

This sequence of nine poems is set between Ballade 100, which constitutes the epilogue, and Ballade 90, which tells a composite, factitious tale about Adonis, who is doomed to die.[28] What part does this *Balade pouetique* play in preparing the conclusion? Help in understanding what Christine meant by *pouetique* is provided by the *Epistre d'Othea*, which appeared about 1400, shortly before the *Livre de Christine* was completed. The *Epistre d'Othea* includes a description of the marriage of Peleus and Thetis "ou la vraye histoire est muciee soubs couverture poetique" [in which the true story is concealed under the covering of poetry]. Earlier in that work Christine had made reference to poets "qui parlent soubz couverture et en maniere de fable" [who talk under the cover and in the manner of a fable] or who have "mucié verite [sic] soubs couverture de fable" [who have concealed truth under the cover of a fable].[29] What then is the truth concealed in Ballade 90?

In his struggle against the gods, Adonis has but one ally, Mercury, whose words cannot be trusted; Venus is powerless to come to his aid. He must face the combined strength of Mars, Vulcan, Pallas, and Apollo, and he must stand trial before Jupiter, with Cerberus taking the role of prosecutor. Juno alone can save Adonis, as we are told in lines 1–2 and reminded in lines 17–18. In the *Epistre d'Othea* the reader is enjoined to be aware of Juno, "deesse d'avoir et de seigneurie" [goddess of wealth and power]: "De Juno ja trop ne te chaille, / Se le noyel mieulx que l'eschaille, / D'onneur desires a avoir, / Car mieulx vault proece qu'avoir" [Do not take great account of Juno if you desire to possess the kernel rather than the shell of honor for prowess is worth more than wealth] (vv. 18–21).[30] Poor Adonis, poor in both senses of the word, is doomed: "Il y morra briefment, au mien cuidier" [In this situation he will soon die, I do believe] runs the refrain of Ballade 90. *Au mien cuidier* is significant: whereas the myth is narrated in a neutral tone, Christine associates herself directly with the refrain. The world of Adonis is a world of cruelty and deceit, where money talks, where love is fickle and impermanent. The world of the *Cent balades* is no different from that of Adonis. Love seems to offer happiness, but, in this fallen world, love's bliss is all too short-lived and ends in disillusionment.

In Ballade 100 Christine stresses that the *Cent balades* are all her own work. Her pride in them is evident from the fact that the refrain incorporates an anagram of her name. She had touched on the function of poetry in Ballade 50, where it was said to provide *esbatement*, "entertainment" or "diversion." When she returns to the topic in her final poem, she again asks her audience to regard her collection as entertainment: "Qu'on le tiengne a esbatement, / Sanz y gloser mauvaisement, / Car je n'y pense se bien non"[Let it be regarded as entertainment, with no evil gloss being put on it, for my purpose is entirely good] (vv. 12–14).[31] It is noteworthy that in both these poems Christine also stresses that her collection has a moral purpose.

Ballades 90–100 stand apart from the main body of the collection, as do Ballades 1–11. These two series of eleven poems provide a symmetrical framework, with Ballade 50, the ballade layée on the choice of poetic themes, set equidistant between them. The rubrics that precede Ballades 12 and 90 support that view, even though they are found in different manuscripts. And yet that symmetry is deceptive, for the introduction also takes in Ballades 12–20: the love narratives that form the main body of the collection begin dramatically at Ballade 21 where the audience encounters a new female voice in dramatic juxtaposition with that of Christine herself.

The introduction prepares for the conclusion, for in the opening poems Christine's plight is set against the background of contemporary France. Her personal experiences inspire more general reflections about life, death, and faith, which look forward to the poems on *belles meurs* in the second half of the collection, and to the conclusion. By setting her love poems in a clear moral framework, Christine makes clear her attitude to love. The *Cent balades* raise questions analogous to those addressed by the earlier *Livre des cent balades*. Like her predecessors, Christine concludes that *Loialté* is to be preferred to *Fausseté* in all its manifestations. Ballade 92 shows that clearly; it is the last of a series of poems that tilt at *faux amans* [false lovers], *faintise* [dissimulation], and *barat* [deceit].[32] What distinguishes the *Cent balades* is that Christine enlarges the debate to show that, when such issues are considered *sub specie æternitatis*, their frivolity and triviality are plain to see.

Christine's formal riposte to that earlier work is also clear: variety of invention is much superior to rigid regimentation. Content and form are blended in the *Cent balades* with the greatest skill, as the foregoing analysis has shown. For a first work, the collection shows remarkable self-confidence. The short decasyllabic poems with envois that dominate the initial section lead her listeners to suppose that she is endeavoring to combine the traditions of Machaut and Deschamps. Hearing the insistent decasyllables arranged in traditional isometric forms, they wonder if she is not a poet of limited range. Only gradually does the audience realize that these have been stratagems, used for specific, limited purposes: the envois were used to direct Christine's plea for support at her patrons; the repetitive rhythms of the opening poems underscore Christine's sorrow and set off Ballades 7 and 11, the two poems which she elaborates to give them prominence. As the love stories develop, later to be combined with the poems *de belles meurs*, Christine begins to deploy the much wider formal range she has at her command. She shows judgment in selecting the places and the subjects that are most appropriate for the ballade layée and other elaborate forms.[33] In short, she fully merits the compliments Deschamps paid to her eloquence: "Muse eloquent entre les •ix•, Christine, / Nompareille que je saiche au jour d'ui, / En sens acquis et en toute dotrine, / Tu as de Dieu science et non d'autruy" [O Christine, o muse whose eloquence rivals the nine (muses), who to my knowledge are today unequalled in sense and experience and in doctrine of every kind, your knowledge comes from God and from no one else] (*Œuvres complètes*, VI (1889), p. 251, vv. 1–4).

What *sens*, what *dotrine* are conveyed by the *Cent balades*? Love, *cette amoureuse rage* [this madness of love], which obsesses Christine's contemporaries as much as it did the gods and heroes of old, is a vain pursuit which must lead to disillusionment, pain, and even death. It cannot be otherwise in this fallen world where treachery and deceit are rife, where virtue goes unrewarded. That contemporary society is sick is shown most eloquently by the king's illness. What is to be done? The answer is to forsake earthly love, to cultivate faith, goodness, and prowess. These are *bonnes balades*, as is indicated by the rubric in the Chantilly Manuscript of the *Livre de Christine*: of good quality, and good in content.[34] Christine has successfully challenged the knightly authors of the *Livre des cent balades* and has won her spurs.

She was too much of a realist, however, to believe that her words would everywhere fall on listening ears. Christine had made that clear as early as the envoi to Ballade 3, which concludes ironically: "Mais je me doubt que perdu soit l'usage / D'ainsi amer a trestoute personne; / Mais grant amour fait un fol du plus sage" [But I doubt whether everyone will quit the habit of loving in this way; but great love makes a fool of the wisest of men] (vv. 25-27).

Notes

1. The Duke's Manuscript was split into five parts, now Paris, Bibliothèque Nationale, fonds fr. 835, 606, 836, 605, and 607. The *Cent balades* are copied in MS 835 on folios 1a-16d, 18a-d. The Queen's Manuscript is now British Library, Harley 4431, in which the *Cent balades* are copied on folios 4a-21b. For a more detailed discussion, see James C. Laidlaw, "Christine de Pizan—A Publisher's Progress."

2. Maurice Roy, ed., *Œuvres poétiques de Christine de Pisan* (Paris: Firmin Didot, 1886), 1:1-100. The text of quotations is taken from that edition, but the punctuation and the capitalization have been revised on occasion. Ballades 1-7, 9, 22, 43, 52, 54, 58, and 64 have an envoi in all the manuscripts of the *Cent balades*. The four ballades which are copied now with, now without an envoi, are: 11 and 72 (envoi in the Duke's and the Queen's Manuscripts, but not in the *Livre de Christine*); 45 (envoi only in the Queen's Manuscript); 86 (envoi in the *Livre* and the Duke's, but not in the Queen's Manuscript). *Balades* is the spelling found in the rubrics of all the collected manuscripts and has been used here in quoting the title of the collection. The modern spelling, *ballades*, is used elsewhere.

3. *L'Avision-Christine*, ed. Mary Louis Towner, pp. 160-61. Punctuation added.

4. Eustache Deschamps, *Œuvres complètes*, 1:243-46; Ernest Langlois, ed., *Recueil d'arts de seconde rhétorique*, p. 12.

5. Suzanne Bagoly, "Christine de Pizan et l'art de 'dictier' ballades."

6. Stanley Sadie, ed., *The New Grove Dictionary of Music and Musicians*, pp. 428-36.

7. It is important to note, however, that the collected manuscripts of Machaut contain musical settings for only a small proportion of his *formes fixes*. The *Louange des dames* contains no music and is followed at some distance by a collection of forty-five *Balades notées*; sixteen of these poems had been included earlier in the *Louange des dames*. See also note 19. For editions of both these collections, see Guillaume de Machaut, *Poésies lyriques*, pp. 16–237, 535–65.

8. Evencio Beltran, ed., *Jacques Legrand*, p. 144, lines 11–15.

9. I. S. Laurie, writing in "Deschamps and the Lyric as Natural Music," put the matter succinctly: "ranging from scenes of criminal life to descriptions of royal châteaux, from the horrors of campaigning in Flanders to toothache, from moralising on ecclesiastical and political disorders to the price of cabbages in Paris" (p. 569).

10. Not all contemporary and later poets adopted the envoi with the same enthusiasm as Deschamps; it was not until the second half of the fifteenth century that the envoi became an indispensable part of the ballade.

11. Guillaume de Machaut, *La Louange des dames*, pp. 19–21. The one example of a *ballade double*, treated by Wilkins as a separate form, is here included among the ballades, increasing his total from 206 to 207. See also the tables in Daniel Poirion, *Le Poète et le prince*, pp. 374–91 (especially pp. 374–75, 385–87).

12. When rhyme schemes are indicated, the refrain is marked in capitals.

13. The *Balades notées* (see note 7) use a range of stanza forms similar to that deployed in the *Louange des dames*. Examples of all the standard forms are included, with the exception of the variety in seven-syllable lines. Thus, if hymns and hymn tunes are taken as an analogy, it is possible to sing many of the poems in the *Louange des dames* to tunes composed by Machaut himself. That is the case, after taking due account of themes and the incidence of masculine and feminine rhymes.

14. Poems 29, 167, and 185 (*La Louange des dames*, 57, 92, and 97).

15. Gaston Raynaud, ed., *Les Cent ballades, poème du XIVe siècle*.

16. Angus J. Kennedy, *Christine de Pizan*, pp. 66–67; Edith Yenal, *Christine de Pizan*, pp. 1–3.

17. See, for example, Kenneth Varty, ed., *Christine de Pisan's Ballades, Rondeaux, and Virelais*, pp. xx–xxii; Leonard W. Johnson, *Poets as Players*, pp. 62–65. Less attention has been paid to poems 17 and 20, but they are also important, as is indicated below.

18. Varty, *Christine de Pisan*, pp. xxii–xxiv, 11–29.

19. See James Laidlaw, "L'unité des *Cent balades*."

20. The envoi is found only in the Duke's and the Queen's Manuscripts. For a more detailed analysis of Ballade 11, see James C. Laidlaw, "Christine de Pizan—An Author's Progress," p. 535.

21. Fol. 3c. The equivalent rubric in the Chantilly copy (fol. 4c) reads *Balade de personnages*, which suggests that the heading applies only to Ballade 12. That the reading of the Paris copy is to be preferred is shown by the presence of only one

personnage in Ballade 12 and by the frequent changes of voice in the poems immediately following.

22. Christine's technique may have been too subtle for some of her listeners or may have been deliberately ignored by others who delighted in spreading rumors that these love poems must be based on the author's personal experience. It is noteworthy that in the passage from the *L'Avision-Christine*, quoted earlier, she refers to "ditz amoureux et gais *d'autrui sentement*" (italics added).

23. The length of the text is identical in all the manuscripts. Laurie cites Ballade 351 as an example of a ballade of four stanzas by Deschamps, in which the fourth stanza serves as an envoi ("Deschamps and the Lyric as Natural Music," p. 563, n. 3). It is difficult to know whether the four examples from Deschamps cited by Poirion are extended ballades or abbreviated chançons royaux; each of them contains four stanzas and an envoi (*Le Poète et le prince*, p. 370, n. 42). The two poems in four stanzas by Philippe de Vitry and Pierre d'Ailly, which Poirion also quotes, are not in fact ballades, since the stanzas do not have a common rhyme scheme or a refrain.

24. That is the literal moral, and it is appropriate in the context of the *Cent balades*. In the *Epistre d'Othea,* Texts 29–30 present Yo as a symbol of written learning. That alternative, loftier interpretation does not seem to be of immediate relevance here. See Halina Loukopoulos, *Classical Mythology in the Works of Christine de Pisan*, pp. 197-99.

25. No analogue for the form of Ballade 65 has so far been discovered. The *Louange des dames* includes one ballade layée in which the shorter line stands sixth (poem 185, p. 97); however, that poem has stanzas of eight heptasyllabic lines. Deschamps composed two ballades layées with stanzas of nine lines with a shorter sixth line (*Œuvres complètes*, 1, pp. 255–56 and 269–70), but neither poem has the same rhyme scheme as Ballade 65.

26. See Ballades 7–8, 10, 12, and 19.

27. These poems are dispersed through the collection; see Ballades 26, 28, 30, 54, 58–60, and 84.

28. The mythological details which Christine combines in her tale are drawn from the *Metamorphoses* of Ovid for the most part. Froissart's poems contain other examples of factitious myths, and Christine no doubt followed his example. See Audrey Graham, "Froissart's Use of Classical Allusion in his Poems" (especially pp. 29–32), and Philip E. Bennett, "The Mirage of Fiction" (especially pp. 291–94).

29. *Epistre d'Othea*, 236:11–12; 162:11; 197:11.

30. *Epistre d'Othea*, 253:21–22; 221:18–21.

31. It is no accident that *esbatement* is not only repeated but is used as a rhyme word on both occasions. It is found nowhere else in the *Cent balades*.

32. See Ballades 4, 22, 30, 52–53, 59–60, 62, 66, 83, 89, and 91.

33. See also "L'unité des *Cent balades*," 102–3.

34. In the Chantilly MS of the *Livre de Christine*, copied under the author's supervision, the collection begins with the rubric "Cy commencent Cent bonnes balades" (Musée Condé, MS 492–3, fol. 2r).

Works Cited

Bagoly, Suzanne. "Christine de Pizan et l'art de 'dictier' ballades." *Moyen Age* 92 (1986): 41–67.

Beltran, Evencio, ed. *Jacques Legrand: Archiloge Sophie—Livre de bonnes meurs.* Paris: Champion, 1986.

Bennett, Philip E. "The Mirage of Fiction: Narration, Narrator, and Narratee in Froissart's Lyrico-narrative *Dits.*" *Modern Language Review* 86 (1991): 285–97.

Christine de Pizan. *L'Avision-Christine.* Ed. Mary Louis Towner. Washington, D.C.: Catholic University of America, 1932.

———. *Œuvres poétiques.* Ed. Maurice Roy. 3 vols. Paris: Firmin Didot, 1886–96.

Deschamps, Eustache. *Œuvres complètes de Eustache Deschamps.* Ed. Marquis de Queux de Saint-Hilaire and Gaston Raynaud. 11 vols. Paris: Firmin Didot, 1878–1903.

Graham, Audrey. "Froissart's Use of Classical Allusion in His Poems." *Medium Aevum* 32 (1963): 24–33.

Johnson, Leonard W. *Poets as Players: Theme and Variation in Late Medieval French Poetry.* Stanford: Stanford University Press, 1990.

Kennedy, Angus J. *Christine de Pizan: A Bibliographical Guide.* London: Grant & Cutler, 1984.

Laidlaw, James C. "Christine de Pizan—An Author's Progress." *Modern Language Review* 78 (1983): 532–50.

———. "Christine de Pizan—A Publisher's Progress." *Modern Language Review* 82 (1987): 35–75.

———. "L'unité des *Cent balades.*" In *The City of Scholars: New Approaches to Christine de Pizan*, ed. Margarete Zimmermann and Dina De Rentiis, pp. 97–106. Berlin: De Gruyter, 1994.

Langlois, Ernest. *Recueil d'arts de seconde rhétorique.* Paris: Imprimerie Nationale, 1902.

Laurie, I. S. "Deschamps and the Lyric as Natural Music." *Modern Language Review* 59 (1964): 561–70.

Loukopoulos, Halina. "Classical Mythology in the Works of Christine de Pisan, with an Edition of 'L'Epistre d'Othea' from the Manuscript Harley 4431." Ph.D. diss., Wayne State University, Detroit, 1977.

Machaut, Guillaume de. *La Louange des dames.* Ed. Nigel Wilkins. Edinburgh: Scottish Academic Press, 1972.

———. *Poésies lyriques.* Ed. Vladimir Chichmaref. Paris, 1909; reprint, Geneva: Slatkine, 1973.

Poirion, Daniel. *Le poète et le prince: L'évolution du lyrisme courtois de Guillaume de Machaut à Charles d'Orléans.* Paris: Presses Universitaires de France, 1965.

Raynaud, Gaston, ed. *Les Cent balades, poème du XIVe siècle composé par Jean le Seneschal avec la collaboration de Philippe d'Artois, comte d'Eu, de Boucicaut le Jeune et de Jean de Crésecque.* Paris: Firmin Didot, 1905.

Sadie, Stanley, ed. *The New Grove Dictionary of Music and Musicians.* Vol. 11. London: Macmillan, 1980.
Varty, Kenneth, ed. *Christine de Pisan's Ballades, Rondeaux, and Virelais: An Anthology.* Leicester, Eng.: Leicester University Press, 1965.
Yenal, Edith. *Christine de Pizan: A Bibliography.* Metuchen, N.J.: Scarecrow, 1989.

~ CHAPTER 3

Last Words: Reflections on a
"Lay mortel" and the Poetics
of Lyric Sequences

BARBARA K. ALTMANN

After the definitive split between lyric poetry and music in the late fourteenth century—which one might posit as occurring somewhere between the completion of Guillaume de Machaut's *œuvre* and Eustache Deschamps *L'Art de dictier* of 1392—the dynamics of the poem as a purely literary artifact gained in freedom. Less constrained by the need to coordinate musical and linguistic structures, the poem could exaggerate the dimensions of its components: the length of its lines, its mixture of line lengths, the number of lines per strophe, all became more flexible elements in the creation of what were often increasingly writerly, in the sense of technically demanding, compositions. The ballade, for example, one of the major *formes fixes* of the late Middle Ages in France, could be notably longer in the works of Froissart, Deschamps, Christine de Pizan, and Charles d'Orléans than it had been in Machaut; not only did the traditional three strophes contain a greater number of lines each, they also collectively acquired an envoi, formerly appended only to the *chant royal*. Within the strophe, the elaboration of the traditional elements of the ballade—*ouvert*, *clos*, and *oultrepassé*, the opening, closing, and continuation—no longer always followed the prescribed formula leading to the refrain. Enjambment destabilized the congruence of syntactic and metrical units. In other words, late medieval poets were at greater liberty to tinker with the tight internal dynamic of the ballade and to challenge the listener's ear with demanding formal variations and linguistic play.[1]

Christine de Pizan, active from the late 1390s until 1431, is one of the poets who pushed the boundaries of fixed form poetry, demonstrating an ability to manipulate these configurations with an elan that has not always met with favor. Daniel Poirion, for example, in his masterful synthesis on late medieval French poetry, compares Christine unfavorably in this regard with contemporaries such as Garencières and Charles d'Orléans. He states: "Chez Christine de Pisan, le rythme subjectif submerge la structure traditionelle. Si elle pousse très loin la virtuosité des rimes, des mètres, du dialogue, et inversement exprime parfois des sentiments nouveaux et personnels, c'est au détriment de l'unité rythmique du poème. Nous assistons chez elle à une grave dissociation du mouvement poétique, la technique se séparant nettement de l'inspiration" [In Christine de Pizan's poetry, subjective choices of rhythm submerge traditional structures. While she attains a high level of virtuosity of rhyme, meter, and dialogue, and, inversely, expresses new and personal emotions on occasion, the rhythmic unity of the poem suffers as a result. In her work we see a serious split in the poetic movement, in which technique is distinctly separated from inspiration] (*Le poète et le prince*, p. 390). Admittedly, technical ingenuity led in some instances to tortured lyric verse, as in a lai written entirely in very rich rhymes [*rimes léonines*], which will be referred to briefly below.

These obvious tours de force aside, however, this breach in the integrity of the poem can be approached from a different angle: what might be considered detrimental to the realization of the individual poem as a symmetrical, perfect, self-contained entity may also, in some cases, result from the growing interest of the day in the dynamics between and among poems, a recognition of the potential of poems to signify beyond their own textual boundaries when placed in conjunction with others of similar or dissimilar form. I am referring here to the aesthetic of the lyric poem sequence, pioneered by Petrarch in his *Canzoniere* and picked up, without attribution, by late fourteenth- and early fifteenth-century French poets. The locus of Christine's challenge to the limits of the lyric models she inherited can often be found within the framework of a larger collection, each individual piece contributing to a larger display of variety in poetic voice, technical expertise, and thematic range. One's appreciation for the bold stylistic strokes of a poem such as the much anthologized *Seulete suis* [A lonely little woman am I . . .] and its anaphora,[2] for example, or of the dialogue poems spoken by lovers in the *Cent ballades d'Amant et de Dame* [Hundred Ballades of a Lover and Lady][3] is greatly heightened by the resonances those poems create within the context of the larger series. To decontextualize them, to remove them from the overarching fiction and metrical patterns formed by a sequence of poems, is to focus on their internal workings at the expense of their movement outward, on a building block rather than on the whole structure.

Clearly a study of the poetics of lyric sequences, Christine's as well as others', is a project of considerable scale which lies well outside the purview of this paper. This essay represents a small foray into that undertaking. Its much more limited purpose is threefold: to explicate the internal workings of the final item in Christine's corpus of lyric poems, a piece entitled *Lay de dame* [Lay of the Lady]; to elucidate its relationship to the larger work onto which it is appended, the *Cent ballades d'Amant et de Dame*; and to use these texts as a test case in beginning to probe the workings of the lyric poem sequence as Christine manipulated it, to expose the interaction of one lyric form with another.

Some background on the *Cent ballades d'Amant et de Dame* will be necessary here in order to set the stage for what follows. This collection of one hundred ballades constitutes the last known lyric poetry written by Christine de Pizan. It is generally assumed to date from 1410 or 1411, largely on the basis that it appears only in the latest of the surviving deluxe presentation copies of Christine's poetic works prepared under the author's supervision for the French queen Isabeau de Bavière.[4] The *Cent ballades d'Amant et de Dame* is the last work in this two-volume manuscript (two volumes as now bound), balancing neatly another collection of one hundred ballades, entitled the *Cent balades,* at the very beginning of the first volume.

In many ways, the second and later group of one hundred ballades represents the culmination of themes, poetic techniques, and authorial strategies adumbrated in the first. Exploiting with consummate skill the narrative potential of a series of lyric poems, Christine creates in the *Cent ballades d'Amant et de Dame* the unfolding story of the love between a knight and lady: the lady is reluctant to accept the advances of a suitor, finally succumbs to his entreaties, enjoys the intense pleasures of love for a short time, and then sees her happiness turn to despair as the relationship sours. Within the one hundred poems, her voice alternates with that of her lover. In the last ballade, she lies close to death, her heart breaking at the demise of the love to which she had given herself completely. There follows, after the explicit signaling the end of the work, a poem of 283 lines in 22 strophes, labeled "Lay de Dame" at its beginning and "Lay mortel" at its end, in which a lady's voice laments the fickleness of lovers, including hers in particular, and inveighs against the inescapable, implacable cruelty of Amours which has driven her to the brink of death.

What is the relationship of the "Lay de Dame," or "Lay mortel," to the ballades that precede it? Obviously, by virtue of its position immediately following the *Cent ballades d'Amant et de Dame* as well as by its similarity of subject matter and voice, the "Lay" is associated with the larger work. Equally obvious, however, is the deliberate positioning of the "Lay" after the explicit and outside the number one hundred which acts as an organizing principle for the collection. As such, it has an analogue in the metadiscursive, prefatory ballade placed at the head of the *Cent ballades d'Amant et de Dame*, in which the author's voice explains the genesis and nature of the work to follow.[5] But the "Lay" is further cut adrift simply by the change of form from ballade to lai, a considerable shifting of poetic gears.

Given the personal supervision to which this and certain other collections of Christine's works were subjected by the author, aspects of the manuscript production can justifiably be invoked to confirm what is found within purely textual boundaries. And indeed, certain elements of layout and ornamentation in the sole manuscript of the work, British Library Harley 4431, reinforce the dual nature of the "Lay."[6] The explicit to the *Cent ballades d'Amant et de Dame*, formally closing that text, and the following rubric (*Lay de Dame*), opening the subsequent one, suggest that the "Lay" be considered a separate work, as do the running titles (which read *Lay de Dame*) on the upper margins of the folios occupied by the "Lay." On the other hand, the "Lay" does not appear as an independent item in the manuscript's table of contents and therefore bears no item number in either its rubric or its running title. Furthermore, in terms of its decoration, it begins with the same kind of two-line decorated capital that marks the first line of each of the ballades in the *Cent ballades d'Amant et de Dame*, rather than with the larger initials reserved for the beginning of each major work.[7] In other words, details in the material realm of codicology again suggest that the "Lay" invites treatment as simultaneously part of the *Cent ballades d'Amant et de Dame* and separate from it, a postscript as well as an autonomous composition.

In an earlier version of this essay, I referred to the "Lay" as a coda to the *Cent ballades d'Amant et de Dame*.[8] In its figurative sense, the notion of coda is particularly well suited to the poem, describing an entity defined in the *Oxford English Dictionary* as of more or less independent character, introduced after the completion of the essential parts of a movement, so as to form a more definite and satisfactory conclusion. Thelma Fenster, translator (with Nadia Margolis) of Christine's *Book of the Duke of True Lovers*, uses the word twice with similar intent in the introduction to her translation to refer to the group of poems appended to that work.[9] Others have found comparable labels or metaphors: Christine's first modern editor, Maurice Roy, described the "Lay de Dame" as a "complément" to the *Cent ballades d'Amant et de Dame* (III, p. xviii), and Jacqueline Cerquiglini, its second and much more recent editor, as an "explicit" for the work (p. 19). The common thread in all these designations, obviously, is a desire to express the parallel movements of the "Lay," one an inward spiral, the other an outward connection to the material that precedes it.

In form, if not in tone, the "Lay" contrasts sharply with the ballades it accompanies. In the terminology of poetic forms used for lyric written in the French vernacular of the later Middle Ages, the *lai* was longer than the other *formes fixes* (such as the rondeau, ballade, and virelai), often running to two or three hundred lines or more. It was therefore relatively open-ended and allowed for a much fuller treatment of the chosen subject than one could manage in a ballade, for example. Machaut composed some two dozen lais, launching a revival of the form that lasted into the fifteenth century. The great majority of his poems of this type correspond to the rules made explicit somewhat later by Eustache Deschamps. Metrically, the lai was subject to relatively few prescriptive rules: the first two strophes established a rhyme scheme and number of syllables per line which were repeated exactly in the last two, but the intervening strophes, often grouped in pairs, could and did follow highly intricate flights of metrical and rhyming fancy.[10]

In a modern treatment of the structural and thematic properties of the lai, Robert Deschaux examines lais composed by the major poets following Machaut to determine how closely they adhered to these prescriptive guidelines.[11] Christine's "Lay mortel," it would seem, manifests the greater liberties taken by fifteenth-century authors in adopting the form. It does conform to the rules of the genre in so far as the last two "couplets" of eight lines (seven syllables per line, with a rhyme scheme of *aaabaaab*) mirror the first two, while the wordplay and manipulation of line length and rhyme in the middle sections stand as a most impressive display of her technical mastery. Within its 283 lines, however, it is difficult to ascertain the exact intended division into strophes. Roy and Cerquiglini, the only two editors to have presented this text for modern readers, divide the text similarly: into twenty-four strophes in Roy's edition, and twenty-five strophes in Cerquiglini's (which splits the last sixteen lines into two blocks of eight, corresponding to a similar division in the first sixteen).[12] The evidence of the manuscript is more than a little ambiguous and therefore open to interpretation, but it would appear that the poem is indeed constructed on the basis of twenty-four discrete sections, sometimes, but not always, grouped in two similar metrical units. It therefore transgresses to some extent the traditional pattern of twelve units, each containing matching halves.[13]

In terms of the thematics of her poem, the choice of the lai form for a poem of despair and sorrow is not unusual, although it was used perhaps more commonly as a template for expressions of joy rather than suffering.[14] Fifty years earlier, Guillaume de Machaut had written two "Lais de plour" [lays of lament] and a "Lai mortel" [lay of death], and there are definite similarities, whether intentional or not, between Christine's "Lay mortel" and Machaut's "Lai" number 5 ("Nul ne doit avoir merveille" [No one should wonder]).[15] Nevertheless, as those who know Christine's poetry might guess, here, as elsewhere, she tailors what is otherwise a conventional poem to make it function in a highly innovative, significant way.

What leaps to the eye immediately in reading the "Lai mortel" is the use of learned examples in the first half of the poem to illustrate the great destructive force of love. The first strophes begin with an apostrophe to the God of Love, "O Amours dure et sauvage" [O Love, harsh and wild] (v. 1), from whom no one can escape. Love lurks everywhere in search of the unsuspecting, she continues (vv. 2–28), as is made apparent by Ovid in his book, who tells of its powers. Herewith follow three groups of examples. First one finds several representatives of "les dieux / Celestes" [the celestial gods] (vv. 52–53), more specifically Pluto, Proserpine, Jupiter, and Apollo, none of whom were immune to love's powers despite their own. Next come representatives of "les vieux / Sages" (vv. 53–54), meaning the wise ancients of history and scripture, David, Solomon, Samson, and Hercules, again equally incapable of escaping Love's arrows. The message is restated as follows: "Il n'est doncques nulz homs mortieulx, / S'il a cuer, pensée, et yeulx, / Qui doubter ne doye en tous lieux / Tes dars" [any mortal creature endowed with heart, eyes, and the power of thought must be wary of Love's arrows wherever he may be] (vv. 62–65).

Finally, the stories of two "sages dames" [wise ladies] (v. 67), Medea and Dido, are treated at some length in two successive strophes. Medea is the main subject in the strophe consisting of lines 67–84, Dido of lines 85–100. The two strophes, containing eighteen and sixteen lines, respectively, are among the longest in the poem and are related metrically, each mixing octosyllabic and four-syllable lines. Their similar length and rhythms reinforce the parallels between Medea and Dido as examples of courtly women helpless and wronged in love. The emphasis remains on the introductory adjective "sage," as both are held up as examples of accomplished, learned women whose knowledge and power were not enough to save them from their fate as helpless prey to both the God of Love and the ill treatment of their respective lovers. Christine provides us here with an example of the filter she employs when invoking biblical figures or the classical pantheon, stripping the Medea and Dido legends of all components extraneous or deleterious to her agenda; unmentioned are the madness and excesses of Dido, purged from the text the magic and infanticide for which Medea is known elsewhere. For the purposes of this poem, they are reduced to and paired as exemplars of noble women constant in love, their experience delimited to the Ovidian arena, just as one finds them in the *Livre de la Cité des Dames* in the company of Thisbe, Hero, and others.[16]

This sampling of illustrious but rejected women works neatly on two levels as a transition from the early, didactic lines of the "Lay" to the much more personal, lyric expression which follows. From Medea and Dido, the topic segues (more or less accurately around line 100) into the experience of the speaking subject, the "I" of this poem: the lady speaking here has herself been abandoned by a lover to whom she is still deeply attached, and it is this deception and disillusionment which are leading her to the grave. Furthermore, Jason and Eneas, unworthy recipients of Medea's and Dido's affections, stand as the first of the false, disloyal lovers against whom a good bit of invective is directed from this point to the end of the poem.

The link established between legendary tragic figures and the narrator of the poem is meaningful on other levels as well, however. On a larger scale, moreover, this technique of self-association with illustrious forebears recalls Christine's rhetorical strategy in the *Livre de la Cité des Dames*, in the *Mutacion de Fortune*, in the *Chemin de long estude,* and even in the *Ditié de Jehanne d'Arc*; in each case, the narrator implicitly or explicitly allies herself with major figures of legend, history, or literature as defining terms in the construction of her own identity and authority.[17] On the more intimate scale of this particular text, the narrator heightens the magnitude of her own tragedy to epic proportions. Despite the modesty topos employed elsewhere—"Moy qui suis simple creature" [I who am a simple creature] (v.115), for example—she succeeds in associating herself with illustrious company, inscribing herself on the list of exempla from which other women should take heed. The reader is reminded of the explicit injunction of the lady in the last ballade of the *Cent ballades d'Amant et de Dame*, who with her dying breath hopes that her fate will serve as an object lesson on the dangers of love. In this instance, the warning is rendered all the more acute by its subtext. As much as Medea and Dido are tamed in the description of them here, the fury and drama of their response to betrayal remain an inescapable if unspoken element of those stories for a knowing audience. They point to the rebellious nature of this speaker's final act: although her exit scene may play out in less spectacular fashion, she no more than they will retreat in silence.

The much more personal lament of the second half of the "Lay" signals a return to the thematic threads of the ballades of the *Cent ballades d'Amant et de Dame* themselves and thus raises another question regarding the relationship between the "Lay" and the larger collection it follows. Is the lady of the "Lay" the same as the female protagonist whose story has just ended? Why a lai to restate the grief already expressed in Ballade 100 by the lady on her deathbed? Answering these questions will uncover the function of this "Lay," imposed as a postscript to a work which achieves a very satisfying level of closure in and of itself.

The first puzzle then, is the identity of the lady speaking in the "Lay." She does not appear to be identical to the woman who has had the last word in Ballade 100. Indeed, if one were determined to hear the same voice in both poems, the fragile lady on the verge of death in Ballade 100 would have to be allowed a major recovery to attain the indignant, somewhat querulous tone of the first half of the "Lay." The lady of the "Lay" also awaits death by the end of her poem, but she seems much more bent on vengeance and/or pique than her resigned sister in Ballade 100. Both Françoise Paradis and Charity Cannon Willard have remarked on the changes in tone from Ballade 100 to the "Lay,"[18] pinpointing the elaboration of historical and mythological examples as the element which seems to "falsify somewhat the emotions of the abandoned lady" (Willard, p. 362). Willard takes this passage as one in which Christine gets carried away by her show of erudition (an interpretation reinforced by the virtuosity of the verse forms in the "Lay"), while Paradis prefers to read it as an indication that the lady can be read as the double of the woman author whose voice is heard in a prologue to the *Cent ballades d'Amant et de Dame*, where she states that love brought many hardships as well as much joy to her characters in the story that follows.[19] Even more pertinent, perhaps, in the prologue, is Christine's statement as author that she writes this work as a fine incurred for encouraging women elsewhere in her corpus to avoid the temptations of love.[20] No matter what the ostensible intent, the *Cent ballades d'Amant et de Dame* is obviously a restatement of the same theme, illustrated this time as an object lesson, and the "Lay" reinforces the warning that a lady can expect misery as the inevitable outcome of courtly dalliance.

Paradis's hypothesis equating the lady of the "Lay" with the author of the prologue is useful, I think, in demonstrating what the "Lay" brings to the *Cent ballades d'Amant et de Dame*. Here I approach the implications of the interaction between a genre such as the lai and an accumulation of examples of the ballade, quite a different type. Poirion points out that whereas the movement of the lyric genres is concentric, the movement of the lai, by contrast, is "excentrique" (*Le poète et le prince*, p. 400), meaning that while it progresses by discontinuous units and remains inherently lyric, it still allows for a development of thought and subject matter much more extensive than possible within the constraints of, for example, the three-strophe ballade with its recurring refrain. This mixture of linear and interrupted movement can lead to greater or lesser degrees of narrativity and lyricism. As Poirion says, "Le lai est comme le commentaire affectif de l'événement ou de l'aventure que raconterait le *dit*, qu'analyserait la prose, que célébrerait la liturgie" (p. 404) [The lai is like the affective commentary on the event or adventure which might be told in a *dit*, analyzed in prose, or celebrated in liturgy]. In the case of the *Cent ballades d'Amant et de Dame*, our "Lay mortel" provides the commentary on a narrative sketched out in a series of ballades, providing a level of reflection which could not be accommodated in the previous one hundred poems, articulating more fully the moral lessons implicit in the situation with which the reader has just been presented.

The one hundred ballades of the main text, spoken as they are by the two protagonists, constitute a very intimate discourse, one which is focused primarily—almost exclusively—on the psychological impact on the two parties of the love they share and then lose. This being vintage Christine de Pizan, however, an element of didacticism does surface: we return to the passage in the last ballade, mentioned above, in which the dying lady states: "De toutes dames soit sceue / Ceste exemple, a fin que leurs / Cuers, si faicte amour, ne mue, / Car ja me deffault li cuers" [Let this example (that is, my example) be known to all ladies, in order that love cannot change their hearts, for already my heart is breaking] (100: 13–16). And of course we have heard the indirect warning of the poet's voice in the introductory ballade. But the "Lay" can supply what the ballades have no room for, the analogies so dear to the heart of any medieval *clerc*, the proof that the text's teachings are grounded in recognized authority. The lai is well suited to such illustration; to quote again from Poirion, "La malléabilité et la mollesse du genre expliquent que la pensée didactique s'y soit trouvée à l'aise" [The malleable and flexible nature of the genre explains why a didactic element can often be found therein] (*Le poète et le prince*, p. 410). In fact, although the lai is at heart still a lyric genre, the passages in the "Lay mortel" which expound on the learned examples resemble closely Christine's narrative texts about love, such as the judgment poems, for example, or the *Epistre au Dieu d'amour* [Letter of the God of Love], to which it is also allied closely by subject matter. Here the "Lay" turns outward the lessons which the lady in the *Cent ballades d'Amant et de Dame* turns inward, glossing the text, making explicit the moral tone implicit in the ballades.

The question remains, however, of whether the voice in the "Lay" is assimilable to that of Christine the poet. Certainly one could assume that this lady is intended at least in part as a mouthpiece for the author. But I would suggest that rather than Christine herself, this woman's voice represents one of her clear-eyed, distinctly anti-courtly female characters who intervene, without participating in the plot, to render a judgment on the topic at hand. Christine has a penchant for building commentary into her love narratives and poetry, either as second-degree narration or simply as extra-diegetic interventions, to correct the notion that she may be promoting the values of the tradition within which her poetry must be evaluated. One thinks of the disclaimers built into poems one, fifty, and one hundred of her first collection of poems, the *Cent balades*. Or of the letter from Sebille de la Tour to her wayward mistress, used twice, once in *Le Livre du Duc des vrais amants* [Book of the Duke of True Lovers] and once in *Le Livre des Trois Vertus* [Book of the Three Virtues]. Or again of the nameless woman invited to accompany the debaters in the *Debat de deux amans* [Debate of Two Lovers], who scoffs at the seriousness of their discussion on the nature of love as the speakers pause between turns. The lady in what begins as the "Lay de dame" speaks as a representative of all the women who have been wronged by unfaithful lovers, much in the same vein as the fictional complaints brought before Cupid in the *Epistre au Dieu d'amour*.[21]

She does it, moreover, in a conspicuously prominent position: at the very end of the very last love poetry written by Christine, the only surviving copy of which occupies the last folios of a major presentation copy of Christine's poetic works. It is not surprising to discover a didactic agenda behind this, the final word on the subject of illicit love. As Nadia Margolis points out with regard to a poem which might be considered a prototype of the "Lay de Dame," Christine manages to exploit the versatile nature of various lyric forms to combine "cris de cour" [cries from the court] with "cris de coeur" [cries from the heart], political protest with more personal expressions of heartache (*Duke of True Lovers*, p. 41). Here the dual nature of the poem is expressed in its two titles: the "Lay mortel" begins as a "Lay de Dame" on behalf of all women before narrowing to the perspective of one particularly unhappy example.

Even the more conventional, more truly lyric portion of the poem corrects the content of similar pieces. Before the *Cent ballades d'Amant et de Dame*, Christine had written two "Complaintes amoureuses" and two other lais, independent of any longer composition, which read like exercises in versification.[22] None is particularly noteworthy except, perhaps, the first lai, which consists entirely of *rimes leonimes*, or very rich rhymes, a considerable technical achievement. Maurice Roy's assessment of it is worth quoting for its tone of dismay: "Malheureusement, les règles étroites auxquelles se trouve assujettie la diction de l'auteur ont pour inconvénient d'obscurcir fortement la pensée et de ne laisser entrevoir le plus souvent qu'un sens à peine intelligible. Car il serait assez difficile de déterminer exactement la raison d'être du premier lai dont le sujet réside tout entier dans une éloge vague de l'amour en générale" [Unfortunately, the strict rules constraining the author's diction have the disadvantage of obscuring to a large degree the thinking behind it, most often permitting one to glimpse only a vaguely intelligible meaning. Indeed, it would be difficult to determine precisely the *raison d'être* of the first lai, the subject of which consists of nothing but vague praise regarding love in general] (I, p. xxxii). Roy's statement is an elegant formulation to say that Christine's preoccupation with the formal properties of the poem largely obscures its contents.[23] While he considers the second lai, consisting of praise for a perfect lover, rather more successful, his opinion of the complaintes is again rather low: he speaks of these poems, both spoken by men who hope to gain the favor of their ladies, as "longues et languissantes tirades de poursuivants d'amour" [long and languishing tirades of those who pursue love] and of their "monotonie douce" [sweet monotony] (1, p. xxxvii). They do have the merit, in his eyes, of leavening the tedium a little with examples taken from mythology, an element which Christine incorporated into the "Lay de Dame" as well, as we have seen.

But what are the topics of these earlier poems? Both of the complaintes are declarations of devotion spoken in a man's voice to the beloved lady. The "Lay mortel" transforms and intensifies these garden-variety entreaties by allowing the lady to adopt the same forum and by raising the stakes to include death as a possible consequence of failed love. In the case of the lais, the subject matter of the two early examples is none other than exactly what she refutes in the "Lay de Dame": the first is in praise of love (beginning: "Amours, plaisant nourriture" [Love, sweet nourishment]), the second an extended song of praise for the speaker's lover, a man of sublime perfection. It will be obvious by now that the "Lay de Dame" following the *Cent ballades d'Amant et de Dame* heaps scorn on the first (that is, love) and doubts the existence of the second (that is, the perfect lover). At the end of her career as a lyric poet, Christine corrects the vision to be found in the commonplaces of her and others' traditional courtly poetry.

The poem in Christine's corpus closest in inspiration to the "Lay de Dame" is the "Complainte," referred to above as a possible prototype, which closes the group of lyric poems appended to *Le Livre du Duc des vrais amans*. The two poems invite comparison not only because they are both tagged onto longer narrative works but also because the *Duc* is supposedly the text to which the *Cent ballades d'Amant et de Dame* replies. As expected according to the rules of lyric genres, the form of the "Complainte" is considerably simpler than that of the "Lay": it consists of ten, regular strophes of sixteen lines, reminiscent of Christine's narrative dits.[24] The tone, however, is much the same as in the later "Lay": the female protagonist of the preceding story (or a character very much like her) expounds upon the grievous wrong done to her by her lover, who has transferred his affections to another lady. Like the "Lay," the "Complainte" contains two distinct parts, the first recalling the early days of the courtship and the lover's dreadful suffering until the lady granted him her attentions, while the second details her despair once he changes his mind.

The poem is significant for an understanding of the "Lay de Dame" because of the inversion it operates on the "dying for love" topos. The first section recounts in a woman's voice the standard male vision of love: her suitor wastes away, lies inert, close to death because the lady has not yet accepted him. She is his "mire," his doctor and remedy. Once their positions are reversed, however, subsequent to the dissolution of their love, her fatal condition is less easily remedied than his. It results from rejection and abandonment, from active ill treatment rather than from a prolonged state of anticipation. The salve of a return visit from the philandering lover would hardly effect a cure, as he has proven himself to be unfaithful, an unworthy object of her constant devotion. Her injury is much more fundamental than his: her trust has been abused, and she has no choice, loyal and virtuous person that she is, but to carry her disappointment to the grave, a passage hastened by her grief. The scenario is the same in the "Lay de Dame," particularly in the desolate second half which evolves into the "Lay mortel." Here the mode of the lai and the complainte merges with the lament; the male model of lovesick languor provides the vocabulary and the figurative language, but the stakes are much higher, and the long-suffering suitor's dissatisfaction is transformed into a dirge. Quite absent is the paradoxical painful pleasure resulting from the deferral of the lover's gratification, that fundamental topos of the love lyric. All reciprocity has been banished from the equation; this is not the sort of delicious despair to which the lady willingly abandons herself because her beloved is similarly afflicted. Here the lady sings of and commemorates her own passing, having adapted the lover's complaint to give voice to a kind of courtly Everywoman, rehearsing her inevitable fate as the victim of a game she is encouraged to play.

As such, the "Lay de Dame" does indeed make a wonderfully resonant "coda" to Christine's corpus of love poems. Extending the metaphor to melodramatic lengths, one might say that the "Lay mortel" sounds a death knell on many levels: a more or less autonomous passage at the end of a composition, it concludes and glosses the *Cent ballades d'Amant et de Dame* but also marks the cessation of Christine's lyric production and constitutes the last entry in one of her principal manuscripts. It also provides a summation of one of the most notable of her preceding themes, an echo recalling many a passage in earlier works. The demise of the solitary and forlorn lady, unremarked but for her own account, forms a suitably bleak closure to an extended challenge of the mores of traditional courtly discourse and its "fatal" nature for the female speaking voice.

With a small shift in focus and metaphor, one might also explain the nature and function of the "Lay" in poetic terms as that of an envoi. As mentioned above, such a short closing passage, intimately linked in theme and form with the greater portion of the poem preceding it, came into its own as an addendum to the ballade in the late fourteenth century. Eustache Deschamps demonstrates and prescribes the appropriate form for the envoi of a ballade in the *Art de dictier*, noting their novelty.[25] Certainly Machaut had already used the envoi in his *chants royaux*, but Christine embraces it wholeheartedly for the ballade, her favorite of the *formes fixes*. She employs it in only seventeen of the one hundred poems in her early *Cent balades*.[26] In the *Cent ballades d'Amant et de Dame*, however, every one of the ballades, including the introductory poem, ends with an envoi, and the flexibility with which the one hundred envois are formulated reflects the technical innovation and playfulness that marks the series of ballades as a whole.[27]

Although in the fifteenth century the exact composition of the envoi could vary, it generally contained no more than half the number of lines in each strophe of the ballade to which it was appended, ended with the refrain, and often began with an apostrophe, either the conventional one to the "Prince" (a vestige of the poetry competitions of the *puys*) or to a more readily identifiable interlocutor of the speaking voice. If we enlarge the scope of the structure, the "Lay" following the *Cent ballades d'Amant et de Dame* conforms to these principles. Even at 283 lines, it is only a fraction of the length of the one hundred ballades taken together and thus reads as a tag to the longer work. With its restatement of the pessimistic, warning note on which the ballades end, and with its reprise of a deathbed scenario as the dramatic situation from which the speaker delivers her diatribe, the envoi most certainly reiterates what one might consider the refrain of the *Cent ballades d'Amant et de Dame* as a whole. Lastly, given its direct address to Amours in its first line, an apostrophe taken up again in line 224 and reinforced through to the end of the poem by repeated deictics referring to the God of Love in the second person, the "Lay" reproduces the vocative with which an envoi usually began. One might say, therefore, that the "Lay" echoes on a larger scale the consistent use of the envoi in the main text, a hallmark of the art of the ballade in this particular collection: that is, the "Lay" is to the *Cent ballades d'Amant et de Dame* as the envoi is to each individual ballade.

This extension of the principle of the envoi to a higher level of poetic organization can be linked, I would argue, to two tendencies in Christine's corpus. The first is her proclivity for glossing any given text, not only the work of others, in accordance with the best medieval tradition, but also her own. We have touched on this feature in relation to the heroines in her love narratives who defy courtly notions by interjecting a dose of cold realism into the discussion. On a broader scale, commentary also comes in the form of the series of poems appended to the *Livre du Duc des vrais amans*; the exhortation of the narrator to "les femmes" in the closing passage of the *Livre de la Cité des Dames*; or the triple layers of meaning exposed for each entry in the *Epistre d'Othea*. Christine likes to have the last word: she reasserts control at the end of a fiction, reinstitutes the focalization through her own narrator's eyes, or plays with perspective in some way so as to broaden—or impose—the final viewpoint on the subject matter of her work.

The second tendency is one she shares with contemporary authors, an aesthetic manifested most obviously in the *Cent balades* penned by Jean le Sénéschal and his collaborators or in John Gower's *Cinkante ballades*, for example, but discernible also in more fluid, heterogeneous groupings of texts. For these authors, the focus of the lyric poem could be turned outward as well as into an individual piece, to capitalize on the formal properties of a genre and the content of any given poem not only as elaborated within the confines of that text but also in its relationship to others. A series of poems linked in some deliberate way becomes more than the sum of its parts. Within the *Cent ballades d'Amant et de Dame*, each ballade gains synergistically from the formal counterpoint and thematic expansion made possible by its inclusion with like poems. In the coupling of the *Cent ballades d'Amant et de Dame* and the "Lay de Dame," both benefit from their differences and similarities. The range of rhythms, strophe size, and sheer length of the "Lay" provide release from the tightly controlled ballade form, allowing for a development of the theme in an expansive mode which highlights the beauty and the limitations of the ballade form. At the same time, the use at both the micro- and macro-levels of an envoi with its direct address is at once especially appropriate for a series that proceeds as epistolary exchange and dialogue and a striking structural device giving symmetry to a combination of dissimilar forms. Christine's lyric may not have lent itself to song, but her deft manipulation of inter- and intrageneric poetic movements gave a new and greater amplitude of voice to the refrains of the late French Middle Ages.

Notes

1. For discussion of the *formes fixes* in general and the ballade in particular, see Daniel Poirion, *Le poète et le prince*, and James Laidlaw, "The *Cent balades*: The Marriage of Content and Form" (included in this volume).

2. This poem is Ballade XI of the *Cent balades* and can be found in *Œuvres poétiques de Christine de Pisan*, ed. Maurice Roy (Paris: Firmin Didot, 1886–96), I, p. 12.

3. Such as "Mon doulz amy, venez a moy parler," *Cent ballades d'Amant et de Dame*: XXXII, Roy, *Œuvres poétiques*, III, pp. 241–42; or *Cent ballades d'Amant et de Dame*, ed. Jacqueline Cerquiglini, pp. 63–64. All quotations will be taken from Cerquiglini's edition.

4. There is some slender evidence to suggest that while Harley 4431 is the only surviving copy of the work, it may not have been the earliest. This information, which I owe to James Laidlaw, is based on details of a lost collection of Christine's works known as the Burgundy Manuscript and of a fragment in Leiden (MS Ltk. 1819), as well as on evidence from MS ex-Phillipps 128, a copy of Christine's *Avision*. For more on the first two manuscripts, see Laidlaw, "Christine de Pizan—A Publisher's Progress," especially pp. 59–60.

5. For the sake of accuracy, it should be noted that the rubric announcing the *Cent ballades d'Amant et de Dame* comes before the prefatory ballade, thus enfolding it to a greater degree than the "Lay de Dame" within the body of the text, although the numbering starts with the second ballade, where the characters themselves begin to speak.

6. In Harley 4431, the "Lay de Dame" occupies folios 396r°b to 398r°b. The *Cent ballades d'Amant et de Dame* in its entirety appears on folios 376 to 398. I am grateful to James Laidlaw for alerting me to the salient codicological features which reinforce the hybrid nature of the text in its relationship to the preceding work.

7. The decoration of the "Lay de Dame" is consistent with that used in Christine's other lais in Harley 4431. They also begin with a two-line ornamented capital and merit their own running title; significantly, however, each of them bears its own item number.

8. My preliminary remarks on this topic were read as a paper in October 1992 at the twenty-sixth annual conference of the Center for Medieval and Renaissance Studies, SUNY Binghamton, entitled "The Roles of Women in the Middle Ages: A Reassessment."

9. Thelma S. Fenster and Nadia Margolis, Christine de Pizan: *The Book of the Duke of True Lovers,* pp. 16 and 27.

10. Eustache Deschamps includes in his *Art de dictier* the following description of how a lai should be constructed: "Item, quant est des laiz, c'est une chose longue et malaisiee a faire et trouver, car il y fault avoir ·xij· couples, chascune partie en deux, qui font ·xxiiij·. Et est la couple aucunefoiz de ·viij· vers, qui font ·xvj·; aucunefoiz de ·ix·, qui font ·xviij·; aucunefoiz de dix qui font ·xx·; aucunefoiz de ·xij· qui font ·xxiiij·, de vers entiers ou de vers coppez. Et couvient que la taille de chascune couple a deux paragrafes soient d'une rime toutes differens l'une couple a l'autre, excepte tant seulement que la derreniere couple des ·xij·, qui font ·xxiiij·, et qui est et doit estre conclusion du lay, soit de pareille rime, et d'autant de vers, sanz redite, comme la premiere couple" [As for lais, they are long and not easy to write and compose, for it is necessary to have twelve strophes in a lai, each one divided in two, which makes twenty-four. The half-strophe sometimes has eight lines, which makes sixteen; and sometimes nine, which makes eighteen; sometimes ten, which makes twenty; sometimes twelve which makes twenty-four whole or truncated lines. It is proper that the measure of each strophe of two stanzas be marked off by a rhyme differing completely from one strophe to the other with the exception of the last strophe of the twelve (which makes twenty-four) which is and must be the conclusion of the lai, and must have the same rhyme scheme, and as many lines, without repetition, as the first strophe], Eustache Deschamps, *L'Art de dictier,* pp. 94 and 96. The *Art* can also be found in *Œuvres complètes de Eustache Deschamps*, vol. 7, pp. 287–88. Christine's *Lay* diverges from these rules in that her strophes are not always arranged in groups of two;

furthermore, the length of some of them exceeds that of the examples Deschamps gives, ranging up to twenty-four lines.

11. For a modern treatment of the structural and thematic properties of the lai (as well as of the complainte), see Robert Deschaux, "Le lai et la complainte," particularly pp. 70–77.

12. Deschaux, by contrast, states that the poem consists of eighteen strophes ("Le lai et la complainte," p. 73). It is unclear how he arrives at this division, which corresponds neither to the blocks of texts as presented in Cerquiglini's edition, which he cites, nor to the manuscript layout itself. On the latter point, see the following note.

13. In Harley 4431, the poem is presented as follows: After the first strophe, in which the initial "O" is a two-line ornamented capital, the prevailing pattern of the layout seems to be a blank line after each strophe and a paragraph mark in the left margin at the beginning of the next. There are anomalies in this scheme, however, which give rise to the ambiguity mentioned above. The twelfth strophic block ("O amorsure," v. 122) is preceded by a blank space but does not have a paragraph mark. In contrast, at two lines where one might expect a break in the text, there are dots in the margin which may or may not indicate that a break was intended. (James Laidlaw, in signaling the presence of these extra-linguistic marks for the benefit of my argument, points out that the problem is compounded by the fact that one cannot be certain when they were inserted and by whom.) The first dot occurs at line 232, in the middle of a block of twenty lines which splits into two similar but not identical halves linked by enjambment from line 231 to 232; a twenty-line strophe is very long for a lai, but there is another in Christine's poem, lines 162–81, which gives no indication of an intended division. One finds the second dot at line 276, halfway through the last block of sixteen lines. If this final passage is intended to mirror the beginning of the poem, according to a rule of the genre Christine seems to respect, one would expect it to be divided into two eight-line blocks just as the first sixteen are.

14. Deschaux identifies "la thématique" of the lai as a genre somewhat differently, by subject matter rather than emotional tenor. He lists the three major topics of the lai as "l'événement politique, la préoccupation morale ou religieuse, le sentiment de l'amour" [a political event, moral or religious concerns, a feeling of love].

15. Machaut's *Lais* are available in the edition by Vladimir Chichmaref, Guillaume de Machaut: *Poésies lyriques*. Number 5 begins on p. 314, the two "Lais de plour" on pp. 434 and 459, respectively. Christine's "Lay" shares the vocabulary of number 5, in which a man laments because his beloved does not accept his entreaties; the first and last two strophes of Christine's poem are metrically similar to those in Machaut's, consisting of eight seven-syllable lines, using one of the same rhymes (in-*endre*) and several of the same rhyme words.

16. See *Le Livre de la Cité des Dames*, Part II, 55 and 56. The *Cité* is available in English translation (Earl Jeffrey Richards, trans., *The Book of the City of Ladies* [New York: Persea, 1982, 1998]) and in modern French (Eric Hicks and Thérèse Moreau,

trans., *La Cité des dames* [Paris: Stock, 1986]). Apart from the passage in which Medea and Dido are cited as ill-treated lovers, both are included earlier in the *Cité* as women of great learning and wisdom (Part I, 32 and 46).

17. I am indebted to Nadia Margolis for her suggestions on this and other points.

18. Françoise Paradis, "Une polyphonie narrative," p. 135; and Charity Cannon Willard, "Christine de Pizan: *Cent ballades d'amant et de dame*," pp. 357–64.

19. Paradis: "Nous affirmerions voluntiers que la voix de la dame protagoniste du récit lyrique s'éteint avec le dernier vers de la centième ballade et que Christine relaye son personnage en prenant à son compte ses malheurs pour refermer son oeuvre sur elle-même du 'commencement' au 'lay de dame'" ("Une polyphonie narrative," p. 135).

20. Perhaps not coincidentally, a lai is among the three poems which Guillaume de Machaut is charged with writing as his punishment at the end of *Le jugement du roi de Navarre*. The "Lay de Plour" of 210 lines following the *Jugement* is written in a woman's voice and laments a death, not her own in this case, but that of her lover to whom she remains constant and whom she wishes to follow to the grave. For the text of Machaut's "Lay," see *Oeuvres de Guillaume de Machaut*, ed. Ernest Hoepffner, I, pp. 283–291; or *Guillaume de Machaut: The Judgment of the King of Navarre*, ed. and trans. R. Barton Palmer, pp. 190–212.

21. This analysis agrees with Cerquiglini's reading, which does not assimilate the voice of the "Lay" to that of the lady in the preceding ballades or to Christine the poet. The voice of the first "s'éteint à la ballade Cent" [dies out in Ballade 100], and Christine herself "ne reprend pas la parole" [does not speak again] in this collection as she does in the last poem of the first *Cent balades*. Cerquiglini labels the "Lay" simply "un jeu formel . . . un poème lyrique très élaborée" [a formal game . . . a very elaborate lyric poem] (*Cent ballades d'Amant et de Dame*, introduction, p. 19), in which she presumably reads the speaking subject as an anonymous, female, third party.

22. The two lays and two complaintes can be found in Roy, I, pp. 125, 136, 281, and 289, respectively.

23. In fact the privileging of technique over content in this poem is not surprising when considered in light of its entry in the manuscript's "Table des dictiez," where it is introduced as, "Item une assemblee de plusieurs rimes auques toutes leonimes en facon de lay a qui vouldroit apprendre a rimer leonimement" [A group of several verses, almost entirely in leonines in the style of a lai, for whoever wants to learn how to compose leonines].

24. See Roy, III, pp. 203–8. Each strophe is composed of four sections of three seven-syllable lines followed by a four-syllable line, giving the rhyme scheme: *aaabaaabaaabaaab*. The complainte as a genre follows a much simpler, linear progression than the lai, in which units of the same structure and rhyme scheme are repeated from beginning to end. While the thematic distinction is, in theory, that the lai treats effusive joy and the complainte, true to its name, provides a frame for lament or complaint on either political matters or matters of love (see Poirion, *Le poète et le*

prince, pp. 399–426), in practice, the two tended to converge, and many a lai by Machaut, Deschamps, or Charles d'Orléans is as gloomy as a complainte in nature.

25. In introducing his own example of a ballade with an envoi, he says of the latter, "[N]e les souloit on point faire anciennement fors es chancons royaulx" [They were not generally used in the past, except in 'chants royaux'], *L'Art de dictier*, p. 78, ll. 339–40. For modern sources on the envoi, see the brief discussion in Poirion, *Le poète et le prince*, pp. 388–89 (in his section on "Chant Royal et Ballade"), and more extensive treatment by Laidlaw in "The *Cent balades*: The Marriage of Content and Form."

26. The exact number of poems in the *Cent balades* containing an envoi varies slightly in the different versions in which the *Cent balades* appear. See Laidlaw, in this volume.

27. For detailed information concerning the formal properties of the ballades in the *Cent ballades d'amant et de dame*, consult the article by Paradis, "Une polyphonie narrative," which diagrams the collection in an appendix, listing meter, rhyme scheme, interlocutors, treatment of the envoi, and the phase of the story ("diégèse") represented in each poem.

Works Cited

Christine de Pizan. *Cent ballades d'Amant et de Dame*. Ed. Jacqueline Cerquiglini-Toulet. Paris: Union Générale d'Éditions, 1982.
Deschamps, Eustache. *L'Art de dictier*. Ed. and trans. Deborah M. Sinnreich-Levi. East Lansing, Mich.: Colleagues Press, 1994.
———. *Œuvres complètes de Eustache Deschamps*. Ed. Marquis de Queux de Saint-Hilaire and Gaston Raynaud. Société des Anciens Textes Français. 11 vols. Paris: Firmin Didot, 1878–1903.
Deschaux, Robert. "Le lai et la complainte." *La littérature française aux XIVe et XVe siècles, Grundriß der romanischen Literaturen des Mittelalters*, VIII/1, pp. 70–85. Heidelberg: Carl Winter, 1988.
Fenster, Thelma S., ed. *The Book of the Duke of True Lovers*. Trans. Thelma S. Fenster and Nadia Margolis. Introduction by Thelma Fenster. New York: Persea, 1991.
Laidlaw, James C. "Christine de Pizan—A Publisher's Progress." *Modern Language Review* 82 (1987): 35–75.
Machaut, Guillaume de. *The Judgment of the King of Navarre*. Ed. and trans. R. Barton Palmer. New York: Garland, 1988.
———. *Œuvres de Guillaume de Machaut*. Ed. Ernest Hoepffner. Paris: Firmin-Didot, 1901.
———. *Poésies lyriques*. Ed. Vladimir Chichmaref. Geneva: Slatkine Reprints, 1973.
Paradis, Françoise. "Une polyphonie narrative: Pour une description de la structure des *Cent ballades d'amant et de dame* de Christine de Pizan." *Bien Dire et Bien Aprandre* 8 (1990): 127–40.

Poirion, Daniel. *Le poète et le prince: L'évolution du lyrisme courtois de Guillaume de Machaut à Charles d'Orléans*. Paris: Presses Universitaires de France, 1965.

Willard, Charity Cannon. "Christine de Pizan: *Cent ballades d'Amant et de Dame*: Criticism of Courtly Love." In *Court and Poet: Selected Proceedings of the Third Congress of the International Courtly Literature Society*, ed. Glynn S. Burgess et al., pp. 357–64. Liverpool: Cairns, 1981.

◌ CHAPTER 4

Tous parlent par une mesmes bouche: Lyrical Outbursts, Prosaic Remedies, and Voice in Christine de Pizan's *Livre du Duc des vrais amans*

JUDITH LAIRD AND
EARL JEFFREY RICHARDS

In examining the religious writings of medieval women, Laurie A. Finke astutely warns that reconstructing a female author's voice in medieval works can be anachronistic: "Any attempt to celebrate medieval mystics as feminist, as self-fashioning subjects, or as the authors of themselves . . . risks applying to medieval texts feminist theories of creativity which have been developed primarily from the study of nineteenth- and twentieth-century realist fiction by women. We should be wary, in particular, of feminist readings of medieval women's writing which privilege, in Patrocinio Schweickart's words, 'the manifestation of the subjectivity of the absent author—the «voice» of another woman.'"[1] Moreover, critics have been quick to speak of the intentional fallacy whenever the question of "voice" in poetry is raised. The viability of "voice" as a critical tool for evaluating Christine de Pizan's lyric remains an open question, especially in light of the important insights of Paul de Man on lyrical voice in general, of James Laidlaw and Nadia Margolis on the different kinds of voices in Christine's ballades and epistles, and of Roberta Krueger on gendered voice in the *Livre du Duc des vrais amans* [Book of the Duke of True Lovers, composed 1403–4].

De Man's observations bear repeating for our consideration of voice since Christine offers a perfect counterexample. She uses "voice" in strict conformity to medieval rhetorical practice (that is, *prosopopoeia*), a practice to which de Man objects, and in so doing Christine seeks to establish neither an aesthetic nor a self-referential, but a historical presence, a recuperation of women's voices. The difference between de Man's and Christine's position could not be more striking, and given the prevalence of de Man's thought among many current readers of Christine, it bears special scrutiny:

> The principle of intelligibility, in lyric poetry, depends on the phenomenalization of the poetic voice. Our claim to understand a lyric text coincides with the actualization of a speaking voice, be it (monologically) that of the poet or (dialogically) that of the exchange that takes place between author and reader in the process of comprehension. Since this voice is in no circumstance immediately available as an actual, sensory experience, the poetic labor that is to make it manifest can take several forms and adopt a variety of strategies. No matter what approach is taken it is essential that the status of the voice not be reduced to being a mere figure of speech or play of the letter, for this would deprive it of the attribute of aesthetic presence that determines the hermeneutics of the lyric.[2]

Roberta Krueger, in turn, examines the tensions she perceives in Christine's speaking for the reticent or tongue-tied Duke. She argues that "by voicing the *livre* as the extended monologue of a man in love, Christine can explore the problem of woman's displacement within the romance's discourse." Krueger skillfully demonstrates in fact that Christine incorporates different, indeed conflicting points of view (which we might call voices) in the *Duc des vrais amans*, and she maintains that this strategy seeks ultimately to replace "deceptive masculine discourse with a feminine voice that gives credence to her own textual and moral authority" (p. 243). Krueger follows a much wider consensus among scholars in treating the *Duc des vrais amans* as a modification of courtly romance. We would argue that while the text bears superficial resemblances to courtly romances as a narrative, it is primarily a dramatized collection of lyric and prose. This distinction helps to avoid reliance on some kind of amorphous and self-contained "romance world" to which Christine may be attempting to refer.

On a more concrete level, James Laidlaw has isolated masculine, feminine, and indeterminate voices in Christine's *Cent balades* and in so doing also has demonstrated a wide range within both masculine and feminine voices that precludes speaking of *a* masculine or of *a* feminine voice per se.³ In a careful refinement of previous investigations, Nadia Margolis has identified voices with rhetorical strategies and in particular identified the stylistically self-conscious "counter-emulative voice" in many of Christine's letters. This use of voices conforms to the model "tu recites, je replique" or "you tell things your way, I'll reply in mine."⁴

As valuable as Krueger's analysis is, it is important to recall that Christine did not view "masculine discourse" as monolithic or inherently deceptive but that, as Nadia Margolis has demonstrated, voice in Christine's works is a function of rhetoric rather than of gender. Authority for Christine stemmed on the one hand from her erudition, which was gender-neutral, and on the other from her innovative coupling of this erudition with women's historical experience, which of course was gender-specific. Although Christine scholars have tended to view the *Duc des vrais amans* as a kind of courtly romance, it actually seems closer in form to lyrical drama (works by Hugo von Hofmannsthal and T. S. Eliot come to mind as modern examples). If one were to dramatize the *Duc des vrais amans*, it would be necessary to have four female and three male actors (for the "parts" of Christine, the Lady, Sebille de Monthault, and an unnamed female companion; and the Duke, his father, and the Cousin). Rather than being a displaced monologue, the work is fundamentally dialogic and ultimately dialectical, but its dialogue and dialectic cannot be reduced to a scheme of deceptive male discourse versus truthful female speech.

The real problem with masculine discourse in the *Duc des vrais amans* is not that men are deceptive when they speak but that they often have trouble speaking to begin with, that they have difficulties finding their voice as it were (the "aw, shucks" syndrome in which men use their silence to manipulate women). Therefore Christine will speak for the Duke, as she quickly assures her readers, just as the Duke told her. A comparable (though somewhat different) situation is repeated within the narrative. At one point, the Lady asks whether she must speak for the Duke, assuring him that whatever she would say would be consistent with what Love would have her say (this question shows that Christine does not identify her rhetorical position only with that of Sebille de Monthault, as many critics have suggested):

Dont pour nous •ii• me convient
Parler, quant ne vous souvient
De riens dire! Et toutevoye,
Je croy bien qu'Amours m'envoye

De ses mets si bonne part
Que je croy que tout ne part!
De ce que je vous cuidoie
Parler ne que dire doye,
N'en saroie un seul mot dire.

[So I must speak for us both since you can remember nothing to say! And yet I think Love sends me such a large serving from his table that I believe that all of it will not show! I will be unable to say a single word of what I thought you would speak or of what I must say.] (vv. 2706–14)

This remark presents an important twist on the "ineffability" topos: while the Duke and Lady are so caught up in love that both are unable to give voice to what they feel, it is the Lady who must do the talking.

A similar pattern emerges when one examines the thirty-seven conversations of the forty-one passages in direct discourse in the *Duc des vrais amans*. While courtly romances are filled with conversational exchanges, Christine's work presents more conversations in a shorter space than courtly romances, lending the conversations an increased rhetorical and narrative prominence that dovetails with the prominence of lyrical monologues throughout the work. Fifteen (the largest number, and over a third of the total) are spoken by the Lady (ten to the Duke, five to the Cousin), as compared to eleven by the Cousin (seven to the Duke, four to the Lady), and to nine by the Duke (six to the Lady, three to the Cousin). The Lady also speaks in a monologue three times. In a concrete sense, the Lady's voice has a prominent place in the verse narrative, but her voice conforms rigorously to the conventions of courtly love. Not surprisingly, Christine looks elsewhere, as in the prose letter of Sebille de Monthault, to recuperate women's voices.

That Christine juxtaposes male and female perspectives on courtly love—with special attention paid to parallel formal structures—has been ably demonstrated by James Laidlaw with regard to the *Cent balades* [One Hundred Ballades] and by Barbara K. Altmann with regard to the *Cent ballades d'Amant et de Dame* [One Hundred Ballades of Lover and Lady]. By the same token we find that in the *Duc des vrais amans* Christine innovatively uses formal heterogeneity in a comparable, though different way in order to present a range of conflicting perspectives on courtly love that do not fall into a simple opposition between male and female voices.

Christine explicitly addresses the question of one gender speaking with a single voice at the beginning of the *Cité des Dames*. She asks Reason why it seems that so many different men are so inclined to speak "from one mouth" when they attack women: "dont ce peut venir que tant de divers hommes, clercs et autres, ont esté et sont si enclins a dire de bouche et en leurs traictiez et escrips tant de deableries et de vituperes de femmes et de leurs condicions . . . semble que tous parlent par une mesmes bouche et tous accordent une semblable conclusion, determinant les meurs femenins enclins et plains de tous les vices" (Richards, ed., p. 42) [(How does it happen) that so many different men—and learned men among them—have been and are so inclined to express both in speaking and in their treatises and writings so many devilish and wicked insults about women and their behavior . . . it seems that they all speak from one and the same mouth. They all concur in one conclusion: that the behavior of women is inclined to and full of every vice] (Richards, trans., pp. 3–4). Misogyny projects a single voice for men when they speak and write about women, whence Christine's valuable insight that all the authors she had consulted "speak from one mouth." Rather than pitting a single female voice against the monolithic voice of misogyny and thus reproducing "univocal" misogyny, Christine creates a series of dialogues among different voices, some naive and conventional (indeed, simultaneously stupid and egotistical), like the Duke's, and some tempered by experience and wisdom, like Sebille's. In her lyrical works Christine frequently chose to write poetry with male speakers, exploiting quite effectively and originally the gender difference between herself as writer and her male characters in order to reveal male hypocrisy. For example, in the *Epistre au Dieu d'amours* [Letter to the God of Love], as Lori Walters has shown, Christine resorted to "an androgynous narrative voice in which a female clerk speaks through the male God of Love."⁵ But Christine did not leave the matter there: she wished to recuperate not "woman's voice" but women's voices. In the *Duc des vrais amans*, she discovered both the limits of the formal play within courtly lyric in the attempt to recover women's voices and the possibilities of using prose to accomplish what lyric could not.

Courtly Lyrical Conventions and Formal Heterogeneity

The formal heterogeneity of the *Book of the Duke of True Lovers* resides in its combination of different kinds of lyrical forms and epistolary prose. The body of the work is in octosyllabic rhyming couplets, interspersed or punctuated by ballades, rondeaux, virelais, complaintes, and prose letters, ending in a veritable lyrical compendium entitled "Balades de plusieurs façons" [ballades of different kinds]. The formal divisions in the *Duc des vrais amans* are listed synoptically in Appendix I. Christine divided her work into fifty-four sections. She speaks explicitly in her own person at the beginning and end of the work. The Duke narrates the remainder of the work, either as indirect description (*style indirect libre* or *erlebte Rede*) or as direct quotations, or with lyrical asides of his own. The statistical breakdown here is important: discounting Christine's thirty-line prologue and the lyrical collection at the end of the *Duc des vrais amans*, the work has a total of 3,557 lines of verse, of which 2,164 lines are rhyming octosyllabic couplets. The proportion of narrative to lyrical verse is roughly three to two. In the narrative portion, 752 lines, a little more than a third of the narrative section and a little more than a fifth of the entire poem are direct citations. The *Duc des vrais amans* has many voices; indeed it is a model of polyphonic composition. Christine stylistically marks her own "voice" with a consistent pattern of alternating masculine and feminine rhymes. This strict alternation of masculine and feminine rhyming couplets in Christine's prologue does not continue in the narrative parts of the Duke's speech.

The octosyllabic rhyming couplets that form the body of the text provide a narrative frame for the lyrical portions which are in direct speech but which rhetorically speaking are monologues. Yet the octosyllabic rhyming couplets also present ostensible citations of direct speech ("ostensible" because normal conversation is usually not rhymed). Since the issue of "voice" is so important in evaluating the *Duc des vrais amans*, it is important to distinguish between narrative descriptions and those passages which, like the lyrical outbursts, are direct speech. The Duke as narrator cites himself, his Cousin, his father, and his Lady. These passages with their respective interlocutors are indicated in Appendix II. A pattern of direct citations emerges, showing on a concrete level that (excluding the brief exchange between the Duke and his father) the work is roughly arranged around three running dialogues: between the Duke and his confidant, between the Duke and the Lady, and between the Lady and Sebille de la Tour. The first two dialogues are utterly conventional exchanges based on the pattern in courtly romances whereas the third dialogue transforms the convention of a lady with her (female) confidante into a discussion by injecting concrete, historical experiences of women in the struggle to preserve their honor into a courtly world in which concrete, historical experiences were otherwise excluded. Here Christine explodes courtly conventions in the name of the "prosaic world" (to use a phrase from Hegel, whose analysis of prose has influenced Romance scholars for nearly two centuries). The Duke's three prose letters always serve to introduce enclosed lyrical compositions. The Lady's letters have no attached lyrics, and Sebille de

Monthault's letter contains an attached ballade on the honor of women. In the lyrical coda or "explicit" attached to the *Duc des vrais amans*, Christine composes ballades, virelais, and rondeaux which roughly alternate male and female speakers, and she concludes with a complainte spoken by a deceived woman.

The opening of the work does not anticipate the formal complexity of what will follow. At first glance Christine does seem to create two central characters not unlike countless conventional others in medieval prose romances: a smitten, persistent knight and his beautiful, forbidden lady, both of whom speak in a style made familiar—perhaps too familiar—by earlier courtly romances composed in both verse and prose. The association of these largely Arthurian tales in prose with the *langue d'oïl* was documented by Dante in *De vulgari eloquentia*, who noted that French literature was known for its prose works presenting, among other things, "the deeds of Trojans and Romans" and "the most lovely adventures of King Arthur."[6] In courtly romances, particularly the prose versions so popular during the fourteenth century, an explicit authorial voice is usually excluded in the name to imbue these romances with the truth of prose. Absent in these prose works, which Christine would certainly have known from the royal library, is the gentle irony of a Chrétien de Troyes or the self-conscious pride in artistic craftsmanship of a Gottfried of Strasbourg. Prosification had wrung much of the art—particularly the voice of a narrator—from these courtly romances in the name of an allegedly higher truth. The influence of these prose romances may be present in the *Duc des vrais amans* in the letters written by the Duke and the Lady, which exhibit the simple syntax and the courtly formulas of their predecessors. The prose letter of Sebille de Monthault, by contrast, is composed in a complex, subordinate prose, organized according to dictaminal rules and dispenses completely with the courtly clichés of the Duke's and Lady's letters.[7]

The prosification movement of the fourteenth century, however, did not displace octosyllabic rhyming couplets as the predominate verse narrative form in Old French literature. While originally found in such different works from the twelfth century as the romances of antiquity and the romances of Chrétien de Troyes and from the thirteenth century as the works of Rutebeuf or the *Roman de la Rose*, poets from the generation preceding Christine such as Guillaume de Machaut and Eustache Deschamps frequently used the octosyllabic rhyming couplet for a wide range of narratives. So widespread was this format that it lacked any automatic inherently "lyrical" or "courtly" associations. Christine herself uses octosyllabic rhyming couplets in the *Chemin de long estude* and *Le Livre de la mutacion de Fortune,* that is, in works far removed in their philosophical allegorical content from earlier examples of courtly romance or extended verse narrative. In other words, the octosyllabic rhyming couplets that comprise the body of the *Duc des vrais amans* do not project in formal terms a "courtly" world in which the narrative plays out. Rather, they supply a neutral background in order to intensify the comparison between the lyrical works (the ballades, rondeaux, and virelais, most of which are spoken by the Duke himself) and the prose letters (written by three characters, two women and one man). It is as though in the *Duc des vrais amans* the women learn to deploy prose against lyric. The underlying issue is the struggle between the "Duke of True Lovers," who employs conventional courtly lyric, and the "historically real" Duchess, Sebille de la Tour, who employs learned dictaminal prose instead.

A Conflict between Lyric and Prose?

Prior to Christine's time, besides being employed to recast Arthurian lore, prose had also been used for the chronicles of the Crusades and of the reigns of French kings. The prose found in these works is generally so simple in both syntax and vocabulary that modern French readers need relatively little help in understanding it. In the *Duc des vrais amans,* the prose letters written by the Duke and the Lady are composed in this simple, nonperiodic prose. In this way Christine marks the competing stylistic registers for prose composition at her disposal: prose set in subordinate syntax (as in the *Cité des Dames*) represents Christine's own voice whereas the simple prose style of the Duke and the Lady shows their remove from the dictaminal arts (not unexpected, given their social estate), and thus, by extension, their remove from a critical intellectual evaluation of their own situation as "courtly" lovers. Put bluntly, the world inhabited by the Duke and the Lady is dominated by uncritically received illusions about love, power, and the position of women and men in the historical world. In showing the shortcomings of this courtly world in light of the new learning of her age, Christine does something provocative, something that remains as provocative today as it was six centuries ago: she asks her readers to think.

Christine was well schooled in the rhetorical and dictaminal arts of her day, more like the authors of the original romances and probably unlike the compilers of the prosified romances that cluttered fourteenth- and fifteenth-century libraries and earned the just scorn of both Italian humanists in the fourteenth century and English humanists in the sixteenth.[8]

What Christine achieves in the verse narrative portions of the *Duc des vrais amans* is to write a series of exercises in prosopopoeia. In this manner, she elevates the style of composition and reshapes what her courtly audience could have expected and enjoyed, combining innovatively both the production and the reception of her work and simultaneously inscribing herself as critical author in the narrative itself.

By examining the lovers in terms of the voice and role that each receives, we can rather easily discern where Christine's voice and views do not reside. The male lover is the speaker, his is a forlorn voice dominating the narrative only in quantitative terms. The crucial question that his presence raises appears not to be "How convincing a heroic lover is he?"—a naive question at best—but rather "How successful would Christine have him be?" The reluctant lady also has a voice, but following convention, hers is not heard as often as her lover's.

In a break with fictional convention, and in a move consistent with the dichotomy between the artificialization of women's experience in courtly romance and Christine's attempt to recover the historical experience of women, it is when the historical character, Sebille de Monthault, the unnamed lady's former governess, speaks, that we hear most directly and strategically Christine's voice in the work. While put in a largely formal register (ultimately indebted to Italian dictaminal arts), her language consistently refers to experience, the key weapon of women against the misogyny of the *auctores* as Christine repeatedly points out at the beginning of the *Cité des Dames*, and avoids the pseudo-metaphysical metaphors sometimes found in courtly lyric. She insists that illicit love cannot be reconciled with virtuous conduct, an assertion that challenges the central preoccupation of courtly romance with extramarital love.

In the voice of the governess, we hear Christine's own low estimation of the courtly tradition. In fact, the governess's advice corresponds so closely to Christine's own opinion that she later cited it in *Le Livre des Trois Vertus* [The Book of the Three Virtues]. In both contexts, the fact that the governess speaks via "the written letter" intensifies the gravity with which her counsel is to be received, as Liliane Dulac has observed.[9] Certainly the parallel between the governess and Christine is strengthened by their respective role as letter-writers and, set within a verse romance whose original context (including, probably, its oral presentation for a largely female courtly public) was far removed from the curial concerns of most late medieval correspondence, lends Sebille's epistle added weight and credibility. Christine has inscribed herself as author into her text—"the writer writing the writer"—in an innovative and serious but also, given Christine's pattern of referring to her own works, no less playful way. Kevin Brownlee has investigated the "tensions between the authorial *je* (female, nonamorous, largely repressed in the course of the story line) and the *je* of her male lover-protagonist" and follows the traditional consensus that "the *je* of Christine-author, speaking in her own voice, appears only twice" in the work.[10] Whereas Brownlee sees the ultimate rhetorical strategy of the work as being an "intradiegetic valorization of courtliness" (p. 177), we would instead maintain that the work shows up the hollowness and superficiality of courtly values against the rising influence of humanistic thought and that the work repudiates courtliness completely. The intradiegetic, or perhaps better put, the self-referential quality of Christine's text that Brownlee correctly identifies is more characteristic of the courtly models that Christine herself chose to criticize and to repudiate. Courtliness as a social ideology and as a literary practice thrived on self-referential paradoxes, which, as C. P. Wormell, a philosopher of logic, has noted, rely on "oscillating statements," that is, "statements which oscillate between different directions and fail to point in any one steady direction."[11] As we will see, Christine will employ self-referentiality in order to transcend it.

Self-Referentiality and Rhetorical Displacement

Christine opens her narrative poem with a forty-line preface explaining that an unnamed patron, who had been living a *vie amoureuse* for many years, had commissioned her to write the work, on the condition that he remain unnamed ("mais ne veult que je le nom") [but he does not wish that I name him] (v. 21).[12] This anonymity departs from Christine's more regular practice of naming patrons, and whether the Duke can be identified with an actual historical person becomes a moot point, because Christine uses his anonymity to contrast with her concrete historical identity as narrator and the equally concrete naming of Sebille de Monthault.

She tactfully submits she would otherwise not have spoken about love ("Je n'eusse ne entencion / A present de dictiez faire / D'amours," vv. 2–4) unless she were quite literally obliged to tell this story of, and for, her patron: "c'est un seigneur / A qui doy bien obeir" [he is a lord whom I must obey] (v. 13) — a claim which contrasts with the central credo of the *Roman de la Rose* of the poets' dying (presumably willingly) in the service of their lord Amor. She will write love ditties [*dictiez d'amours*] but only because she has been asked to, so that she clearly foregrounds that her own authorial intention [*m'entente*] lies elsewhere. She explains that she was at the same time absorbed in her work on a serious matter far more delightful to her, which I would argue, was her biography of Charles V, "en autre affaire / Ou trop plus me delictoie / Toute m'entente mettoie" [I was wholly intent upon another matter that delighted me much more] (vv. 5–7). The ideal king presented in the biography of Charles V contrasts pointedly with the would-be "Duke of True Lovers." Thus speaking *in propria persona* at the outset in what amounts to an example of *praeteritio*, Christine disavows any endorsement of courtly love, skirting an explicit condemnation of the lovers themselves. At the same time, this allusion to the conditions under which the work was composed constitutes a textbook example of "self-referentiality" whose functions Jonathan Culler precisely described: "Self-referentiality opens a gap, between the enunciating I and the I of the statement . . . or between the enunciating poem and the poem described. . . . In general, self-referentiality does not create a self-enclosed organic unity where a work accounts for itself or becomes the things that it describes but rather produces paradoxical relations between inside and outside and brings out the impossibility of a discourse to account for itself. A work's self-description does not produce closure or self-possession but an impossible and therefore open-ended process of self-framing."[13] Culler's insights lend themselves well to the *Duc des vrais amans*: Christine's self-referential remark opens the gap between herself and the "courtly love" she describes precisely because courtly poets had created a discourse unable to account for itself. Christine was searching for a discourse that could account for itself, that could counter "the dissolution of the referent" so typical of courtly poetry, a dissolution that supported and endorsed misogyny outside the text.

Her first rhetorical tack is to adopt an utterly conventional stance by announcing at the outset that she will tell the story "just as he told it."[14] She is not inventing anything: "Si lui plaist que je raconte, / Tout ainsi comme il me conte" [thus it pleases him that I tell the story just as he told it to me] (vv. 5–6). In order to establish that she as poet is not necessarily a proponent of such affairs, she assumes the persona of the principal love, the Duke himself. The last three lines of her preface quite firmly establish how she masks her identity: "Et par son assentement / Je diray en sa personne / Le fait si qu'il le raisonne" [and with his consent I will speak in his person the matter just as he tells (or conceives of) it] (vv. 36–40). The term *raisonner* (which can mean both "to tell, recount" and "to conceive of") emphasizes the Duke's subjective and limited perception of love. Christine portrays courtly love from one male perspective by literally quoting the Duke quoting himself and others and thus shows how little the Duke has understood the women whom he quotes to Christine. While critics are correct in speaking of a displacement of women in the courtly world, the issue here is far more profound: Christine has displaced the Duke's *raisonnement*—his reasoning, his telling, his conceptualization—into a formally heterogeneous work that subverts it.

This device represents a "truth claim" similar to the kind of "truth claims" that Christine makes in *Le Livre de la mutacion de Fortune* [The Book of the Mutation of Fortune], as analyzed by Jeanette Beer.[15] While it indicates the author's seriousness, it also solves a difficult rhetorical problem by freeing her from two constricting roles: that of the purveyor of courtly ideology and that of the critical judge of that ideology and, by extension, of her patron. Simultaneously as the device lays claim to truth, it is consistent with the rhetorical figure of *fictio personarum* or more properly, of prosopopoeia, the act by which poets and historians alike portray personages and attribute fictional discourse to them.[16] Nor is invoking the figure of *fictio personarum* inappropriate when speaking about Christine's practice as a lyric poet, because she of course also wrote "balades de personnages" that epitomize this rhetorical figure. Here, speaking as the Duke, Christine can recount "les griefs ennuis et les joyes" [the heavy pains and joys] (v. 27) wholly sympathetically, since a first-person narrator is expected to be immersed, often uncritically, in his own experience. By definition, as a lover he lacks, or has forsaken temporarily, a rational identity, even when he "reasons" about his experiences.

This specifically willful and irrational voice suits precisely Christine's ultimate purpose,[17] and speaking through it, she can disclose the haphazard, damning course of love without explicitly blaming the Duke. As narrator, the Duke will reveal his own piteous plight as a young and therefore naive lover who quite simply could not help himself. His is the language typical of courtly love. The Duke's pronouncements could be turned into a veritable catalogue of the verbal formulas that delighted readers of romance, including many members of Christine's courtly audience. But rather than suggesting approval for such conventional thought and language, the elaborate banality of the Duke's speech confirms "Christine's dissatisfaction with such artificiality."[18]

For example, the Duke's very first ballade, strategically placed only thirty lines into his poetic narrative, recalls the standard invocation of Cupid and Venus in much courtly literature. It comes as no surprise to readers familiar with the *Roman de la Rose* that the "true god of Love" [vray dieu d'Amours] answers the Duke's prayers when he is hunting near a castle inhabited by a lady of "noble estat" [noble estate] and "royal personne" (vv. 155–56). As even the most superficial reader of Christine must gather, she invariably questions the privileges of inherited nobility by invoking, if only at times implicitly, the truer nobility of virtue. Thus, any sensitive reader of Christine would automatically recognize the problematic nature of any reference to *noble estat* and realize that the courtly landscape of this speech only undercuts the presumed nobility of its speaker. Nor would a courtly audience (itself probably a little bored by the whole situation) be astonished at, much less share, the Duke's surprise when Amours, the pleasant archer [archier plaisant] shoots him unawares [ne m'en donnoie regard] (v. 263) with the obligatory arrow of—what else?—Sweet Look [la fleche de Doulz Regard] (v. 264). And so, predictably, the Duke's *maladie* began, at least so he tells us, as though this were something new. Speaking in stock terms of "amoureux lians" [the bonds of love] and "doulz yeulx rians" [sweet laughing eyes] (v. 277), he recounts his moment of capture and the ensuing conversation, typically stressing repeatedly, five times in fifty lines (as though he were perhaps not only naive but slightly slow on the uptake), the power of—again, what else?—the power of his lady's eyes. We must remember that if these stock elements, dating back to Ovid and Co., were already well worn in the twelfth century, they were definitely threadbare by the early fifteenth century. Christine can manipulate the clichés as deftly as the best of the love poets and still communicate her dissatisfaction with them. Thelma Fenster has demonstrated the subtle power of Christine's humor, and the Duke's speech hides much of Christine's often missed irony. That Christine could turn courtly conventions upside down, as in her description of male (rather than female) beauty in the *Dit de Poissy*, has been superbly documented by Barbara K. Altmann.[19]

Also conventional is the role of the obligatory go-between played here by the Duke's Cousin who accompanies the Duke on the hunting expedition and who indeed first introduces him to the Lady. The Cousin alternately advises, arbitrates, and consoles the Duke throughout the romance, never once discouraging him in his *aventure*. As accomplished a pander as Ami in the *Roman de la Rose*, the Cousin convinces the love-struck and lovesick Duke that he must take comfort in his hope [*esperance*] and immediately reveal his feelings to his Lady or be found a fool: "Fol est l'amant qui repont / Et cele l'amour a dame / Dont il l'aime, car par m'ame! / L'atente lui peut trop nuire" [The lover is foolish who hides his love from his lady, for by my soul, the delay will greatly hurt him] (vv. 1967–70). Here the Cousin makes the same point that Sebille will later note, though with a completely different intention: at issue always is the lover's, not the lady's, well-being. The Cousin's endorsement of male egotism makes him the instigator of the affair itself, eagerly promising to take charge: "Ains esleeciez / Vostre cuer et me laissiez / Faire" [Let your heart rejoice and leave matters to me] (vv. 1994–96).

In romance, as a matter of convention, a lover's youth often serves to make him seem blameless and more intensely vulnerable as the naive victim of Love's power (Paolo and Francesca come to mind, to show the rhetorical power and deception of these conventions), but youthfulness appears here among a compendium of obligatory parallel traits—nobility, riches, beauty, agility, physical strength, and so on. In this work, the Duke's youth must be emphasized—in fact, the Duke protests his childishness (rather than his youth) too much. It opens the narrative ("Jone et moult enfant estoye" [I was young and much of a child], v. 41) and is mentioned (perhaps as an over-deliberate example of *amplificatio*) no fewer than a dozen times.[20] This emphasis clashes with Christine's own preference for the modesty topos in describing herself, and in this context, Christine's foregrounding of the Duke's *enfance* functions transparently as a deflector or apology shielding the Duke from responsibility for his reckless behavior. Christine even has the Lady pointedly comment on his youth as she urges the Cousin to discourage him: "par l'Apostre / Saint Paul! . . . ce fait Enfance, qui boute / Son cuer, et trop grant jonesce, / En amer—autre riens n'est ce" [By the Apostle Paul! childishness which makes his heart bloom and very great youth in loving, and nothing else, cause this (his infatuation)—it is nothing else] (vv. 2065–66, 2071–74). The allusion here to Paul's remarks on true love and putting off childish things in 1 Corinthians 10–11 can hardly be overlooked. But of course the Duke has been encouraged by his experienced friend ("Et tant le monde ay hante / Que je vois, congnois et sçay vostre mal" [I have experienced the world so much that I perceive and know your malady], vv. 1686–88), who in turn points to the Duke's *enfance* as the obstacle to his success in finding true love: "Mais Enfance vous tenoit, / Certes, je dis de ce voir" [But childishness holds you back, I'm telling you the truth about this] (vv. 1983–84). The irony here is patent: the foolish lover who wants to be called the "Duke of True Lovers" mistakes the nature of "true love" because he is a child. The Duke probably missed the allusion to Paul.

Like the Duke, the Lady is described following all the literary commonplaces of romance, as Alice Colby-Hall identified them.[21] As the Duke tells it, she is gray-eyed, the most beautiful and honorable of all women, a sweet flower, the mistress who commands and orders him in everything. But in her portrayal, as in the Duke's, Christine has subtly also altered convention by personalizing the character and thereby suggesting exoneration. The jealous and vicious enemy of this Lady is not her husband or some moral worthy, but one of her retainers, an interfering *veillart*, full of *punaisie* who threatens her. She curses him ("Dieu Maudie!"), rather than her husband, as the source of *jalousie*. Thus Christine is once again able to sustain the general imagery without condemning the particular players. Like the non-specific Cousin, the anonymous spy functions as the agent of the wicked and wanton dynamics of courtly love, thereby displacing any blame from her real, historic ducal patron and any actual lover he might have.

Courtly Prose and Dictaminal Prose: Two Worlds at Odds with Another

Just as the portraits of the Duke and the Lady closely resemble one another both in their conventionality and in their exceptions to it, so too do the language and style of their prose letters reveal a marked similarity. As expected, both speak in clichés. In his *doloreuse complainte*, the Duke insists that his life is in her hands ("car, se je y fail, vous verrés ma mort" [for if I fail, you will see my death]) since, naturally, it is her fault that he loves her in the first place (he piles on every stock adjective at his disposal: "je vous dis que ce ont fait voz tres doulx, plaisans, beaulx, rians et amoreux yeulx" [I tell you that your most sweet, pleasing, beautiful, laughing and lovely eyes have done this], p. 138). She responds to her "fair and gracious knight" [bel et gracieux chevalier] that she will grant him her love ("sachiés que je suis celle qu'Amours a ad ce menee, qui vous vueil amer trés or et trés ja" [know that I am she whom Love has led to this, who will value you always]) only if she can rely upon his honorable intentions ("si que je voye continuer vostre amoureux propos et bon vouloir" [if I see your loving purpose and good will continue], p. 148).

The diction in the Duke's letter is abstract and general, a characteristic that enhances the vagueness if not triteness of his speech and underscores its indebtedness to the threadbare clichés of courtly love. He speaks of the "nom de vaillant" [valiant name] and "toutes choses honnourables" [all things honorable] that he would win if she would simply acquiesce to his wishes. She need give only her "sweet confort" [doulx reconfort] and risk merely her "esteem and high reputation" [valeur et haulte renommee]. The Lady's response also relies heavily on general and abstract terms. She agrees to be the "cause" of his "enhanced valor" [exaulcement en vailliance] and urges him to dispense with melancholy (what a contrast to Christine's melancholy at the beginning of *Cité des Dames*, a melancholy based on her failure to recognize women's true contributions to human history) and to be happy: "Si vueil que vous chaciés de vous tout merencolie et tristece, et soiés liez, jolis et joyeux" [So I want you to chase away all your melancholy and sadness, and be happy, gay and joyous] (p. 142). The tone of the Lady's letter, however, is more guarded than that of her would-be Lover. She is more guarded, using more conditional clauses than he does, and more admonitory, using more imperatives not introduced by the formulaic *vueillez* that accompanies all the Duke's entreaties. Clearly she is more cautious than her male suitor, which would suggest that Christine's sympathies lie more with her than the Duke.

The Lady's all-too-modest reservations ultimately fail to protect her from the appeal of clandestine love and the ruin that accompanies it. Once she has succumbed to her Lover and met him secretly, she has reduced herself to folly. Her very own maidservant puts it best (a stock convention, of course) when she wryly observes, "Sage compaignie a cy! / Vous voy je en ce point ja sy! / Bien voy qu'Amours le plus sage / Fait foloyer, ce bien sçay je" [A wise company is this! I see that you now have come to the point where Love makes the most wise commit folly, as I know well] (vv. 2719–22).

Such folly alarms the prudent Sebille de Monthault and prompts her to write the Lady a long letter—one could almost say in light of the dictaminal skill behind its composition, a proper letter—that strikingly (and deliberately) resembles a didactic prose treatise warning her of the dangers and consequences of such love. In strict formal terms, the letters of the Duke and the Lady do not reveal the same level of epistolary sophistication as that of Sebille de Monthault. In terms of content, Sebille's letter does not rehash courtly commonplaces but introduces practical matters into the discussion. Sebille's voice is the voice of practical experience itself to which Christine so frequently appeals in refuting received authorities, that declare the real-life horrors of misguided, adulterous love. While Christine knew that marriage was no guarantee of happy love, she was convinced that adultery only brought on misfortune. Those familiar with Christine's earlier *jugement* poems will recall a similar pragmatism on the part of the poet. Barbara K. Altmann has observed that in those debates, Christine "is not concerned with the intellectual aspect of the courtly game, but rather with the rules, making sure that the players behave honorably, and with the effect that love's disappointments might have on the participants."[22] Certainly these concerns parallel those of Sebille in her letter, with the difference being that Christine—and here we begin to distinguish her voice more clearly—no longer reserves judgment. No longer subtly reticent on the wrongs of courtly love, Christine here competently exploits the rhetorical strategies at her disposal, even allegorizing the voice of wisdom. And if the name Sebille (that is, Sibyl) were not a sufficient guarantee of her wisdom, the profound advice offered by Sebille issues from somewhere on high, and the onomastic plays on her surnames ("Monthault" = "high mountain" and "de la Tour" = "from the tower") confer a universalizing status on her pronouncements. In the ostensibly courtly setting of a book about true lovers, Christine has welded together the strategies contained in letter-writing manuals, the *ars dictaminis*, the conventional techniques of medieval rhetoric (*amplificatio, praeteritio, prosopopoeia*) and allegorical practice.

The letter's format is painstakingly organized, its language vivid, its tone unremittingly castigating. Unlike Christine's impersonations of a male lover and a passionate mistress, Sebille speaks in Christine's voice, employing the stylistic registers that Christine employed on other occasions for serious purposes. It is characterized, as Thelma Fenster says, by "Latinate learned-sounding periodic constructions" more typical of *Le Livre des Trois Vertus* where Christine "reprints" Sebille's advice on conduct for all women.[23] The same periodic style in *Cité des Dames* marks the development in French of a "suitable linguistic vehicle for argumentation in the vernacular."[24]

We can trace the inception of this periodic prose style to Christine's biography of Charles V, *Le Livre des fais et bonnes meurs du sage roy Charles V*, her first work in prose, which she was probably composing when commissioned to write *Duc des vrais amans*. In that biography she employs a Latinate prose, stylistically indebted both to Scholastic prose and the *style clergial*, appropriate to her subject. In order to honor the wisdom of Charles the Wise she frequently names his virtues with abstract nouns and evaluates them in terms of metaphysical causes. Within this elevated and intricate moralistic framework, she incorporates detailed, concrete historical descriptions. She has shaped Sebille's letter in a similar fashion, successfully blending concrete and abstract nouns, grounding her advice in the real world with the real dangers faced by women rather than situating it in the fictitious world of courtly romance, dominated by androcentric ideals. Sebille warns that a woman may become recalcitrant, ingracious, and quarrelsome [*rechignee, malgracieuse, tenseresse*], vivid adjectives replete with negative connotations. She reminds the Lady that the legitimacy of heirs and all of the concrete ramifications of legitimacy are volatile issues tied directly to a woman's conduct. Sebille even suggests that women are better advised to tolerate their husbands' infidelities rather than imitating their husbands and thereby ruining their reputation. As homely and submissive as this counsel might appear on first view, Christine repeats it, in hardly less controversial form, at the end of *Le Livre de la Cité des Dames*. It is based on a pragmatic assessment of women's abilities to exercise power in the real world dominated by men and takes the first step by refusing to play the fool to men in the romance world.

Sebille's periodic syntax and use of subordination echo Christine's syntax at the beginning of the work. The opening sentence covers twenty-four lines of verse and begins with a subordinate clause governing an imperfect subjective that in turn governs another subordinate clause which in turn governs a third subordinate clause before it comes to the main verb in the seventh line: "Combien que occupacion / Je n'eusse ne entencion / A present de dictiez faire / D'amours, car en autre affaire / Ou trop plus me delictoie / Toute m'entente mettoie, / Vueil je d'autrui sentement / Comencier presentement / Nouvel dit..." [Although I had neither occupation nor intention to write love poetry at present, *for* I was putting all my effort in another matter *in which* I delighted much more, I want to begin now a new work of someone else's feelings...] (vv. 1–9). One would be hard pressed to find a comparable opening in earlier courtly romances. If we do not recognize how provocative Christine's use of subordination must have been for her contemporaries, we can easily miss the point. Certainly Charity Cannon Willard is right to decry the "deplorable Latin of the notaries and royal secretaries [who] exercised a very great influence on the written language of the period,"[25] but if Christine wished to be heard and understood, she had little choice but to use the linguistic and rhetorical weapons otherwise used by contemporary males. Just as Christine's prose would surely have earned the respect of her audience, her prose would have caused her readers to wake up and pay attention. Her prose departed from the style of the prose romances and chronicles. By endowing Sebille with these rhetorical skills, Christine enhances Sebille's authority and reinforces the dual identity—Sebille/Christine—behind the voice of the governess.

By the same token, Sebille relies heavily on lists and categories, the penchant for which, while widespread in the prose of the period, Christine almost surely acquired from Egidio Colonna (Gilles de Rome), who was one of her major sources for her biography of Charles V. Many copies of Egidio Colonna's *De regimine principum*, both in Latin and in French translation, were owned by members of the royal family.[26] Whether she imitated her source or whether she independently shared Egidio's preference for lists, her audience would not have missed the similarities, specifically the tripartite organization prevalent in Egidio Colonna. Sebille's three-part organization of her letter fits the expectations of a learned (rather than courtly) public.

The letter begins with the modest reverence suitable to a princess, as Sebille often refers to the Lady, but quickly establishes that its author will not grant the Lady's wish to come to her because her own daughter is too gravely ill to leave ("ma fille est tres griefment malade que je ne la pourroie laissier nullement").[27] One cannot ignore the implicit contrast between the two younger women in need especially because the Lady earlier calls Sebille "dear mother and friend" [chiere mere et amie] and refers to herself as "fair daughter" [belle fille]. The one malady requires Sebille's physical presence while the other can be remedied by sound counsel, which Sebille wastes no time in delivering. After a relatively succinct *apologia* (contained in only one, rather than several, of Christine's lengthy complex sentences), in which she explains that the Lady's "noble reputation and honor" [noble renommee et honneur] have moved her to write, whereby the concept of "true nobility" for Christine was always a question of virtue rather than birth, Sebille announces abruptly that she has heard rumors about the Lady's conduct. She seems especially grieved by the gossip since the Lady had been in her charge since childhood [gouvernance depuis enfance jusques a ore (p. 171)], thus indirectly alluding to the "childhood" or *enfance* that previously had made the Duke so reticent to court her, and now she fears a decline in the Lady's good name [decheement de vostre bon los].

At this point Sebille lays out her code of conduct for princesses and highborn ladies, a kind of mirror for princesses in the tradition of Gilles de Rome's mirror for princes. Next she offers a vividly accurate account of the Lady's recent conduct ("vous estes devenue trop plus esgayee, plus emparlee et plus jolie que ne souliés estre" [you have become much merrier, more talkative and gayer than you used to be]), illustrating the truth of the adage that looks change when hearts change ("c'est ce qui fait communement jugier les cuers changiez quant les contenances se changent" [p. 173]). Lovers, Sebille observes, give themselves away by withdrawing from people and speaking in innuendos, the very behavior exhibited by the Lady, of course, during her affair with the Duke.

Once Sebille has presented this mirror for princesses and asked the Lady to look into it, she proceeds with her argument by imploring her to change her behavior. Thus, more than half the letter is devoted to exclamations and exhortations. The voice we hear "from the Tower"—Sebille's and Christine's—is a polemical voice intent upon order and reason, directed specifically to a female audience. For example, Sebille formulates hypothetical responses to the three reasons a lady might seek love: that she is young and therefore naturally seeks pleasure; that she can love truly without "villenie" or sin; and that she can make a man valorous ("Tu es jone, il ne faut fors que plaisance. Tu pues bien amer sans villenie. Ce n'est point de mal quant il n'y a pechié. Tu feras un vaillant homme" [p. 175]). Sebille systematically rebuts each of these reasons, showing their fallacies one by one. She argues first that pleasure brings with it a thousand times more grief, especially for women, "par especial du costé des dames." Second, she cautions against certainty in one's own resolve (specifically in judging sinfulness) when it comes to love, and she emphasizes her overriding concern here with women by using the feminine pronoun: "ne soit nul ne nulle si asseuree de soy qu'elle se rende certaine" [no one, man or woman, may be so sure of herself that she become certain]. She demonstrates cogently that the third claim, that loving a man makes him valorous, is preposterous: "certes je dis que c'est trop grant folie de soy destruire pour accroistre un autre" [Certainly I say that it is great folly to destroy oneself in order to enhance another (p. 176)]. Here, as throughout the letter, Sebille/Christine dispenses with the irony and humor present in the earlier, ostensibly more courtly, portion of the work and sets out unambiguously to destroy the chivalric myth that women are bound to dedicate themselves to men pledged to serve them.[28]

Elsewhere in the letter, Sebille lists many of the all-too-numerous perils that, again, quite specifically women face in such affairs. At risk first is the wrath of God, then the loss of reputation if husband or family discover the love. At one point, in an intriguing passage, Sebille takes up the hypothetical case of a love affair remaining secret in order to discuss lovers who are loyal, discreet, and truthful. But then, as though unable to restrain herself, Christine immediately interjects her own observations, discounting the possibility of such a positive situation since lovers are notoriously deceitful: "ains scet on assez que communement sont faints et pour les dames decevoir dient ce que ilz ne pensent ne vouldroient faire" [yet it is known well enough that these men commonly are pretenders and, in order to deceive women, they say things they neither think nor intend to do (p. 178)].

Throughout the letter, the presumed or inscribed audience is explicitly female. It extends from the specific Lady as addressed by Sebille to all women as invoked by Christine. On no fewer than ten occasions does the correspondent comment that she offers her wisdom for the benefit of women in general, and the phrases *toute femme* and *vous et toutes femmes* recur intermittently. Christine, however, not only doubles up with the Sebille as speaker, she doubles up her audience as well by extending the remarks supposedly intended for the Lady to all women. This remarkable shift comes when Sebille replaces the singular *ma dame* of address employed consistently throughout the letter with the plural *mes dames* within the context of a scathing attack on men and a severe warning to women: "car Dieux scet comment ilz en mentent, et pleust a Dieu qu'entre vous, mes dames, le sceussiés bien, car cause ariés de vous en garder" [for God knows how they lie, and may it please God that you, ladies, know it well in order to protect yourselves (pp. 178–79)].

Once Sebille has completed her reasoned but impassioned treatise, interspersed for good effect with a half-dozen "ha's" and as many invocations of heaven, the futile nature and outcome of the romance are hardly in doubt. The Duke resumes the narrative and immediately regrets Sebille's advice because his Lady temporarily rebuffs him on account of it. Finally, though, it is not Sebille but love itself that he laments as the predicted rumors and ills begin to take their destructive course. Notably it is the Lady's voice that we hear last. Bereft of hope, filled with doubt and bitterness, she begins her complaint. This concluding position privileges the female perspective, in this case, the dismal suffering forecast by the wise Sebille/Christine. It may have been the Duke's story, told in the Duke's words, but the Lady here has the final word, the final haunting echoes commenting on the Duke's love. *Hers* is the ruin, the Lady now cries—just as Sebille had counseled, just as Christine knew, just as Christine knows— as we close the book. The Lady is, at least in part, exonerated as victim, for Christine here, as elsewhere, "does not condemn such women; rather she condemns their illicit love."[29]

By degrading the lovers' standards and behavior without condemning her patron and his lover, and by elevating the prudent, chastising voice of the governess, Christine unmasks and discredits the conventional male heroics of the romance. The misguided first-person narrator fails in his quest, and his lover fails with him, their empty rhetoric symbolic of the futility of their code. Referring to Sebille's letter in the *Livre des Trois Vertus*, Liliane Dulac has succinctly analyzed the role of the governess: "Beyond delivering a moral lesson, the lady knows how to use her speech to influence actions, modify certain situations, and in general, direct the life of the young princess."[30] Certainly, in the *Duc des vrais amans*, Sebille's speech functions similarly. In the latter work, moreover, Christine's framing this distinctly uncourtly prose letter with the narrative verse of the two distraught lovers amplifies the didacticism and implicit humanism of the letter itself. Thus both in the straightforward erudite prose put in Sebille's mouth and in the verse portions informed by the traditions of medieval rhetoric, especially prosopopoeia, the faults and limits of courtly love and values are shown up.

Courtly love, inasmuch as it is "courtly" in the original sense of the term, belonged to the public realm—in the very least as it was presented in readings before a court public—even if, in the romance world it projected for this court public, the intimacies of love it described were private. Christine's rhetorical and ethical assumptions embrace both spheres, consistent with the ideal advanced by Brunetto Latini, one of Christine's sources, that the rhetorician addresses both public and private issues.[31] Egidio Colonna, another one of her sources, held that art serves to guide human actions; as the French text available to Christine's public says, "rhetorique . . . enseigne une maniere d'argüer grosse et par essample es sciences qui determiner des euvres humaines" [rhetoric teaches a manner of arguing broadly and by example in the sciences that direct human deeds].[32] These are the "practical" sciences—ethics, economics, politics. For Christine, then, artistic virtuosity and moral probity were inseparable. She finds in the worn-out genre of the courtly romance in verse another forum in which to denounce the earlier courtly tradition that she abhors in literature and in practice. In its stead, she offers a profile of virtue embodied in a character whose ethical agenda is Christine's own. The author's control of voice is most impressive as it moralizes from within the very world it condemns.

Appendix I. Formal Divisions in the *Livre du Duc des vrais amans*

1. vv. 1–40: octosyllabic couplets, frequent semi-learned words in rhyming position; consistently alternates masculine and feminine rhymes; Christine speaks as author; subordinate constructions predominate;

2. vv. 41–70: octosyllabic rhyming couplets, syntax is either simple or compound, few subordinate constructions, narrative;

3. vv. 71–82: decasyllabic apostrophe addressed to the "true god of Love," rhyming *ABBA*, conventional ballade syntax (that is, phrase length corresponds generally to line length) but entitled "Rondel";

4. vv. 83–476: octosyllabic rhyming couplets, syntax either simple or compound, narrative;

5. vv. 477–504: ballade (three stanzas *ABABBCBC*, envoi *BCBC*, all feminine rhymes), addressed to the God of Love;

6. vv. 505–606: octosyllabic rhyming couplets, narrative;

7. vv. 607–34: ballade (three stanzas *ABABBCBC*, envoi *BCBC*), addressed to the beloved "princess";

8. vv. 635–824: octosyllabic rhyming couplets, narrative;

9. vv. 825–36: rondeau, *ABBA, ABA, ABBAA;*

10. vv. 837–1234: octosyllabic rhyming couplets, narrative;

11. vv. 1235–46: rondeau, *ABBA, ABA, ABBAA;*
12. vv. 1247–1402: octosyllabic rhyming couplets, narrative;
13. vv. 1403–27: octosyllabic ballade, three stanzas *ABABBCC*, envoi *BBCC*;
14. vv. 1428–73: octosyllabic rhyming couplets, narrative;
15. vv. 1474–1501: ballade, a lament that the Duke addresses to himself ("how can I say farewell to you?"), each stanza composed in decasyllabic verses with the exception of the fifth line composed in five syllables, rhyming pattern *ABABCCDD*, envoi *CCDD*, all feminine rhymes;
16. vv. 1502–63: octosyllabic rhyming couplets, narrative;
17. vv. 1564–88: ballade, addressed as a farewell to the beloved, every line begins with "A Dieu" (literally "to God" or "adieu"; the anaphora here may involve a pun on the "God of True Lovers"), rhyme scheme *ABABBCC*, all feminine rhymes;
18. vv. 1589–1622: octosyllabic rhyming couplets, narrative;
19. vv. 1623–50, ballade;
20. vv. 1651–1858, octosyllabic rhyming couplets, narrative;
21. vv. 1859–87: ballade, octosyllabic *ABABBCBC*, addressed to Love;
22. vv. 1888–2283: octosyllabic rhyming couplets, narrative;
23. Prose intercalation: "Lettres closes en proses" [prose letter]: Duke writes to his Lady, undated, intended as an introduction to two enclosed ballades;
24. vv. 2284–2308: ballade, decasyllabic with every fourth line in five syllables, *ABABCCDD*, two-line envoi *DD*;
25. vv. 2309–28: ballade, decasyllabic *ABABCC*, two-line envoi *CC*;
26. vv. 2329–59: octosyllabic rhyming couplets, narrative;
27. Prose intercalation: "Response de la Dame aux lettres devant dictes" [The Lady's answer to the previous letter];
28. vv. 2360–2409: octosyllabic rhyming couplets, narrative;
29. Prose intercalation: letter from the Duke to his Lady;
30. vv. 2410–15: octosyllabic rhyming couplets, narrative;
31. vv. 2416–40: ballade, all in five-syllable lines, all feminine rhymes *ABABBCC*, envoi *BBCC*;
32. vv. 2441–2956: octosyllabic rhyming couplets, narrative;
33. vv. 2957–81: virelai, *AABAA;*
34. vv. 2982–97: octosyllabic rhyming couplets, narrative;
35. vv. 2998–3025: ballade, decasyllabic *ABABBCBC*, envoi, *BCCB*;
36. vv. 3026–61: octosyllabic rhyming couplets, narrative;
37. vv. 3062–89: ballade, decasyllabic *ABABCCDD*, fifth line five syllables;

38. vv. 3090–97: octosyllabic rhyming couplets, narrative;
39. vv. 3098–3125: ballade, lines of varying length, *ABABCCDD*, envoi, *CCDD*;
40. vv. 3126–63: octosyllabic rhyming couplets, narrative;
41. Prose intercalation: Lady's letter to Sebille, "La Duchece," dated January 8;
42. vv. 3164–71: octosyllabic rhyming couplets, narrative;
43. Prose intercalation: the Sebille's letter, dated January 18;
44. vv. 3172–99: the Sebille's ballade, on women's honor (as contrast to the two ballades sent by the Duke with his first letter);
45. vv. 3200–3219: octosyllabic rhyming couplets, narrative;
46. Prose intercalation: Lady's letter to the Duke;
47. vv. 3220–43: octosyllabic rhyming couplets, narrative;
48. Prose intercalation: Duke's letter to his lady;
49. vv. 3244–49: octosyllabic rhyming couplets, narrative;
50. vv. 3250–77: ballade addressed to Death;
51. vv. 3278–3307: octosyllabic rhyming couplets, narrative;
52. Prose intercalation: Lady's letter to the Duke;
53. vv. 3308–3557: octosyllabic rhyming couplets, narrative;
54. vv. 3558–end: "explicit": commentary on the rhymes in the work and introduction to "Balades de plusieurs façons" (9 ballades, 3 virelais, 4 rondeaux, 1 complainte): all of these lyrical works are presented by "her, who made this poem" [celle ... qui ce dictié dicta].

Appendix II. Examples of Direct Speech Cited in the *Livre du duc des vrais amans* and Interlocutors

1. vv. 164–67: Lady to Cousin
2. vv. 168–75: Cousin to Lady
3. vv. 177–78: Lady
4. vv. 308–11: Cousin to Duke
5. vv. 369–97: Cousin to Duke
6. vv. 404–20: Duke
7. vv. 443–46: Father to Duke
8. vv. 679–81: Lady to Duke
9. vv. 741–42: Duke to Lady
10. vv. 861–64: Lady to Duke
11. vv. 867–76: Duke to Lady
12. vv. 879–99: Lady to Duke
13. vv. 1211–12: Lady to Duke

14. vv. 1213–14: Duke to Lady
15. vv. 1674–1714: Cousin to Duke
16. vv. 1743–1858: Duke to Cousin
17. vv. 1898–1945: Cousin to Duke
18. vv. 1946–1965: Duke to Cousin
19. vv. 1967–2010: Cousin to Duke
20. vv. 2063–2133: Lady to Duke
21. vv. 2139–73: Cousin to Lady
22. vv. 2174–2220: Lady to Cousin
23. vv. 2346–51: Lady to Cousin
24. vv. 2382–83: Duke to Cousin
25. vv. 2560–65: Lady
26. vv. 2570–73: Lady to Cousin
27. vv. 2574–78: Cousin to Lady (not marked in text)
28. vv. 2579–81: Lady to Cousin (not marked in text)
29. vv. 2582–87: Cousin to Lady
30. vv. 2597–2602: Cousin to Duke
31. vv. 2673–74: Duke to Lady
32. v. 2675: Lady to Duke
33. vv. 2686–94: Lady to Duke
34. vv. 2696–2703: Duke to Lady
35. vv. 2707–15: Lady to Duke
36. vv. 2719–22: Lady's Companion
37. vv. 2723–78: Lady to Duke
38. vv. 2781–2858: Duke to Lady (end of speech not marked in text)
39. v. 2890: Lady to Duke
40. vv. 2920–22: Cousin to Duke
41. vv. 3207–17: Lady (end of speech not marked in text)

Notes

1. Laurie A. Finke, *Feminist Theory, Women's Writing*, p. 98.
2. Paul de Man, "Lyrical Voice in Contemporary Theory," p. 5.
3. James C. Laidlaw, "L'unité des *Cent balades*."
4. Nadia Margolis, "'The Cry of the Chameleon,'" p. 42.
5. Lori Walters, "The Woman Writer and Literary History," p. 2.
6. *De vulgari eloquentia*, ed. A. Marigo and P. G. Ricci, I.x.2: "Allegat ergo pro se lingua oïl . . . quidquid redactum sive inventum est ad vulgare prosaycum suum est: videlicet Biblia cum Troianorum Romanorumque gestibus compilata et Arturi regis ambages pulcerrime et quamplures alie ystorie ac doctrine" [The *langue d'oïl*

claims for itself whatever has been written or composed in vernacular prose, that is, biblical compilations with the deeds of Trojans and Romans and the most fair adventures of King Arthur and several other histories and textbooks].

7. See Earl Jeffrey Richards, "'*Seulette a part*'—'The Little Woman on the Sidelines' Takes Up Her Pen"; and Nadia Margolis, "'The Cry of the Chameleon.'"

8. This phenomenon is best documented by Robert P. Adams, "Bold Bawdry and Open Manslaughter."

9. Liliane Dulac, "Feminine Speech in *Le Livre des Trois Vertus*," p. 20.

10. Kevin Brownlee, "Rewriting Romance," p. 173.

11. C. P. Wormell, "On the Paradoxes of Self-Reference," p. 271.

12. All French citations are from Christine de Pizan, *Le Livre du Duc des vrais amans*, ed. Thelma Fenster. All translations are our own.

13. Jonathan Culler, "Changes in the Study of Lyric," p. 52.

14. Christine is thus adopting the role of compilator, as described by A. J. Minnis, in his *Medieval Theory of Authorship*, as a way of disavowing responsibility for treatment of the "highly controversial subject" such as "human love" which "was supposed to be potentially dangerous and conducive to sin" (p. 195).

15. Jeanette Beer, "Stylistic Conventions in *Le Livre de la mutation de Fortune*," p. 128.

16. According to Edmond Faral in *Les arts poétiques du XIIe et du XIIIe siècle*: "La prosopopée . . . est nommée de façons diverses: *fictio personarum, conformatio, deformatio*, ou *effiguratio*. C'est une figure d'application étendue. Prise en son sens le plus large, celui des paroles prêtées à des personnes mortes ou absentes, ou à des objets inanimés, elle n'est pas seulement l'ornement accidentiel d'un discours: elle peut constituer, à elle seule, un discours entier. Quintilien considère comme de véritables prosopopées les *suasoriæ* où l'on s'exerçait, dans les écoles, à faire parler César, ou Cicéron, ou Caton, ou tel autre: exercice excellent pour les poètes et les historiens qui ont à peindre des personnages et qui leur prêtent des discours supposés" [Prosopopoeia is called by various names: *fictio personarum, conformatio, deformatio* or *effiguratio*. It is a widely applied figure of speech. Taken in its broadest sense—the made-up speech of persons dead or absent or that of inanimate objects—it is not merely an incidental ornament of discourse: It can constitute, in itself, an entire discourse. Quintilian considers as true instances of prosopopoeia the *suasoriæ* (persuasive speeches) practiced in the schools by which one made Caesar, Cicero or Cato speak—an excellent exercise for poets and historians who have to portray characters and attribute presumptive speeches to them] (p. 72).

17. Fenster has noted the emphasis on youth in her superb introduction to her's and Nadia Margolis's translation of the work. Here and elsewhere we are grateful for their insightful reading and analysis. See their translation entitled *The Book of the Duke of True Lovers* (New York: Persea, 1991).

18. Earl Jeffrey Richards, "Christine de Pizan, the Conventions of Courtly Diction and Italian Humanism," p. 253.

19. Barbara K. Altmann, "Reopening the Case."
20. Fenster, "Did Christine de Pizan Have a Sense of Humor?"
21. Alice M. Colby[-Hall], *The Portrait in Twelfth-Century French Literature: An Example of the Stylistic Originality of Chrétien de Troyes.*
22. Altmann, "Reopening the Case," p. 144.
23. Fenster, introduction to *The Book of the Duke of True Lovers*, pp. 15 and 21.
24. Richards, in "Christine de Pizan and the Question of Feminist Rhetoric," discusses in detail the development of Christine's prose style in his comparison of her work with male contemporaries. See also his essay in this volume.
25. Charity Cannon Willard, *Christine de Pizan, The Livre de la paix, A Critical Edition* (The Hague: Mouton, 1958), p. 50.
26. Richard Firth Green, *Poets and Princepleasers*, p. 144.
27. One is reminded of Sheila Delany's discussion of Christine's creation of "mothers for herself: woman as mistress of discourse" (p. 196). Sebille functions here both as the literal mother of one daughter in need and as the figurative daughter of another, and by extension, of all women desirous of instruction. See Delany's *Women Writers and Women in Literature, Medieval to Modern*.
28. Christine's skepticism toward courtly and chivalric values has not been accepted by Sylvia Huot, who in "Seduction and Sublimation" argues that Christine "never abandoned her belief in chivalric values, whereby women would be honored and protected by men and would in turn inspire them to great deeds."
29. Allison Kelly, "Christine de Pizan and Antoine de la Salle," p. 183.
30. Dulac, p. 20.
31. Brunetto claimed in the *Livre dou tresor*, 3.2.1, "rectorique est une science ki nous ensegne bien, plainement et parfaitement dire es choses communes et es privees, et toute sa entention est a dire paroles en tele maniere que l'en face croire ses dis a ceaux ki les oient" [rhetoric is a science that teaches us well, plainly and perfectly to speak in matters public and private, and its whole purpose is to make speeches in such a way as to produce belief in those who hear them]. Brunetto took his cue from the Pseudo-Ciceronian *Ad Herennium* 1.2.2, "Oratoris officium est de iis rebus posse dicere quae res ad usum civilem moribus et legibus constitutae sunt, cum adsensione auditorum quoad eius fieri poterit" [The task of the public speaker is to discuss capably those matters which law and custom have fixed for the uses of citizenship and to secure as far as possible the agreement of his hearers].
32. Gilles de Rome (i.e., Egidio Colonna), *Li Livres du gouvernement des rois (De regimine principum)*, ed. Samuel Paul Molenaer, p. 200. This edition gives the text of Henri de Gauchy's translation.

Works Cited

Adams, Robert P. "Bold Bawdry and Open Manslaughter: The English New Humanist Attack on Medieval Romance." *Huntington Library Quarterly* 23 (1959–60): 33–48.

Altmann, Barbara K. "Reopening the Case: Machaut's *Jugement* Poems as a Source in Christine de Pizan." In *Reinterpreting Christine*, ed. Earl Jeffrey Richards with Nadia Margolis, Christine Reno, and Joan Williamson, pp. 137–56. Athens: University of Georgia Press, 1992.

Beer, Jeanette. "Stylistic Conventions in *Le Livre de la mutacion de Fortune*." In *Reinterpreting Christine*, pp. 124–36.

Brownlee, Kevin. "Rewriting Romance: Courtly Discourse and Auto-Citation in Christine de Pizan." In *Gender and Text in the Later Middle Ages*, ed. Jane Chance, pp. 172–94. Gainesville: University Press of Florida, 1996.

Burnley, J. D. "Christine de Pizan and the So-Called *style clergial*." *Modern Language Review* 81 (1986): 1–6.

Christine de Pizan. *The Livre de la paix: A Critical Edition*. Ed. Charity Cannon Willard. The Hague: Mouton, 1958.

———. *Le Livre du Duc des vrais amans*. Ed. Thelma Fenster. Binghamton, N.Y.: MRTS, 1994.

———. *La Città delle dame / Le Livre de la Cité des Dames*. Bilingual ed. Ed. Earl Jeffrey Richards. Trans. Patricia Caraffi. Milan: Luni Editrice, 1997.

———. *The Book of the City of Ladies*. Trans. Earl Jeffrey Richards. 2d ed. New York: Persea, 1998.

Colby[-Hall], Alice M. *The Portrait in Twelfth-Century French Literature: An Example of the Stylistic Originality of Chrétien de Troyes*. Geneva: Droz, 1965.

Colonna, Egidio (Gilles de Rome). *Li Livres du gouvernement des rois (De regimine principum)*. Ed. Samuel Paul Molenaer. New York: Columbia University Press, 1899; reprint, New York: AMS, 1966.

Culler, Jonathan. "Changes in the Study of Lyric." In *Lyric Poetry: Beyond New Criticism*, ed. Chaviva Hošek and Patricia Parker, pp. 38–54. Ithaca: Cornell University Press, 1985.

Dante. *De vulgari eloquentia*. Ed. A. Marigo and P. G. Ricci. Opere di Dante, 6. Florence, 1968.

Delany, Sheila. *Women Writers and Women in Literature, Medieval to Modern*. New York: Schocken, 1983.

de Man, Paul. "Lyrical Voice in Contemporary Theory: Riffaterre and Jauß." In *Lyric Poetry: Beyond New Criticism*, ed. Chaviva Hošek and Patricia Parker, pp. 55–72. Ithaca: Cornell University Press, 1985.

Dulac, Liliane. "Feminine Speech in *Le Livre des Trois Vertus*." In *Reinterpreting Christine*, pp. 13–22.

Faral, Edmond. *Les arts poétiques du XIIe et du XIIIe siècle*. Paris: Champion, 1962.

Fenster, Thelma. "Did Christine de Pizan Have a Sense of Humor?" In *Reinterpreting Christine*, pp. 23–36.

———. Introduction to Christine de Pizan, *The Book of the Duke of True Lovers*, pp. 15–38. New York: Persea, 1991.

Green, Richard Firth. *Poets and Princepleasers*. Toronto: University of Toronto Press, 1980.
Huot, Sylvia. "Seduction and Sublimation: Christine de Pizan, Jean de Meun, and Dante." *Romance Notes* 25 (1985): 361–73.
Kelly, Allison. "Christine de Pizan and Antoine de la Salle: The Dangers of Love in Theory and Fiction." In *Reinterpreting Christine,* pp. 173–86.
Laidlaw, James C. "L'unité des *Cent balades.*" In *The City of Scholars: New Approaches to Christine de Pizan,* pp. 97–106. Berlin: De Gruyter, 1994.
Latini, Brunetto. *Li Livres dou tresor*. Ed. Francis James Carmody. University of California Publications in Modern Philology 22. Berkeley: University of California Press, 1948.
Margolis, Nadia. "'The Cry of the Chameleon': Evolving Voices in the Epistles of Christine de Pizan." *Disputatio* 1 (1996): 37–70.
Minnis, A. J. *Medieval Theory of Authorship*. London: Scolar Press, 1984, 1988.
Richards, Earl Jeffrey. "Christine de Pizan and the Question of Feminist Rhetoric." *Teaching Language through Literature* 22 (1983): 15–24.
———. "Christine de Pizan, the Conventions of Courtly Diction and Italian Humanism." In *Reinterpreting Christine,* pp. 250–71.
———. "'*Seulette a part*'—'The Little Woman on the Sidelines' Takes Up Her Pen: The Letters of Christine de Pizan." In *Dear Sister, Medieval Women and the Epistolary Genre,* ed. Karen Cherewatuk and Ulrike Wiethaus, pp. 139–70. Philadelphia: University of Pennsylvania Press, 1993.
Walters, Lori. "The Woman Writer and Literary History: Christine de Pizan's Redefinition of the Poetic *Translatio* in the *Epistre au Dieu d'amours.*" *French Literature Series* 16 (1989): 1–16.
Wormell, C. P. "On the Paradoxes of Self-Reference." *Mind* NS 58 (1958): 267–71.

∾ *The Limits of Lyrical Self-Representation*

∽ CHAPTER 5

Clerkliness and Courtliness in the Complaintes of Christine de Pizan

NADIA MARGOLIS

I shall begin by confessing straightaway my intention to stretch the boundaries of the concepts of clerkliness [*clergie*] and courtliness [*courtoisie*] to some extent, which is not to say that I will abandon them in the conventional sense either. I shall attempt to provide traditional working definitions of these antithetical, though not *a priori* incompatible, terms. In addition, I hope to show how the convergence or divergence of these two concepts may serve to define the lesser-appreciated genre of complainte as re-created by Christine. I also hope to show that modern as much as fifteenth-century versions of these concepts, specifically in the monumental editing of her lyric poetry by Maurice Roy, affect how we read her complaintes and their relationship to her other poems.[1]

Clerkliness is the closest English translation of what Christine herself refers to as the *stile clergial* [clerkly style] as well as the more frequent *clergie* in her epistle to Eustache Deschamps.[2] As a concept, it connotes all that is learned, usually from classical antiquity, for the eventual practical purpose of implementing enlightened government and diplomacy in the spirit of civic virtue. At least since Chrétien de Troyes's allusion to it in a famous passage beginning his *Cligés*,[3] whichever people possessed this sacred cultural attribute, together with *chevalerie* [courtliness plus feats of arms], stood to inherit the next Golden Age. Certainly by Christine's time more than two centuries later, it became a nation's literate weapon, as powerful in its own way as those on the battlefield. In fact, as Christine was well aware, *clergie*'s scholarly spirit even enhanced chivalry by codifying it as military science and conduct.[4] Clerkliness in many ways can be perceived as a medievalization of Cicero's *studia humanitatis* ("study of the humanities" as enunciated in his oration in defense of Archias) and, as an ethereal ideal, can be said to be transmitted via a transfer of culture or *translatio studii*, as we saw in Chrétien (which in turn is closely linked to a transfer of political power or *translatio imperii*). By the early fifteenth century, as scholars from Ernst Robert Curtius to George H. Bumgardner, Jr., have demonstrated, *clergie* was the highest attribute of curial culture, itself the summit of national culture.[5] The intellectuals of Christine's milieu thus did not suffer from feeling marginalized. As a style, then, the clergial did not wear its learning lightly—especially as practiced in France, the eager cultural rival of Italy in the late fourteenth through early fifteenth centuries.[6] It strove to include as many classical allusions as possible not only in its content but also in its structure and vocabulary, both often becoming overblown parodies of Latinate legalese, except via the elegant pens of a few early Parisian humanists. Such adept examples as Jean Gerson, Jean de Montreuil, and Alain Chartier could compose in Latin verse, for pleasure, in addition to the official prose required of their positions in Church and lay government. Even in more intimate correspondence, the personal feelings of late medieval French notaries were mediated by the Ciceronian epistolary model.

Of course, one of the major conflicts within the clerkly mode of writing emerged from the authors' admiration of classical antiquity, with its inherent paganism, versus the requisite Christian piety of their own time. Another conflict lay in what we now call "gendered writing": the clerkly style was inevitably and inextricably male, by virtue of its origins and milieu. Instead of treating women in more enlightened fashion, the humanist *cléricature* [clerkly milieu] could deploy classical citation and rhetoric to defame them more authoritatively than their vernacular counterparts, who at least attempted some sort of courtly finesse.

Coming from the other end of the literary spectrum, the courtly style is more familiar to medievalists and thus requires less expatiation. Courtliness functions as the peacetime component of chivalry. Let us just remember that, while the clerkly ethos derives from the study and emulation of ancient Rome, the courtly one grew out of a series of vernacular, mystical, and lyrical traditions—all converging on its own exalted ideal of *joie* or joy. This elevated goal, while often seen to have been merged with the cult of the Virgin, is nonetheless not purely Christian—especially in its fostering of extramarital sexuality. Courtliness inspired its own brand of paganism: worship of Amor, the God of Love, sometimes uncontrollable, to whom one prayed nevertheless to intervene in favor of worthy lovers. And it inspired its own pagan authority: not Cicero this time, but Ovid. Put more simply, if clerkliness responds to all that is public, rational, and deliberate in the human spirit, then, for our purposes here, courtliness cultivates the private, emotional, and uncontrollable or inexplicable. To this, however, we hasten to add that much of this is authorial persona, for as Chrétien advocated in his romances, the lover must study as hard as the cleric, in his own way.[7] Although courtly literature also can be described in modern terms as "male-oriented," female intelligence and psychology did at least receive some favorable attention.

As an established professional woman writer by the time she was producing the great manuscript volumes to be discussed later, Christine had quickly perceived the value of mastering both clerkly and courtly modes and incorporating them into her literary arsenal as a prerequisite to her being taken seriously as an author. While we are becoming increasingly aware of her success at the clerkly style in such better-known works as the *Livre de la Cité des Dames* [Book of the City of Ladies], *Epistre Othea* [Epistle of Othea], and the *Livre de la mutacion de Fortune* [Book of the Mutation of Fortune], not to mention her talent for lyric in the various sequences of ballades, rondeaux, and virelais, what she does in her three specifically labeled complainte poems (the two "Complaintes amoureuses" and the final poem of the *Livre du Duc des vrais amans* [Book of the Duke of True Lovers]) has yet to be examined.[8] What I shall attempt to show here is that these three poems are unique and yet highly representative examples of Christine's development as lyric poet—and female polemicist. Toward this end I shall also reveal Christine's alternating deployment of clerkliness and courtliness in these poems—first, by taking each in isolation, then by studying their meaning within the context of Christine's total oeuvre in the four main manuscript collections supervised by her[9]—as she develops a final statement of her vision of the woman's real place in *fin'amors* [courtly love].[10]

If Deschamps provides no rules for the complainte in Christine's time in his *Art de dictier*,[11] modern preeminent scholars of later medieval poetry, such as Daniel Poirion, Jean-Claude Mühlethaler, and, most recently, Robert Deschaux, define it as a lyric genre whose more flexible structure, while highly conventionalized, also permits more creativity than the fixed forms of ballade, rondeau, and virelai.[12] It is allied with both the lai[13] and the epitaph and also with religious devotional poetry. Constructing, for example, sixteen-line stanzas containing a predominant rhyme governing the four-and ten-syllable verses (usually, although other verse lengths exist in this genre), each quatrain of which would be "cut" by a trisyllabic verse in another rhyme, the poet of the complainte could add any number of independent stanzas, each carrying only two rhymes in the same scheme (so that rhyme "a" for each different stanza could be different, and likewise with the "b" rhyme). This becomes clearer upon reading the opening stanzas of Christine's "Complaintes amoureuses," containing lines of ten and four syllables, rhyming schematically, *aaabaaab bbbabbba*:

(1)   Vueillez oÿr en pitié ma complainte,
Belle plaisant pour qui j'ay douleur mainte
Et que j'aour plus que saint ne sainte,
    Chose est certaine;   4
Et ne cuidez que ce soit chose fainte,
Trés doulce flour dont je porte l'emprainte
Dedens mon cuer pourtraicte, escripte et painte.
    Car la grant peine   8
Du mal d'amours qui pour vous me demaine
Me grieve tant, de ce vous acertaine,
Que plus vivre ne puis jour ne sepmaine,
    Dont par contrainte   12
Dire me fault a vous, ma souveraine,
Le trés grant faiz dont ma pensée est plaine,
Bonne, belle, tout le vous dis je a peine
    Et en grant crainte.   16

[Please take pity and hear my complainte, lovely one for whom I suffer pain and whom I adore more than any saint. One thing is certain; believe this not a ruse, sweetest flower, whose imprint I bear portrayed within my heart, both written and painted. For the great pain of love's malady that wracks me because of you so afflicts me—of this I assure you—that I cannot live a day or a week. Through this constraint I must tell you, my sovereign, of the grave subject that fills my thoughts. My beauty, fair one, I can hardly tell you, such is my fear.] (Ed. Roy, I, pp. 289–95)

(2)   Doulce dame, vueillez ouÿr la plainte
De ma clamour; car pensée destrainte

Par trop amer me muet a la complainte
    De mon grief plour   4
Vous regehir, si ne croiez que fainte
Soit en nul cas; car friçon, dont j'ay mainte
Et maint grief dueil me rendent couleur tainte
    Et en palour.   8
Chiere dame, dont me vient la douleur,
Par qui Amours trembler, en grant chaleur,
Me fait souvent, dont j'ai vie et couleur
    Par fois estainte.   12
Mon piteux plaint ne tenez a folour,
Pour ce qu'en vous il a tant de valour;
Car je sçay bien, du dire n'ay coulour,
    Mais c'est contrainte.   16

[Gentle Lady, please hear the complaint of my cries; for my mind's distress, from loving too much, moves me toward complaint, to tell you of my grievous weeping, so think this not a pose by any means; for many a shiver and much profound grief make me both livid and pale. Dear lady, through whom pain comes to me, and for whom Love makes me often tremble feverishly; by which I've at times had my life and looks destroyed. Do not ascribe my piteous plaint to folly, since it has placed so much in value in you; for I know well that I've no flair for speaking, but that's what I'm constrained to do.] (Ed. Roy, 1, pp. 281–88)[14]

One is tempted, in light of the requirements of such extremely confining genres as the rondeau and virelai, to imagine the fifteenth-century poet reveling in what might appear as the new freedom of the complainte, because of its more flexible length and subject matter. However, when one studies their structure more closely and considers how few true complaintes were written by the *grands maîtres*, or leading poets, of the period, the unusually demanding nature of their composition becomes apparent.[15]

As its name indicates, the complainte, like the lai and prière [prayer], functions as a distinctly nonnarrative genre, often used by such authors as Machaut to heighten the emotional power of key moments in the otherwise narrative *dit* or tale. Repetitive and incantatory, the complainte seeks to persuade the listener by re-creating sadness within him or her rather than by any kind of dialectic and is also akin to the melopoeia in ancient Greek lyric, as Liliane Dulac has pointed out.[16] At the same time, it can exert a calming effect on the bereaved narrator, as "the act of composing this tirade seems to assuage him."[17]

But this amorous complainte is only the so-called feminine-style complainte, to use Poirion's terminology (p. 415), more typical of courtly lyric. There also existed the more exclusively clerkly political complainte, in which the poet decried the moral and political situation around him. Actually, we could probably discern a class rather than gender basis for this typology (as Poirion does also, p. 418) and suggest that the first belongs more to the late medieval French aristocracy, which felt itself increasingly threatened and helpless, while the more polemical style of the complainte manifests the insolent aspirations of the rising bourgeoisie—the yuppie class of their day. Christine, as a member of both classes in a sense, and never one to accept women or worthy leaders as helpless, will come to infuse both types in at least one of her complaintes.[18] Another example of a more strictly "clergiale" complainte would be Jean de Meun's "Confession of Nature" episode in the *Roman de la Rose* [Romance of the Rose], inspired by Alain de Lille's twelfth-century *De planctu naturæ* [Complaint of Nature].

What I would surmise to be Christine's first attempt at writing the complainte begins "Doulce dame, vueillez ouÿr la plainte / De ma clamour" (see above). It appears in the so-called Book of Christine or *Livre de Christine* (Paris, Bibliothèque Nationale de France, fonds fr. 12779), in the Duke of Berry's Manuscript, Paris, Bibliothèque Nationale de France, fonds fr. 835, and in the Queen's Manuscript, British Library, Harley 4431. The longest of the three (240 vv. divided into fifteen stanzas), this complainte is also the most clerkly in its style of supplementing the familiar courtly motifs in this plea of a male lover to win over his lady.

After clearly echoing Machaut's "Douce dame, vueilliez oïr la vois / De ma clamour" [Sweet Lady, please listen to the voice of my clamor],[19] Christine displays her lyric aplomb from the beginning, as she has the *-ainte* rhyme from "plainte" dominate the entire first stanza (each quatrain of which is *aaab*), thus generating rhymes to echo her thematics: his constraint, the taint of tear stains or love's pain upon his mind [*pensee distrainte*], and his alternatingly livid or pallid face. From the first stanza as well, Christine advocates the primacy of the word—especially the juridical-confessional—as a direct link with the lover's heart, leaving no chance for deception via the mind (*fainte* [feint]), including allusion to rhetorical flourish (*couleur* as used in v. 15). Hence the recurrent terms for speaking and especially confessing or pleading: along with *plainte* and *complainte*; *regehir, clamour*. Again in the first two verses, we note the primacy of the word as the lover introduces the poem not as *ma complainte*—my complaint—but pointedly as *la complainte de ma clamour*: a tautological ploy that one might translate as "my clamorous claim," to echo both Christine's forceful use of redundancy and her play upon legalistic versus lyric clamor as "claim,"[20] in conjunction with more narrowly juridical terms as *distraint*—an old term connoting control in English law enforcement as much as the "distress" of love—along with the more open implications of words like *contrainte* [constraint]. We may even affirm that Christine juggles and exploits the courtly/clerkly registers—here, lyric/legalistic—motivating these terms more than does Machaut. In so doing, she marshals the discourse too often devoted to ruse (the clerkly) toward serving her lyric ideal of sincere, spontaneous feelings.

Christine's lover underscores the theme of confinement and inward turning in the second stanza, together with the Ovidian lover's malady, for which only the lady's love is the cure. His inner torment at the sight of her is represented in the third stanza by the metaphor of raking leaves (vv. 39–40), instead of happily being able to gather her favors.

Fear is another aspect gradually expounded upon in the succeeding stanzas: the lover is afraid to complain too fervently lest he lose her attention completely, yet he is also aware of her fear of losing her honor should she consent to his advances. To her concern he can respond only by repeatedly averring his utter lack of false intent, as underscored by the many terms for fraud and evil gossip [*faintise, boisdie*],[21] juxtaposed with an even greater number connoting the praise and honor he hopes to bestow upon her as his "revered goddess" and "sovereign princess" (vv. 65–66). Also within the courtly register we find the lover's professed desire to serve her or to have her rule him. Verses 85–86 in particular play on the concept of bail: his desire to deliver his heart to her in bondage. Thus whether physically or socio-interactively, the man continually represents himself as frail and the woman as powerful. As we read this, we are struck by Christine's successful mimicry of the male courtly poetic voice. Is it merely a demonstration of her ability or is it a form of satire? Or perhaps she is attempting to do the male complainte one better by having something more emerge through the veil of tears. It would appear in this respect that she is attempting to make her lover more engaging—not out of sheer helplessness but by clerkly initiative.

Such might be the case in stanzas seven through twelve, in which we find a small but effective array of male wish-fulfillment exempla: Pygmalion; Pyrrha and Deucalion; and the True Lover (also, it seems, from antiquity) function as an inserted moral tale.

It all begins after the Lover, made desperate by his lady's unyielding impassivity, prays to the God of Love, who answers him by recounting, "in most sweet language" (v. 106), the Pygmalion and Galataea story: "Que jadis ot Pymalion de l'ymage / De pierre forte / Vray reconfort de l'amoureux malage, / Par lui servir de trés loial corage, / Et vraye amour, ouquel trés doulz servage /Tout bien enorte" [In ancient times did Pygmalion take from an image / of solid stone / True comfort from love's afflictions / By serving her with a most loyal heart / And true love, to which / All good things exhort us] (vv. 107–12).

The association between the lady's stony reception of the lover's pleas and the evocation of a slab of stone on a pedestal transformed into an amorous woman is only drawn afterward, as is that of Christine's lover-complainant—a wordsmith—with Pygmalion, a stonecutter, both of whom sought aid from Amor upon realizing that their own mortal talents did not suffice. Although Christine might not appreciate our noting this, her borrowing of the Pygmalion story in the above context strongly recalls Jean de Meun's account in his part of the *Roman de la Rose*,[22] not only for the story itself but also its lapidary context, since Jean inserts his version right after relating how Venus attacked the Tower of Shame, the tower being of ivory. Jean's text is of course more playful and licentious—that crudely flippant side of the curial brotherhood Christine found hard to bear. Yet, as on other occasions, she saw the potential value of Jean's often questionable cornucopia of material, filtered through the more courtly version in Machaut's *Fontaine amoureuse* [Amorous Fountain] (vv. 963–64, 1392 ff.), and adapted it to the tighter morality of her own works.

The warmer potential of stone informs the story immediately following: "Aussi Pyrra et Deücalion, / Ains que fondé fust le noble Ylion, / Amolierent / Pierres dures..." [So too did Pyrrha and Deucalion, / When noble Ilion was founded, / They softened / Hard stones...] (vv. 113–17). The amorous-moral message in lines 117–22 may be summarized and paraphrased, "so soften up your own heart toward me [n'ayez cuer de lyon / Et sanz pitié vers moy] that we may live and love, our hearts entwined, faithfully ever after." What strikes us in this passage—aside from the abrupt shift from stone hearts to lion hearts, and thus the lover's identification from Pygmalion/Deucalion momentarily to Androcles—is Christine's careful "courtly" distillation of a more "clerkly" foundation story.[23] Which is to say that nothing is mentioned of Deucalion's Noah-like adventures, and even Christine's brief allusion, inspired by the Promethean episode of the couple's sowing the mother's bones to create men and women, serves only the immediate needs of love poetry. By contrast, in a learned, didactic work such as the *Mutacion de Fortune* (1403) — from which this particular story is curiously absent, in favor of other creation and ship-of-life myths — she would have exploited such material more fully in true clerkly fashion.

The third and most developed exemplum resembles those in Boccaccio's *Decameron* in substance, style, and intent, even in excerpted form: "Et vous vueille, ma dame, souvenir / Que de ce fait ainsi ne puist venir . . . / Que il avint / D'un vray amant qu'Amours si voult tenir / En ses durs las et tant lui maintenir, / Que hors du sens lui convint devenir . . . / A la parfin que morir lui convint / Par trop amer . . . " [And may I remind you, my Lady . . . of what happened to a true lover whom Love wished to hold / In his cruel shackles so much / that he duly went mad / To such a degree / That he finally died . . . of loving too much] (vv. 129–38).

As the rest of the tale goes, we are shown the pitiless lady who had rained angry curses and insults upon the poor fellow who, as he lay dying of her ill treatment, prayed to the Gods to avenge his suffering. Once again, the stone has been romanced, for at this point (v. 155) he compares his lady's cruelty to "hard stone" [*pierre dure*], in fact, he begs that her intransigent body become a statue [*estature*]: "Dont les dames en ycelle aventure / Se mirassent, qui n'ont pitié ne cure / Des amoureux" [A statue, / in which women in this story might mirror themselves / those who have neither pity nor care / for lovers] (vv. 157–60) — in other words, the lady thus conjured is a reverse Galataea. His orison is answered: the previously heartless woman, upon seeing his corpse on the bier, is suddenly seized with such pity that "with the force of lightning" she is struck and turned into white marble, which can be seen to this day. The moral *expositio* to this tale beginning stanza twelve is predictable enough, as the lover returns to his usual praise, promises, and pleas — not without some nicely wrought verses — for four more stanzas.

Could it be that this third story receives the most space because it is here that Christine has had the Lover create his own exemplum with all the trimmings?[24] And that she, like Stendhal toying with Julien Sorel, pokes gentle fun at his grand aspirations to exegesis and prophecy, beginning with his current situation and foretelling what will happen to him and her?[25]

Whatever the intent, Christine's interweaving of these exempla demonstrates a rare finesse often abandoned in her weightier, more outwardly erudite, didactic volumes, in which such insertions are far from seamless. In this poem she manages to prove her *clergie* without allowing it to encumber her courtly lyrical message.

The *complainte* concludes in stanza fifteen with our lover's final requests:

first to his "sweet flower" to take pity on his lovesickness, and second, to God (not Amor), to "avenge" him, but very gently: while wishing a long life and good health to his lady's body, he asks God to levy a "light penalty" [*legiere amende*] against her soul. The quiet drama of this dualistic "sentence" is emphasized by the trisyllabic line "*legiere amende*" coming at the very end, thus completing the fusion of court of love and court of justice.

The second "Complainte amoureuse" repeats the opening imperative of the first ("Vueillez oÿr en pitié ma complainte") and its overall rhyme schemes and structure, but the later poem is generally more spontaneous and optimistic in tone. Shorter by almost fifty verses, it contains none of the exempla—indeed none of the classical allusions found in "Doulce dame . . . " This complainte thus maintains a more unified, courtly ethos and thematic development. Because it is less ambitious—Christine appearing content to take up conventional themes while focusing on style—it reads more fluidly: the octosyllable seems less taxed, the rhymes less forced.

Yet the poem is neither bland nor banal. In depicting the oscillating emotions of the self-denigrating lover before his exalted lady, its transitions, heralded by interjections (*Hé! Helas!*), resound more sharply from stanza to stanza: first meditative, then outraged, then back to restraint. The imagery, if conventional, is more starkly drawn as it moves from the most refined repetition from the first complainte, "Sweetest flower whose imprint I bear / Within my heart portrayed, inscribed and painted" (above, vv. 6–7—in which *painte* strategically rhymes with *complainte*), to the sight of her "Que si trés doulx ymage fust peü / De fiel amer" [That this sweetest image might have been nourished on bitter bile] (vv. 71–72). As in the earlier poem, the dualism of the lady's body and soul underlies the more prominent topics of love's suffering, the lady's lack of pity and fear of vile rumors: if her body is more yielding because the lover can derive pleasure at least from seeing it, her soul, as reflected in her gaze, remains unattainable. It is her soul, the fortress to her heart, that he seeks to move by his words, as he reiterates throughout the poem.

Failing this, his words (*parler, clamour*) must rise even higher to reach Amor, who in turn must inspire Pity to aid the lover (stanza ten) and "redress" his tormented heart. The lover also asks Amor to permit the lady's heart no rest until she "unleashes" the lover's heart and bestows joy upon him. In return (stanza eleven) he pledges eternal service and loyalty to her, promising her goods equal to "all of Burgundy" if such be her desire. The twelfth and final stanza begins with an impossibilia topos: "Plus ne vous sçay que dire, belle née" [I no longer know what to say to you, highborn one] (v. 177). Once again, he makes his final lines a renvoi to God, but less directly than in "Doulce dame . . . ," as he begs not for judgment but that Amor bind their hearts together forever.

The reference to the greatness of Burgundy—the only specific one of its kind—brings us to an even more interesting aspect of this second amorous complainte, which devolves from its codicological existence. This second complainte is found only in the British Library, Harley 4431, the so-called Queen's Manuscript, presumed to have been not only supervised by Christine, as were the earlier collectanea (Chantilly 492–93, BnF 12779, BnF 604), but also copied in the author's own hand. We recall that the queen to whom it was destined was Isabelle (Isabeau) of Bavaria, wife of Charles VI and ally of John the Fearless, Duke of Burgundy. Duke John and various members of the house of Burgundy were and would be generous patrons for Christine throughout her career. But perhaps the ultimate confirmation of the dominance of this house in Christine's career lies in the existence of a "Burgundy Manuscript," now lost, of Christine's works, as listed in one of the ducal library catalogues.[26]

In Queen Isabelle herself, Christine tried to envision not only a patron but also a peacemaker during France's all too frequent political crises. In this collection and in her later work not contained in this manuscript, the *Lamentacion sur les maux de la guerre civile* [Lamentation on the Evils of Civil War] (1410), she pleads with the Duke of Berry to act as peacemaker. This strikes us more as an example of Christine's clerkly pragmatism, by now well honed after more than a decade of fighting off creditors and striving to establish herself as an author worthy of patronage, than of the political idealism evident in her treatises, since both the queen and the duke themselves proved to be consistently menacing to the welfare and unity of France.

We can therefore assume that Christine composed "Vueillez oÿr . . . " for this "command performance" manuscript for the queen, placing it after the majority of *formes fixes* sequences, among which the famous *Cent balades*, ending with the *Balades de divers propos* [Ballades on Different Subjects]. The rubric introducing "Vueillez oÿr" reads: "Ci commence une complainte amoureuse" [here begins an amorous complainte]. After the text of the poem come *Encore autres balades* [Still More Ballades] and the first polemical piece in the volume, the well-known *Epistre au Dieu d'amours* [Epistle of the God of Love] (1399). There then follows the first "Complainte amoureuse," "Doulce dame," rubricated as "une autre complainte amoureuse" [another amorous complainte].

At this juncture arises another manifestation of *clergie*, a modern one this time. For unnoticed by scholars of Christine's publishing career,[27]

Maurice Roy, in his canonical edition of Christine's lyric poetry, while including both complaints, misleadingly placed the "Doulce dame" first, without reproducing the rubric of either the Paris or the Queen's Manuscript. In so doing he made the Queen's Manuscript's "Vueillez oÿr" come second, instead of first, thus subtly relegating to secondary status the Queen's Manuscript itself. We might interpret this as symptomatic of French *fin-de-siècle* nationalism, with Roy, having based his three-volume edition on the now separate codices of the Parisian Duke's Manuscript, exercising his clerkly initiative to defend its primacy over the Queen's Manuscript, dedicated to a Bavarian and now in England. Fortunately, Roy's judgment on manuscript primacy has since been conclusively overturned, without necessitating another Hundred Years' War.

After reproducing this text, Christine continues with the same sequence of works as she does in the *Livre de Christine* and the Duke's Manuscript, except for situating the *Rose* Debate epistles later in the volume. In the Queen's Manuscript, these appear three titles after the *Duc des vrais amans,* while in the Duke's Manuscript and the *Livre de Christine*, they come much before, the *Duc des vrais amans* having been placed farther on in the Paris collection. It would appear that Christine made more of an effort to unify the various "courtly polemical" works—those debating, arguing against, or satirizing it—in the Queen's Manuscript, although she does insert the major compendium of moral tales, the *Epistre Othea,* among them, perhaps to avert monotony and royal ennui. The *Duc des vrais amans*, an epistolary, lyric-narrative anti-romance and source of our third complainte, follows the *Othea*.

The two complaintes just treated stand as independent works within Christine's lyric corpus. The third one, by contrast, she specifically intended to conclude the coda poems—themselves a somewhat disjointed lyric finale—to the longer lyric-narrative work, the *Livre du Duc des vrais amans*, first composed between 1403 and 1405 and included in both the Duke's and Queen's Manuscripts.[28] This complainte is the only one written by Christine for a female speaker. Its verses differ from the previous two in that they now contain seven and four syllables (instead of ten and four). Christine's choice of the heptasyllable for this complainte helps to relate it to the *Livre du Duc des vrais amans*, as Laidlaw suggests, in which she also used this meter for the narrative sections. For these reasons, and for its position within the volume and content, I suggest that this complainte, though an integral part of one work, may also be read as a rebuttal to the earlier amorous complaintes and as a portent of the *Lay de dame* [Lady's Lay] or *Lay mortel* [Lay of Death], also written in seven and four syllables, concluding Christine's final lyric sequence, the *Cent ballades d'Amant et de Dame* [One Hundred Ballades of Lover and Lady] (1409–10), which exists only in the Queen's Manuscript.

The *Livre du Duc des vrais amans* complainte commences lugubriously, builds upon inner torment, and ends with a death wish, all to reflect the fate of the honorable lady who yields to a *fin'amors* relationship—that is, who has succumbed to the man's complaintes! However, we should not forget that, within the story line of the romance, both lover and lady feel betrayed. That Christine has taken the woman's part indicates another symmetry of rebuttal besides the mode just suggested above: that of gendered universal justice, since the woman's side in these affairs has never been adequately represented.[29] Following the same structure as the two others, this is the shortest of the three examples at only 160 lines over ten stanzas, yet it is perhaps the most original and most powerful. While at first displaying the elegant, controlled octosyllable and rhyme of the earlier efforts, Christine here appears to attempt to re-create the lady's unheralded suffering by straining verse convention: what might in other contexts qualify as excessive use of enjambement here effectively mirrors the deceived woman's nervousness and desperation as she seeks to survive from day to day. It is as though the abuse inflicted upon her by this affair justifies Christine's (slight) abuse of poetic practice.

The tense phrasing and often percussive, rather than playful, repeated rhymes help to refute and gradually demolish each and every tenet of the previous male complaintes. Yet each refutation is surprisingly methodical in substance, despite the emotional tone. Stanza by stanza, she takes up each of the lover's themes: first, her supposedly sovereign status, now transformed into a lone, supreme martyr to the man's love (she addresses the God of Love as *tu* here, while the men address their ladies in the *vous* form). As for his lovesickness, hers is now worse, since she has no one even to complain to. To answer the customary exchange metaphor of love, hearts, flowers, and rewards, she emphasizes repeatedly that the "wages" of illicit love are death (*si mortel rente*, v. 16), or a desire for it (vv. 159–60).

After the first stanza, she recounts the process of her downfall, in a manner reminiscent of Dante's victims of lust in the *Inferno* 5: how all this sorrow came to be; the growing force of her inner *dure clamour* (75). In particular she relates how she was deceived by his near-death act, confronted because of Amor's intervention, which aroused within her a fear of losing him and her honor, as well as seducing her with his physical beauty and, once she first tried to comfort him, his idyllic courtly behavior. She even takes up the play on *amende* noted at the end of "Doulce dame," to show that she could not *amender* [help] herself. She devotes much description to his outward signs of being the ideal lover, only to set us up, just as she had been made vulnerable, for the shocking change.

This turnabout is abruptly introduced in stanza seven: "Helas! Mais il est changié / A present et estrangié" [Alas! But now he's changed and from me estranged] (vv. 97–98). He had hidden his true heart from her. She too becomes confined, imprisoned—not by love but rather by its cruel consequences—and has only her own heart into which to retreat, "par dur pourpris" [by harsh enclosure]—no *locus amoenus* for her. Her last stanza is also centered on an impossibilia motif, but it differs from the man's in that she does know what to say but realizes that it is all to no avail, since he will never love her, and only a lover could care about a complainte. Her strategic -*ainte* rhymes in the last stanza imitate the openings of the man's complaintes: once again *complainte*, *tainte*, and *fainte* appear, but this time to mock the lover's pleas. The poem ends in rhymes that seem to hammer one's ears with the feeling of hopelesness to counter the conventional lover's softer-sounding *clamour* for *espoir*: "Et il clamera / Autre dame et reclamera / Et en elle s'affermera, / Dont mon las cuer en semera / Ha! larme mainte" [He'll keep deceiving women, claim another as his fiancée, all of which—alas!—will sow many a tear in my heart] (vv. 152–56). Only death will free her from this recurrent cycle of shame, jealousy, and pain.

In conclusion, we have come to see Christine's first complaintes as artistic experiments in writing in the male voice. I do not believe that in these she is yet satirizing the double standard of courtly love. However, in the final one being treated here, she seems to be speaking her own mind, if perhaps only because she can take shelter in the fictional lady's persona in the *Vrais amans*. She may well have composed the "Vueillez oÿr" after the *Vrais amans* complainte to fill out her own symmetrical plan for the Queen's Manuscript. She did not need to worry about the impact of her final, anti-*fin'amors* message, since her last lyric work, the *Cent ballades d'Amant et de Dame* ends, we recall, with the woman-centered "lay mortel."[30]

More detailed study of these relatively neglected complaintes remains to be done, particularly concerning how they reflect Christine's intensifying answers to her authorities: to Machaut's *Fontaine amoureuse*, for example.[31] We hope, however, to have supplemented Poirion's assessment that this genre opened itself more to social and personal influences as the complaintes embody the fundamental tendencies of courtly literature: "artistique, morale et amoureuse" [artistic, moral and amorous] (p. 422), and that our closer reading of the complaintes has elucidated a more universal Christine, the developing poet and feminist ideologue, as they exemplify her appropriation of clerkly and courtly ideals in unique combination.

Notes

I first presented this material in a paper bearing a similar title at the September 1993 SEMA Conference in New Orleans, for which I thank E. J. Richards; and in a shorter French version, "Les Complaintes de Christine: Tradition et refus," at the International Medieval Congress, Leeds, July 1994, for which I thank B. Ribémont. In between these occasions, my work has greatly benefited from discussions with Lori Walters and especially from the many suggestions offered by James C. Laidlaw in two e-mails from June 1994. All references to Laidlaw not otherwise specified are from this correspondence. I am also indebted to Christine Reno for her comments and for the loan of essential microfilms of the relevant manuscripts.

1. In his three-volume Œuvres poétiques, I.281–95; see also Roy's preface, xxi–xxiv, for scheme of ordering of all works in the MSS. All references to Christine's poetry are from this edition unless otherwise noted.

2. Ed. Roy, II, pp. 296–97, vv. 21, 57 resp.

3. Ed. Alexandre Micha (Paris: Honoré Champion, 1970), 2, vv. 28–37 (italics mine):

> Ce nos ont nostre livre apris
> Qu'an Grece ot de *chevalerie*
> Le premier los et de *clergie.*
> Puis vint chevalerie a Rome
> Et de la clergie la some,
> Qui or est an France venue.
> Dex doint qu'ele i soit maintenue
> Et que li leus li abelisse
> Tant que ja mes de France n'isse
> L'enors qui s'i est arestee.

[This our books teach us: that Greece was the first to be blessed with chivalry and learning. Then chivalry came to Rome, and with it all the learning which now has come to France. God granted that, for as long as it is preserved and cherished in this place, this honor should never leave France, wherein it has come to rest.]

4. In 1410, Christine composed the *Livre des fais d'armes et de chevalerie*, a respected manual in England as well as in France during the fifteenth century. See Charity Cannon Willard, "Christine de Pizan's Treatise on the Art of Medieval Warfare," in *Essays in Honor of Louis Francis Solano*, ed. R. J. Cormier and U. T. Holmes, UNC Studies in Romance Languages and Literatures, 92 (Chapel Hill: University of North Carolina Press, 1970), pp. 179–91.

5. Ernst Robert Curtius, *European Literature and the Latin Middle Ages*, pp. 384 ff.; George H. Bumgardner, Jr., "Tradition and Modernity from 1380 to 1405," passim.

6. For an excellent definition and discussion of the *clerkly* or *curial* style of this period in England, highly applicable to the French while citing Christine explicitly, see J. D. Burnley, "Christine de Pizan and the So-Called *style clergial*," pp. 1–6, and "Curial Prose in England."

7. Perhaps the most explicit representation of Chrétien's ideal of the *estude* to counteract *folie* [foolishness, madness] and *vilenie* [evil deeds] is found in the prologue to his *Erec et Enide*, although most of his romances are shaped around lessons in love relationships, whether courtly or anti-courtly, as is well known.

8. That is to say, the three labeled "complaintes" that follow the rules of versification for the complainte, to which we refer by this spelling to distinguish the formal genre from the looser mode of complaint. Two notable examples of "complaintes" by Christine that must be considered more properly ballades are the *Autres balades* 42 (Roy II, pp. 255–56) and the *Cent ballades d'Amant et de Dame* 9 (ed. J. Cerquiglini-Toulet, Paris: 10/18 / UGE, 1982), p. 40. The former is a political lament on the death of Duke Philip of Burgundy, and thus more clerkly, while the latter belongs to the courtly tradition, resembling in theme and development her *Complaintes amoureuses*. Yet another example might be *Balades d'estrange façon*, "Balade a vers a responces" (Roy, I, pp. 122–24), beginning "Amours, escoute ma complainte?".

9. These would be, according to James C. Laidlaw, in the following chronological order: (1) The *Livre de Christine* (Paris, Bibliothèque Nationale de France, fonds fr. 12779; and Chantilly, Condé 492–93 — copied under Christine's supervision ca. 1399–1402. Paris, Bibliothèque Nationale de France, fonds fr. 604, completed after 1407, is a copy of the Chantilly manuscript); (2) The Duke's Manuscript (Paris BnF mss. fr. 835, 606, 836, 605, and possibly 607), supervised by Christine for, eventually at least, the Duke of Berry, who acquired it in 1408–9; and (3) The Queen's Manuscript (British Library, Harley 4431), made by Christine for Queen Isabelle of France and given to her 1410–11. See Laidlaw's discussion of these in "Christine de Pizan — An Author's Progress," and "Christine de Pizan — A Publisher's Progress."

10. Johanna C. Schilperoort, *Guillaume de Machaut et Christine de Pisan (Étude comparative)*, p. 16, singles out the same three complaintes, only to assert harshly their inferiority to Machaut's: "Tandis que les complaintes de Machaut sont assez riches de contenu, les complaintes de Christine ne sont intéressantes que comme adroits jeux de rimes" [While Machaut's complaintes are rich in content, the complaintes of Christine are interesting only as clever rhyme games].

11. Schilperoort, p. 15, in observing this absence in Deschamps, rightly implies that Machaut's complaintes already sufficed as models for Christine and her contemporaries.

12. Daniel Poirion, *Le poète et le prince,* chap. 10; Jean-Claude Mühlethaler,

Poétiques du quinzième siècle, esp. pp. 18–19, 49; Robert Deschaux, "Le lai et la complainte."

13. We recall that Granson's "Complainte de Granson" was also known as the "Lay en complainte" in Arthur Piaget, *Oton de Grandson, sa vie et ses poésies,* esp. p. 283; see also, in same work, the full text of the "Complainte," pp. 259–66. Laidlaw underscores the resemblance of this lai to the complainte form due to the twelve (four-part) stanzas = 192 vv.: the same pattern and length of Christine's second "Complainte amoureuse" ("Vueillez oÿr . . . "), as is Machaut's in Vladimir Fedorovich Chichmaref [Shishmarev], ed., *Guillaume de Machaut. Poésies lyriques,* pp. 256–61.

14. Text slightly emended according to BL Harley 4431, fol. 58d.

15. Confirmed by Laidlaw, who, with Poirion, cites among the few examples of this period: Machaut, *Remede de Fortune* (ed. J. Wimsatt and W. Kibler, pp. 219–49), that in ed. V. F. Chichmaref, pp. 251–56 (to which we can add the *Fontaine amoureuse,* pp. 47–100); Granson, "Lay en complainte" / "Complainte de Granson" (pp. 259–66, 283); and Deschamps, No. 1357 (No. 1397 in prose and distinctly "clergial"; all other of Deschamps's "complaintes" being really ballades). See Deschaux, "Le lai et la complainte, p. 77, who adds a few from Froissart and Garencières, all of which nonetheless attest the relative rarity of this genre in Christine's time. For the fun of the *formes fixes,* see Michel Zink, "Le lyrisme en rond."

16. Liliane Dulac, "Christine de Pizan et le malheur des vrais amans," p. 232.

17. Maureen Boulton, *The Song in the Story,* p. 189, on a lai by Machaut preceding the complainte in the *Remede de fortune,* most recently edited in Guillaume de Machaut, *"Le jugement du roy de Behaigne" and "Remede de Fortune,"* ed. Wimsatt and Kibler, pp. 219–49.

18. Christine also penned at least one clerkly complainte in ballade form, notably *Autre balades,* No. 42, lamenting the death of Philip the Bold (1404), which won enough respect to have been plagiarized by Jean Petit for another cause later on. See Alfred Coville, "Sur une ballade de Christine de Pizan."

19. *La Fontaine amoureuse,* vv. 235–36, p. 46.

20. Both Greimas's *Dictionnaire de l'ancien français* (Paris: Larousse, 1968), pp. 116–17, and Peter Rickard's *Chrestomathie de la langue française au quinzième siècle* (Cambridge: Cambridge University Press, 1976), p. 385, for example, present evidence for continuing legalistic usage of *clamer* and its various forms throughout the Middle Ages. Christine herself would note the power of "mos et termes actisans" in the "clamour" of the epistles in the debate on the *Romance of the Rose.* See *Le Débat sur le Roman de la Rose,* ed. Eric Hicks (Paris: H. Champion, 1977), p. 16. For a formidable exposition of the role of *clamour* and *mos actisans* within Christine's clerkly involvements, see Helen Solterer, "Flaming Words."

21. As the sole woman writing courtly romances and lyrics, Christine is uniquely sensitive to the tragic consequences awaiting women who consent to *fin'amors* because of the *losengiers* [malicious gossips]. This recurs as a major courtly theme

in her love poetry, particularly as elaborated upon when the Dame de la Tour advises the lady against her liaison in the *Duc des vrais amans*, while the deploration of fraud and falsehood can also be found in such clerkly works as the *Mutacion de Fortune*. See *Le Livre du Duc des vrais amans*, pp. 171–80; and *Le Livre de la mutacion de Fortune*, ed. Suzanne Solente, 4 vols., SATF (Paris: Picard, 1959–65), e.g., the Path of Ruse (*Grant Barat*) attached to Fortune's Castle (I, pp. 114–16) and the falsehood of clerics through deceptive language (II, pp. 60–65).

22. Ed. Poirion, vv. 20815 ff.

23. This first appears in Apollodorus's first- to second-century *Bibliotheca* I, 46–47, though Christine's source derived more closely from Ovid's *Metamorphoses*, I, 318 ff.

24. In this paragraph I embellish on a suggestion by Laidlaw.

25. Allusion to the scene in *Le Rouge et le noir*, in which Stendhal has Julien, poised on a rock, contemplating a soaring sparrow hawk as symbolic of Napoleon's destiny, wondering if it would be his own (ed. H. Martineau [Paris: Pléiade/Gallimard] I, pp. 276–77).

26. Laidlaw, "Christine de Pizan—A Publisher's Progress," p. 59, cites the 1487 Brussels inventory's description of this manuscript as it existed in the Duke of Burgundy's library, which contained many of Christine's major works, including a copy of the *Cent balades* and *Cent ballades d'Amant et de Dame*.

27. See Laidlaw, "Christine de Pizan—A Publisher's Progress," pp. 62–63, 74–75, who has rightly noted the unusual form of that particular quire.

28. All citations have been taken from the critical edition by Thelma Fenster.

29. Since my formulation of this premise, Roberta Krueger independently discusses a similar notion in "A Woman's Response."

30. For Christine's *lay mortel*, see Barbara K. Altmann, "Reflections on a 'Lay mortel' and the Poetics of Lyric Sequences," in this volume.

31. This in light of Jacqueline Cerquiglini-Toulet's comments on the *Fontaine amoureuse*, such as when she notes how the poem "réduit au maximum la distance clerc-chevalier" [reduces to the utmost the distance between clerk and knight] and cites Paris's sneering at clerkliness and other gifts of Pallas and Juno in the poem: "Gardés vos tresors amassés, / Vostre scens et vostre clergie . . . " [Keep your treasures amassed, / Your wisdom and learning . . .] (vv. 2130 ff.), in *"Un engin si soutil,"* p. 125. See also her introduction to her edition of the *Fontaine amoureuse*, esp. p. 13, when along with her discussion of Machaut's Pygmalion legend, she also remarks on Machaut's quotation (*Fontaine*, v. 131), "Qui se veut mirer, si se mire," and Christine's (*Autres balades*, no. 17, v. 22) echo in her "Qui s'i vouldra mirer s'y mire," both of which mean "Whosoever wishes to observe himself, may he observe himself." Christine, thus inspired by Machaut, is arguably trying to construct her own mirror, as in almost all of her works.

Works Cited

Boulton, Maureen. *The Song in the Story: Lyric Insertions in French Narrative Fiction, 1200–1400*. Philadelphia: University of Pennsylvania Press, 1993.

Bumgardner, George H., Jr. "Tradition and Modernity from 1380 to 1405: Christine de Pizan." Ph.D. diss., Yale University, 1970.

Burnley, J. D. "Curial Prose in England." *Speculum* 61 (1986): 593–614.

———. "Christine de Pizan and the So-Called *Style Clergial*." *Modern Language Review* 81 (1986): 1–6.

Cerquiglini-Toulet, Jacqueline. *"Un engin si soutil": Guillaume de Machaut et l'écriture au XIVe siècle*. Paris: Honoré Champion, 1985.

Christine de Pizan. *Le Livre du Duc des vrais amans*. Ed. Thelma Fenster. Binghamton, N.Y.: MRTS, 1995.

———. *Œuvres poétiques*. Ed. Maurice Roy. 3 vols. Paris: Firmin Didot, 1886–96; reprint, New York: Johnson, 1965.

Coville, Alfred. "Sur une ballade de Christine de Pisan." In *Entre camarades*, pp. 181–94. Paris: Félix Alcan, 1901.

Curtius, Ernst Robert. *European Literature and the Latin Middle Ages*. Trans. Willard Trask. New York: Bollingen/Harper & Row, 1963, 1990.

Deschaux, Robert. "Le lai et la complainte." In *Grundriß der romanischen Literaturen des Mittelalters*, VIII/1: *La Littérature française aux XIVe et XVe siècles*, ed. Daniel Poirion et al., pp. 70–85. Heidelberg: Carl Winter, 1988.

Dulac, Liliane. "Christine de Pizan et le malheur des vrais amans." In *Mélanges de littérature médiévale offerts à Pierre Le Gentil*, ed. Jean Dufournet and Daniel Poirion, pp. 222–33. Paris: SEDES, 1973.

Krueger, Roberta. "A Woman's Response: Christine de Pizan's *Le Livre du duc des vrais amans* and the Limits of Romance." In *Women Readers and the Ideology of Gender in Old French Verse Romance*, chap. 8. Cambridge: Cambridge University Press, 1993.

Laidlaw, James C. "Christine de Pizan—An Author's Progress." *Modern Language Review* 78 (1983): 532–50.

———. "Christine de Pizan—A Publisher's Progress." *Modern Language Review* 82 (1987): 35–75.

Machaut, Guillaume de. *La Fontaine amoureuse*. Ed. Jacqueline Cerquiglini-Toulet. Paris: Stock, 1993.

———. *"Le Jugement du Roy de Behaigne" and "Remede de Fortune"*. Ed. James I. Wimsatt and William W. Kibler. Music ed. Rebecca A. Baltzer. Athens: University of Georgia Press, 1988.

———. *Poésies lyriques*. Ed. Vladimir Fedorovich Chichmaref [Shishmarev]. Paris: Honoré Champion, 1909; reprint, Geneva: Slatkine, 1973.

Mühlethaler, Jean-Claude. *Poétiques du quinzième siècle*. Paris: Nizet, 1983.

Piaget, Arthur. *Oton de Grandson, sa vie et ses poésies*. Lausanne: Payot, 1941.

Poirion, Daniel. *Le poète et le prince: l'évolution du lyrisme courtois de Guillaume de Machaut à Charles d'Orléans*. Paris: Presses Universitaires de France, 1965.

Schilperoort, Johanna C. *Guillaume de Machaut et Christine de Pisan (Étude comparative)*. The Hague: H. P. De Swart, 1936.

Solterer, Helen. "Flaming Words: Verbal Violence and Gender in Premodern Paris." *Romanic Review* 86 (1995): 357–78.

Zink, Michel. "Le lyrisme en rond: esthétique et séduction des poèmes à forme fixe au moyen âge." *Cahiers de l'Association internationale des études françaises* 32 (1980): 71–90.

◈ CHAPTER 6

Translatio Studii: Christine de Pizan's Self-Portrayal in Two Lyric Poems and in the *Livre de la mutacion de Fortune*

LORI WALTERS

At the beginning of her *Livre des fais d'armes et de chevalerie* [Book of Deeds of Arms and Knighthood], a handbook written in 1410 on the art of warfare, which includes sections on the distinction between just and unjust wars, Christine de Pizan proclaims "O Minerve, deesse d'armes et de chevalerie! . . . je suis comme toi femme ytalienne" [O Minerva, goddess of arms and chivalry! . . . I am an Italian woman like you]. The Roman deity Minerva corresponded to the Greek Athena, goddess of warfare and wisdom. Athena acquired the right to give her name to the city of Athens when she won the contest with Poseidon as to who should rule Greece by offering the citizens of Athens an olive bough, symbol of peace and prosperity.[1] In comparing herself to Minerva, Christine implicitly presents herself as the fulfillment of the *translatio studii*, the transmission of learning from Greece to Rome and then to France.[2] A learnèd woman, Christine came to France from Italy at the age of four to join her father, Tommaso di Benvenuto da Pizzano, who three years previously had assumed the position of astrologer and physician to Charles V. Later she interpreted this geographical displacement as indicative of her true nature and destiny as a writer. Although a commonplace, the theme, which Christine developed throughout her career, reveals a great deal about the way that she viewed herself and her poetry.[3] It also gives insights into the transformation of the lyric in the late medieval period. My study will examine Christine's use of the *translatio studii* topos in two lyric poems, Ballade 2 of the *Cent balades*, where the focus is on Rome, and Ballade 37 of the *Autres balades*, where Christine concentrates on Greece, and in the *Livre de la mutacion de Fortune* [Book of the Mutation of Fortune] (1403),[4] which includes a universal history stretching from the beginning of time to the establishment of the Roman Empire and an epilogue that describes conditions in present-day France.

In the *Cent balades*, Christine's first collection of lyric poetry begun in 1399 and completed in 1402, she invokes the *translatio studii* topos in Ballade 2 (ed. Roy, I, pp. 2-3). The refrain here refers specifically to a crown of laurel that honors princes and poets (as we will see, a veiled reference to Petrarch's being crowned as the *poeta laureatus*).[5] For a clearer understanding of Christine's use of the theme of *translatio studii*, it is important to consider its most well-known appearance in the Old French vernacular in the prologue to *Cligés*,[6] where Chrétien de Troyes, pairing *studium* and *imperium* [learning and political supremacy], assigns the greater importance to the transfer of culture. Chrétien declares that *chevalerie* and *clergie*, after having migrated first from Greece to Rome, had now settled definitively in France where they were, God willing, destined to remain forever. He goes on to say that they had only been on loan to Greece and Rome. Under his tutelage, he hopes to keep the locus of supremacy, at least literary supremacy, in France.[7] In his earlier romance, *Erec et Enide*, linked to *Cligés* in the first line of its prologue ("Cil qui fist d'Erec et d'Enide" [he who wrote of Erec and Enide]), the author had boasted that the ultimate worth of vernacular literature was connected to the survival of Christianity by virtue of his very name, "Chrétien." Christine goes Chrétien one better in the *Mutacion de Fortune* with her paronomastic play on her name (ed. Solente, vol. I, vv. 371-78), in which she likens herself in her transformed state, following the model of *imitatio Christi*,[8] to Christ himself.

Addressing herself to unspecified "princes" in the envoi to Ballade 2, Christine claims that present-day France is not living up to its duty as continuator of Rome because the right people are not being rewarded: people with money or good blood lines are getting ahead rather than those who perform noble and virtuous deeds. Here one must recall that Christine, in *Le Livre de la Cité des Dames* and elsewhere in her work, held virtue, not inherited position, to be the basis of true nobility, whence her insistence that all women, thanks to the exercise of their virtue, could become veritable "ladies."[9] Christine implies that France has lost the position of cultural supremacy that it had occupied in Chrétien's time and, more immediately for her, during the reign of the model king, Charles V. In his study of the *translatio* topos, Ernst Robert Curtius pointed out that the transfer of dominion from one empire to another was the consequence of the unlawful exercise of that dominion, that is, in a loss of "true nobility" based on virtue.[10] Christine documents the troubles plaguing the French realm in Ballade 95: Charles VI's mental illness prevents him from exercising the monarch's necessary function as intermediary between his subjects and God. In verses 7–8, Christine sets forth her contention that Charles's mental disability has been visited on him by God as punishment for the sins of his subjects: France is being punished for its widespread failings in the interconnected realms of knightly prowess and human relationships, particularly in love relationships.

In the second stanza of Ballade 2, in her reference to the proper celebration of heroes returning from military campaigns in Carthage, Christine proposes a first step in setting things right again, which she will develop in her reworking of the *translatio* theme in the *Mutacion*. The refrain of Ballade 2 refers to those returning from the Carthaginian wars as "digne[s] d'estre de lorier couronné[s]" [worthy of being crowned with laurel], an allusion both to Cicero's story from the *De re publica* [On the Commonwealth] of Scipio Africanus as recounted by Macrobius in his *Commentary on the Dream of Scipio* and to Petrarch's reworking of Cicero and Macrobius in the *Africa*, his epic poem on Scipio. Macrobius's commentary on Cicero's sixth book represented a compendium of knowledge and philosophy as well as one of the most important sources for Platonism in the Latin West. By reworking Macrobius and Cicero in the *Africa*, Petrarch extended and disseminated an imposing corpus of classical learning. The *Africa* is the product of a whole line of textual refashioning, which introduces another meaning of the term *translatio*, namely the series of recastings of earlier texts that constitutes the foundation of literary tradition in the Middle Ages and afterward. The sixth book of Cicero's *De re publica*, the only part known to medieval authors as preserved in Macrobius's commentary, retells Plato's myth of Er.[11] Just as Cicero received inspiration from Plato's use of this legend about a man who reports on his experiences in the otherworld, so Petrarch in turn took his inspiration from Cicero's work and Macrobius's extended commentary that frames it.

Petrarch's creative transformations of Cicero included his having the elder Scipio, who experiences the dream rather than Scipio the Younger, be inspired in his pursuit of wisdom and glory by a reading of the Sixth Book of Cicero's *De re publica*. Petrarch thereby affirms the capacity, indeed the duty, of literature to inspire real-life figures to perform heroic deeds.¹² According to Aldo Bernardo, Petrarch's choice of Scipio as the epic hero par excellence can be explained by Petrarch's active involvement in attempts to improve the political situation in Europe (p. 121), an aspect of Petrarch's humanism that clarifies part of the *Africa*'s appeal for Christine. In Ballade 2, Christine echoes the concern that Petrarch expressed in his second letter to his friend Pierre Bersuire, written after his visit to Paris in 1361, that the answer to current political problems in Italy and France was the revival of the example of Roman military and civic virtues.¹³ Pierre Bersuire's Christianized version of Ovid's *Metamorphoses* begins with an introduction "De forma et figuris deorum" [On the form and figures of the gods], for which Petrarch had lent Bersuire a copy of the *Africa*.¹⁴ Petrarch's *Africa*, then, was a focal influence in the tradition of the moralized Ovid from which Christine borrowed heavily in the *Mutacion*.

Christine, like Petrarch, would have found substantiation for her own views in the anticipations of Christian purgatory in Cicero's work (Bernardo, p. 117). Petrarch also repeats Cicero's interdiction of suicide, a notion that underlies Christine's treatment in the figure of Hero in Ballade 3 of the *Cent balades*. In some sense envious of Hero's gesture that allowed her to follow Leander to the grave, Christine nonetheless rejects suicide as a solution to her own despair following the death of her husband, Étienne de Castel. As an alternative to self-destruction, Christine adopts a stance endorsed by the tradition of Cicero, Macrobius, and Boethius where she observes the world as a detached observer of events but, again like Petrarch, allows herself to comment on them in the hope of changing the course of history.

In Ballade 2 of the *Cent balades*, Christine offers the implied example of Petrarch's celebration of the deeds of Scipio Africanus as the basis for her own role as praisegiver to those who are indeed "digne[s] d'estre de lorier couronné[s]," a role that she hopes will function as an alternative to the poor leadership shown by many other French poets.¹⁵ The refrain of Ballade 2 inevitably recalls Petrarch's crowning as Rome's first *poeta laureatus* in twelve centuries on Easter Sunday, 1341, some fifty years prior to the composition of the *Cent balades*. Petrarch had been awarded the laurel wreath in large part for his work on the *Africa*. Through her use of the Petrarchan subtext, Christine implicitly calls for a revival of French letters through the adoption of illustrious Italian models like Petrarch and Dante, who besides giving a large place to Christian morals and civic responsibility, promoted the vernacular as a literary language on the level of Latin. As Kevin Brownlee has shown, in the *Chemin de long estude* [Path of long study], Christine "translates" Dante's *Commedia* into the Middle French vernacular.[16]

This last comment leads us to consider another meaning of *translatio*, adaptation, and especially the adaptation of a work into another language. In the *Mutacion* Christine creatively adapts elements from Petrarch's *œuvre*, first by proposing the historically informed advice that she was to develop as the only available remedy for all fortunes,[17] and second, by adapting the paradigm of gender transformation utilized by the Italian poet in poem 23 of the *Rime sparse* [Scattered Verse], his famous song of metamorphosis based on Ovidian legends, for didactic purposes that would certainly have won Petrarch's approval. Here Petrarch's poetic persona alternately assumes the characteristics of the man and the woman in the love dialogue.[18] Unlike her many quotations of Dante's name, Christine may have refrained from referring to Petrarch directly in the *Cent balades* because Petrarch had claimed that poets and orators should not be sought outside of Italy,[19] a declaration that had understandably won him the enmity of many Parisian humanists in Christine's circle.[20] Ezio Ornato explains how around 1395 French humanists found themselves in the contradictory position of desiring "French" solutions to cultural problems while feeling bound to invoke nonnative, and typically "Italian" remedies.[21] Jean Gerson, Chancellor of the University of Paris and Christine's principal ally in the literary quarrel over the moral worth of the *Roman de la Rose* [Romance of the Rose], prepared the terrain for Christine's proposed solution to France's predicament by declaring that only up to now had the French lacked poets and historians capable of celebrating properly its renowned thinkers and warriors (Ouy, p. 144).

Before arriving at the proposal that Christine presents in the *Mutacion*, it is important for our study of the *translatio studii* theme to consider her relationship to her Greek heritage as set forth in poem 37 of the *Autres balades* (ed. Roy, I, p. 250; see also Margolis, p. 366). We have already seen how Christine, in comparing herself to Minerva as a representative of *clergie* and *chevalerie* in the *Livre des fais d'armes et de chevalerie*, laid claim simultaneously to her heritage as a modern Italian, a Roman, and a Greek. In Ballade 37, a poem headed by the verses, "Jadis avoit en la cité d'Athenes / Fleur d'estude de clergie souvraine" [At one time there used to be in the city of Athens / A flowering of study of sovereign learning], Christine establishes her intellectual pedigree by comparing the defamation to which she was subject during the quarrel of the *Rose* (1401–2) to the persecution of the Greek philosophers Socrates and Aristotle for having foretold the coming of Christ: "On est souvent batu pour dire voir" [One is often beaten for speaking the truth] affirms the refrain. In the dispute over the *Rose*, Jean de Montreuil had compared Christine to Leontium, the Greek prostitute who had dared to criticize Theophrastus. Christine responded to this criticism in the *Cité des Dames*, I.30.3, by redefining Leontium as a philosopher: "Et femmes de grant science te pourroie dire assez. Leonce qui fu femme grecque fu autresi si tres grant philosophe que elle osa par pures et vrayes raisons reprendre et redarguer le philosophe Theophraste qui en son temps tant estoit renommez" [I could tell you a great deal about women of great learning. Leontium was a Greek woman and also such a great philosopher that she dared, for impartial and serious reasons, to correct and attack the philosopher Theophrastus, who was quite famous in her time (trans. Richards, p. 68)]. If Christine portrays herself as a Leontium figure in the *Cité*, she goes even further in poem 37 where she presents herself as an avatar of Athena/Minerva—indeed, I am tempted to say, as a kind of precursor of the Blessed Virgin Mary—whose character and wisdom outshine the beleaguered male philosophers for whom Christine proposes female counterparts.

In the *Livre de la mutacion de Fortune*, Christine frames a universal history greatly indebted to the *translatio imperii* topos with an allegorized version of her own life in which the events of her biography show her to embody concretely the *translatio studii* theme.[22] In the conclusion to the fourth part, as well as to the fifth, sixth, and seventh ones, Christine presents a universal history that places special emphasis on the history of the Greeks, the story of the Trojan War, and the founding of Rome by Aeneas and Brittany by Brutus. Christine's own interest in Scipio's career is evident here in her lengthy description of the Carthaginian wars. The *translatio imperii* underlying the universal history is doubled by the *translatio studii* of Christine's personal history: in the beginning verses of the work she informs us that she was born "near Lombardy in a city founded by the Trojans"; in verses 4754–4833 (ed. Solente, vol. 2), she specifies that the city in question is Venice on which she lavishes abundant praise. Venetian by birth, she was then brought to France as a consequence of her father's newly acquired position as physician and astrologer to Charles V.

According to Christine, the main event of her life was her transformation into a man brought about by the unpredictable workings of Fortune, the *mutacion* of the work's title. Christine explains how she came to undergo such a bizarre but intriguing gender change, itself a type of *translatio*, through her recourse to yet another meaning of the term *translatio*, what Douglas Kelly refers to as allegorical or extended metaphorical discourse (p. 291). In the metaphorical rendition of the circumstances of her birth,

Christine contrasts her father, who desires a male heir capable of inheriting the riches of his formidable erudition (vv. 382–83), with her mother, identified as Dame Nature, who wants a female child. Since her mother is the stronger of the two parents, her choice prevails. A girl is born who nonetheless resembles her father in everything but her gender, a point on which Christine insists (vv. 394–400). Christine tells us that during her childhood she was reduced to scavenging the scraps of her father's immense treasury of knowledge. Christine represents the source of her father's wealth as two precious stones, the first signifying his gift of seeing into the future, the second his capacity to heal.[23] The child's education was left incomplete; although Tommaso did devote time to Christine's instruction at home, her mother encouraged Christine to engage in specifically feminine pursuits, and it is certain that she did not receive her father's formal education in medicine, astrology, and Latin.[24] The unexpected change brought about by Fortune, that is, that she had to assume the function of family breadwinner, authorized Christine to accede, albeit in a limited way, to her father's role, in effect to undertake the "chemin de long estude" that enabled her to become a writer who would increasingly address political and social concerns as her career progressed.

Christine's change of gender "en homme naturel parfait" [into a natural, complete man] (v. 145) allowed her to circumvent some of the limitations usually imposed on women by society. Christine's attitude toward her acquisition of her father's learning was twofold: on the one hand, she realized that as a woman lacking formal credentials she would never be a court advisor as her father had been; on the other hand, her comparison of herself with the Cumaean Sibyl in the *Chemin de long estude* and with Tiresias's gender change in the *Mutacion*[25] implies that she possessed the gift of prophecy that made her the equal of her father, who could read the future in the stars. Many of the contributions to the recent collection of essays edited by Margaret Brabant, *Politics, Gender and Genre: The Political Thought of Christine de Pizan,* insist on the political import of a great number of Christine's works, especially those composed after 1405. In "Authority in the Prose Treatises of Christine de Pizan: The Writer's Discourse and the Prince's Word," Liliane Dulac remarks that Christine wanted to establish her competence in the political realm before undertaking the *Livre des fais et bonnes meurs du sage roy Charles V* [Book of the deeds and good character of wise King Charles V] (1405), her first political treatise (p. 129). In its opening pages, Christine presents her commission to write the biography of Charles V for the Duke of Burgundy, the brother of the deceased monarch, as a direct result of the presentation of the

Mutacion to the Duke. From this statement, it appears that the universal history in the *Mutacion* served as proof that Christine had acquired the learning necessary to be of service to present-day princes; her grasp of the movement of civilization demonstrated that she was qualified to continue in a limited way the services that her father had rendered to Charles V. Besides containing several anecdotal recollections of her own concerning his reign, the biography of the wise king Charles V gives testimony to what her father had witnessed during his fourteen-year career as advisor to the king.[26]

In the *Livre de la mutacion de Fortune*, Christine employs the *translatio studii* theme to imply that it is through her, poet and historian, that literary and cultural legitimacy can be restored to France. The unique facts of her personal history make her ideally suited to her dual role as historian of the past and problem-solver for the future. The *translatio studii* theme operates in several ways in the *Mutacion*. First, it justifies Christine's suitability as a learnèd woman despite the unusual circumstances of her birth, both in terms of her national origin and her gender. Christine's use of the topos asserts the primacy of the vernacular, the mother language, over Latin and Greek and confirms her status as *clergece* (the explicit term Christine first uses in the *Cité des Dames*) or female *clerc* even though she, unlike her father and her Italian models Dante, Boccaccio, and Petrarch, would never compose works in Latin.[27] She then turns this apparent weakness to her own advantage: the analogies between her personal history and the *translatio studii et imperii* topos authorize her to transform herself from a poet of light verse into a commentator on political and social issues who applies lessons drawn from history to contemporary problems. This shift is, I think, what Christine implies at the end of the *Mutacion* when she asks princes if they indeed understand the "mutacions" taking place around them. After offering her life story as proof that it is possible to survive the worst effects of evil fortune (vv. 23595–98), she insinuates that they would benefit from the advice of a counselor capable of analyzing the "mutacions" of the past in order to be able to comprehend the course of current events.

In portraying herself as the incarnation of the *translatio studii*, Christine suggests that she animates or provides the motor force behind the topos. She is the living answer to France's problems. Christine takes Chrétien de Troyes, who had boasted that the art of composing works in the vernacular would flourish under his leadership, one step further in appropriating for herself the regenerative power of the *translatio studii*. It is noteworthy that the truthfulness of the universal history is guaranteed by the authority of the first-person voice that recounts its personal history, rather than the other way around. In employing the metaphor of her transformation into a man in the *Mutacion*, Christine proves herself to be the ultimate translator (in the medieval sense) in that she treats her former self as an extant *materia* to be constantly redone at her will (Kelly, p. 291), becoming a female Pygmalion who with each subsequent work fashions a slightly different rendition of her authorial persona.

The *Livre de la mutacion de Fortune* traces the evolution of Christine's conception of herself as a *clergece*. First admitting that she is powerless before the change of Fortune that has made her metaphorically into a man, Christine then assumes the power to transform her narrative persona and the discursive forms in which she expresses that change, a stance that paradoxically opens up the possibility for her to exert some control over events through the advice that she offers to royal figures. The implicit political and social recommendations of the *Cent balades* give way to the explicit counsel of her late prose works. To take just two related examples, in the *Epistre à la reine* [Epistle to the Queen] (1405), addressed to Isabeau de Bavière, and in the *Livre de la paix* [Book of Peace] (1412–13), addressed to Louis de Guyenne, Christine makes impassioned pleas to establish and maintain peace. Besides the many meanings already mentioned, Christine's *translatio studii* takes the form of generic transformation that follows the development of personal and universal themes through the discursive forms of lyric poetry, extended allegorical discourse, and the prose treatise as she comes to assume a characteristic humanist stance. Christine shows herself to be the consummate translator by borrowing the primary means of effecting the *translatio studii*, the paradigm of narratological and gendered metamorphosis, from Petrarch,[28] her Italian compatriot who had a half-century earlier so emphatically denied that the locus of literary culture could ever move to France.

Notes

1. For Christine's treatment of Minerva in the *Livre de la Cité des Dames*, see Eleni Stecopoulos and Karl D. Uitti, "Christine de Pizan's *Livre de la Cité des Dames*," p. 56, especially their comment that "Christine truly and ingeniously found in her [Minerva] the fulfillment of the *translatio imperii et studii*."

2. Douglas Kelly, *"Translatio Studii"*; Jacqueline Cerquiglini, "L'étrangère."

3. My treatment of the *translatio studii* theme is indebted to George M. Bumgardner's unpublished dissertation, "Tradition and Modernity from 1380 to 1405: Christine de Pizan," pp. 105–31, 169–213, and Nadia Margolis's superb article "Christine de Pizan."

4. This allegorical narrative contains 23,636 verses of octosyllabic rhyming couplets and a section concerning Jewish history in prose. Christine explains that she was sick with fever when she composed the latter.

5. See my "Chivalry and the (En)gendered Poetic Self."

6. *Cligés* was present in the library of Jean, Duc de Berry, a collection to which Christine had access. See Léopold Delisle, *Recherches sur la librairie de Charles V, roi de France, 1337–1380*, vol. 1, p. 40.

7. See Michelle A. Freeman's treatment of the topos of *translatio studii et imperii* in *The Poetics of Translatio Studii and Conjointure*. Freeman claims that Chrétien may be implying that only clergie came to France, a viewpoint that anticipates the later polemics of Alexander von Roes in the thirteenth century, that *ecclesia, imperium*, and *studium* resided in Italy, Germany, and France respectively.

8. See Dina De Rentiis, "'Sequere me.'"

9. The classic discussion of the nature of "true nobility" is found in Dante, *Convivio*, Book IV. See the discussion of this topic in Alexander Murray, *Reason and Society in the Middle Ages* (Oxford: Clarendon, 1978), pp. 277–78.

10. *Europäische Literatur und Lateinisches Mittelalter*, p. 38; *European Literature and the Latin Middle Ages*, p. 29.

11. Aldo S. Bernardo, *Petrarch, Scipio and the "Africa,"* pp. 113–21. See also William Harris Stahl's useful introduction to Macrobius, *Commentary on the Dream of Scipio*. The surviving fragments of Cicero's work have been critically edited by K. Ziegler in M. Tullius Cicero, *De re publica librorum sex quae manserunt septimum recognovit*.

12. The story of Christine's complex response to Petrarch has yet to be fully investigated. The two most promising studies to date are those of Bumgardner and of Earl Jeffrey Richards, "Christine de Pizan, the Conventions of Courtly Diction and Italian Humanism." Joël Blanchard, "Christine de Pizan," makes some suggestive remarks about Petrarch's influence on Christine (pp. 218, 233) while downplaying (incorrectly, I believe) the relations that existed between Parisian and Italian humanistic circles (in his notes 25 and 76). My article "Chivalry and the (En)gendered Poetic Self" is the first attempt to document Christine's use of Petrarch as a model for her lyric poetry and for the transformations of her poetic persona.

13. Willard, "Christine de Pizan's Treatise on the Art of Medieval Warfare," p. 190.

14. *Dictionnaire des lettres françaises (Le moyen âge)*, ed. Geneviève Hasenohr and Michel Zink (1964; Paris: Fayard, 1992), pp. 1093, 1162. This work constitutes Book XV of Bersuire's *Reductorium morale*, which was influenced by the verse edition of the *Ovide moralisé* in the last of its three revisions (completed around 1350).

15. Numerous are the poems in which Christine praises a knight or regent. See Ballade 92 of the *Cent balades* and Ballades 2 and 3 of the *Autres balades*, among many other examples.

16. See his "Literary Genealogy and the Problem of the Father."

17. Christine's treatment of Fortune in the *Mutacion* is, on one level, a response to the *De remediis utriusque fortunæ*, Petrarch's most popular work in France (Bumgardner, p. 175). Jean Daudin translated this work into Middle French for Charles V in 1377 or 1378.

18. See my "Chivalry and the (En)gendered Poetic Self" for Christine's use of Petrarch as a model for her lyric poetry. This study includes an explanation of the ways in which Christine could have become acquainted with the *Rime sparse*.

19. "Oratores et poete extra Italiam non querantur"; see Gilbert Ouy, "La dialectique des rapports intellectuels franco-italiens et l'humanisme en France au XIVe et XVe siècles," pp. 138, 144–45.

20. See Alexander Peter Saccaro, *Französischer Humanismus des 14. und 15. Jahrhunderts,* chapter 6, "Zur Polemik Petrarcas gegen die französische Kultur," pp. 148–77.

21. *Jean Muret et ses amis Nicolas de Clamanges et Jean de Montreuil,* pp. 31–32. See also Bumgardner, pp. 176–77, for Nicolas de Clamanges's twofold response to Petrarch: he affirmed the *translatio studii* while imitating Petrarch in an eclogue.

22. See Kevin Brownlee, "The Image of History in Christine de Pizan's *Livre de la mutacion de Fortune.*"

23. See Andrea Tarnowski, "Maternity and Paternity in *La mutacion de Fortune.*"

24. Christine often notes that she acquired her education only relatively late in life. For example in the *Livre du chemin de long estude* (ed. R. Püschel, 1887; reprinted, Geneva: Slatkine, 1974), vv. 1673–80, she remarks, "Monter ou firmament te fault, / Combien qu'autres montent plus hault, / Mais tu n'as mie le corsage / Abille a ce: toutefois say je / Que de toy ne vient le deffault, / Mais la force qui te deffault / Est pour ce que tart a m'escole / Es venue . . . " [You must ascend to the heavens, just as others rise higher. But you do not have the body proper for this. However, I know that the fault does not come from you, but that the strength you lack is because you came late to my school].

25. Margolis, p. 369, notes that in Christine's version, Tiresias is able to foresee the future because of his sex change.

26. For specific references, see pp. lxxii-lxxiv of Suzanne Solente's introduction to her edition of the *Livre des fais et bonnes meurs du sage roy Charles V.*

27. On Christine's knowledge of Latin, see Liliane Dulac and Christine Reno, "L'humanisme vers 1400, essai d'exploration à partir d'un cas marginal." See also Thelma Fenster, *"Perdre son latin."*

28. Charity Cannon Willard, "Christine de Pizan's Treatise on the Art of Medieval Warfare," pp. 189–90, suggests that Petrarch had a greater influence on the *Fais d'armes* than Vegetius.

Works Cited

Bernardo, Aldo S. *Petrarch, Scipio and the "Africa": The Birth of Humanism's Dream.* Baltimore: Johns Hopkins University Press, 1962.

Blanchard, Joël. "Christine de Pizan: Tradition, expérience et traduction." *Romania* 111 (1990): 200–235.
Brownlee, Kevin. "The Image of History in Christine de Pizan's *Livre de la mutacion de Fortune*." *Yale French Studies, Special Edition: Contexts: Style and Values in Medieval Art and Literature*, ed. Daniel Poirion and Nancy Freeman Regalado, pp. 44–56. New Haven: Yale University Press, 1991.
———. "Literary Genealogy and the Problem of the Father: Christine and Dante." *Journal of Medieval and Renaissance Studies* 23 (1993): 365–87.
Bumgardner, George M. "Tradition and Modernity from 1380 to 1405: Christine de Pizan." PhD. diss. Yale University, 1970.
Cerquiglini, Jacqueline. "L'étrangère." *Revue des Langues Romanes* 92 (1988): 239–51.
Cicero, M. Tullius. *De re publica librorum sex quae manserunt septimum recognovit*. Ed. K. Ziegler. M. Tulli Ciceronis, *Scripta quae manserunt omnia*, Fasc. 39, Bibliotheca Teubneriana. Leipzig: BSB B. G. Teubner, 1969.
Curtius, Ernst Robert. *Europäische Literatur und Lateinisches Mittelalter*. Berne: Francke, 1948; *European Literature and the Latin Middle Ages*. Trans. Willard R. Trask. Bollingen Series 36. New York, 1953; reprint, Princeton: Princeton University Press, 1983, 1990.
Delisle, Léopold. *Recherches sur la librairie de Charles V, roi de France, 1337–1380*. 2 vols. 1907; reprinted, Amsterdam: van Heusden, 1967.
De Rentiis, Dina. "'Sequere me': *Imitatio* dans la *Divine Comédie* et dans le *Livre du chemin de long estude*." In *The City of Scholars: New Approaches to Christine de Pizan*, ed. Margarete Zimmermann and Dina De Rentiis, pp. 31–42. Berlin: De Gruyter, 1994.
Dulac, Liliane. "Authority in the Prose Treatises of Christine de Pizan: The Writer's Discourse and the Prince's Word." In *Politics, Gender and Genre: The Political Thought of Christine de Pizan*, trans. E. J. Richards, ed. Margaret Brabant, pp. 129–40. Boulder: Westview, 1992. Subsequently in French as "L'autorité dans les traités en prose de Christine de Pizan: Discours d'écrivain, parole de prince." In *Une femme de lettres au moyen âge: Études autour de Christine de Pizan*, ed. Liliane Dulac and Bernard Ribémont, pp. 15–24. Orléans: Paradigme, 1995.
Dulac, Liliane, and Christine Reno. "L'humanisme vers 1400, essai d'exploration à partir d'un cas marginal: Christine de Pizan traductrice de Thomas d'Aquin." In *Actes du Colloque "Pratiques de la culture écrite en France au XVe siècle,"* ed. Monique Ornato and Nicole Pons, pp. 161–78. Louvain-la-Neuve: Fédération internationale des Instituts d'Études médiévales, 1994.
Fenster, Thelma. "*Perdre son latin*: Christine de Pizan and Vernacular Humanism." In *Christine de Pizan and the Categories of Difference*, ed. Marilyn Desmond, 91–107 Medieval Cultures 14. Minneapolis: University of Minnesota Press, 1998.

Freeman, Michelle A. *The Poetics of Translatio Studii and Conjointure: Chrétien de Troyes's Cligés.* French Forum Monographs, 12. Lexington, Ky.: French Forum, 1979.

Kelly, Douglas. "*Translatio Studii*: Translation, Adaptation and Allegory in Medieval French Literature." *Philological Quarterly* 57 (1978): 287–310.

Margolis, Nadia. "Christine de Pizan: The Poetess as Historian." *Journal of the History of Ideas* 47 (1986): 361–75.

Ornato, Ezio. *Jean Muret et ses amis Nicolas de Clamanges et Jean de Montreuil: Contribution à l'étude des rapports entre les humanistes de Paris et ceux d'Avignon (1394–1420).* Hautes Études Médiévales et Modernes, 6. Paris: Droz, 1969.

Ouy, Gilbert. "La dialectique des rapports intellectuels franco-italiens et l'humanisme en France au XIVe et XVe siècles." In *Rapporti culturali ed economici fra Italia e Francia nei secoli dal XIV al XVI.* Atti del colloquio italo-francese, febbraio 18–20, 1978. Rome: V. Ferri, 1979.

Richards, Earl Jeffrey. "Christine de Pizan, the Conventions of Courtly Diction and Italian Humanism." In *Reinterpreting Christine de Pizan*, ed. Earl Jeffrey Richards with Joan Williamson, Nadia Margolis, and Christine Reno, pp. 250–71. Athens: University of Georgia Press, 1992.

Saccaro, Alexander Peter. *Französischer Humanismus des 14. und 15. Jahrhunderts.* Munich: Fink, 1975.

Stahl, William Harris. Introduction to Macrobius, *Commentary on the Dream of Scipio.* New York: Columbia University Press, 1952.

Stecopoulos, Eleni, and Karl D. Uitti. "Christine de Pizan's *Livre de la Cité des Dames*: The Reconstruction of Myth." In *Reinterpreting Christine de Pizan*, ed. Earl Jeffrey Richards with Joan Williamson, Christine Reno, and Nadia Margolis, pp. 48–62. Athens: University of Georgia Press, 1992.

Tarnowski, Andrea. "Maternity and Paternity in *La mutacion de Fortune.*" In *The City of Scholars: New Approaches to Christine de Pizan*, ed. Margarete Zimmermann and Dina De Rentiis, pp. 116–26. Berlin: De Gruyter, 1994.

Walters, Lori. "Chivalry and the (En)gendered Poetic Self: Petrarchan Models in the *Cent balades.*" In *The City of Scholars: New Approaches to Christine de Pizan*, ed. Margarete Zimmermann and Dina De Rentiis, pp. 43–66. Berlin: De Gruyter, 1994.

Willard, Charity Cannon. "Christine de Pizan's Treatise on the Art of Medieval Warfare." In *Essays in Honor of Louis Francis Solana*, ed. Raymond J. Cormier and Urban T. Holmes, pp. 179–91. University of North Carolina Studies in the Romance Languages and Literatures, 92. Chapel Hill: University of North Carolina Press, 1970.

∽ CHAPTER 7

Lyrical Conventions and the Creation of Female Subjectivity in Christine de Pizan's *Cent ballades d'Amant et de Dame*

CHRISTINE McWEBB

Traditionally since the Greeks, lyrical poetry has been assigned a more personal or subjective character than epic or drama because lyrical poets themselves are frequently subjects in their works. In discussing the poetic "I" in the thirteenth-century poems of Rutebeuf, Nancy Freeman Regalado demonstrated that "the question of Rutebeuf's appearance in his poetry cannot be reduced . . . to a struggle between sincerity and convention, but involves the medieval idea of self and subjective experience."[1] Male medieval French poets created for themselves a specific, trademark personality as a kind of heraldic blazon or motto, though the "personal" consistently represents a "convincing and expert treatment of conventional theme, not an artistic transposition of historical reality" (p. 270). When Christine de Pizan, however, wrote her *balades de personnages* [ballades in character], she alternated, as James Laidlaw has shown, between male and female singers. Christine also includes noncourtly female characters, such as the widow and the nun, in her lyric, characters that she does not identify as conventional (like the betrayed lady) but as historical (she is the widow, her daughter is the nun). Here Christine clearly and skillfully departs from the earlier lyrical tradition by offering a "transposition of historical reality," indeed of her own personal historical experience. We do not confront the substitution of a female poet for a male poet as in the medieval Provençal tradition of the *trobairitz*, in which the female adaptation of a male genre entails a series of displacements in gender and class relationships, as Marianne Shapiro and Laurie A. Finke have carefully examined.[2] Instead, we confront the creation of a female subjectivity through the inclusion of women's historical experience itself. This female subjectivity is created specifically when Christine explores lyrical conventions in her attempt to make lyric refer to women's experiences and emotions. Here I shall take my cue from Finke's suggestion that, following Émile Benveniste, "the individual is constructed out of the languages available to the subject in her culture; subjectivity, that is, is primarily semiotic" (p. 111). Christine wrests courtly lyric away from its empty formalism in order to make it refer to women's concrete experiences, and in so doing she creates a female subjectivity that is innovative in both its form and content.

The revisions in the courtly lyrical tradition undertaken by Christine occur, I will argue, at what Benveniste refers to as the "site of utterance" or *scène de l'énonciation*. This linguistic approach to courtly lyric offers new purchase on old problems: how can a literary work, especially lyric, actually refer to experiences outside the literary work itself? How can a literary work do more than manipulate formal conventions in creating meaning? How do literary conventions depend on unspoken assumptions about the roles of women and men in society?

In order to explore the changes that the female poet makes in courtly discourse, I shall compare Christine's last lyrical work, the *Cent ballades d'Amant et de Dame*, with two highly conventional ballades of one of her contemporaries, Jean Froissart, drawn from his collection of poems, *Ballades et rondeaux*. These two poems, in which women are lent a speaking voice, can be usefully compared with Christine's ballades. However, although several of Froissart's poems are spoken or enunciated in a female voice, they remain representative of a masculinist courtly paradigm.[3] I shall demonstrate that the female speaker acts as a mere disguise for the lover's androcentric and self-absorbed discourse. As Rae S. Baudouin states in the introduction to Froissart's work: "His first concern was doubtless to pour a traditional subject matter into pre-existing molds" [Sa préoccupation première était sans doute de couler dans des moules déjà existants une matière traditionelle] (introduction, *Ballades et rondeaux*, p. xl). It is important to stress here that Christine did not believe that all male speech is inherently false: the point is that courtly lyric had situated male discourse in a context that ended up by denying women their own voice, and by extension, their own experience.

With the exception of the few female poets, Marie de France, Christine, and the *trobairitz*, medieval courtly poetry was primarily a domain reserved for noble males, in which noble males spoke primarily to other noble males about love. A personalized female individuality within this lyrical world was neither possible nor desired: it was the male's role to court the lady and to woo her and the lady's to acquiesce or to refuse the man's advances. The lady was, by convention, cast as silent for the most part. As Erich Köhler noted in his classic study "Observations historiques et sociologiques sur la poésie des troubadours": "The lady takes the front spot, ever desirable, inaccessible, sitting on her throne well above the lover, object of all his hope and despair, frequently apostrophied but always silent" [Au premier rang (est) la dame, toujours désirable, inaccessible, trônant bien au-dessus de l'amant, objet de tous les espoirs et de tous les désespoirs, apostrophée maintes fois, mais toujours muette] (p. 43). The lady was the desirable object of the poet who praised her and tried to win her favor. Köhler's terms clarify the nature of the woman's role in courtly poetry: "she is never described in an individualized manner, first because it was enough to say that she was the fairest, noblest, most courtly, and especially because she was the beloved, the mistress and the ideal of all men" [elle n'est jamais décrite de façon individualisante, d'abord parce qu'il suffit de dire qu'elle est la plus belle, la plus noble et la plus courtoise, et surtout parce qu'elle est la bien-aimée, la maîtresse et l'idéal de tous] (p. 43). The idealized lady was a passive object rather than an acting subject. Deprived of all individuality, she was an incarnation of feminine perfection, of the ultimate virtue whose source was the Virgin Mary, a perfection linked to submission to the Word of God (as the Gospel account has Mary say, "Ecce ancilla Domini, fiat mihi secundum verbum tuum" [Behold the handmaiden of the Lord, let it be done to me according to your word, Luke 1.38]). Christine seizes upon the linguistic submission of women (*fiat mihi secundum verbum tuum* is perhaps a motto for the linguistic starting point of women—since doubting the Angel's message can lead to being struck dumb, as with Zechariah, the father of John the Baptist) to create a voice for the hitherto silent.

From a linguistic point of view, in courtly discourse the traditional speaker, or "enunciating subject"—*sujet de l'énonciation* to use Benveniste's term—is a masculine "I," whereas the content or "enunciated subject"—*sujet de l'énoncé*—is the beloved lady herself. By definition and by convention, the enunciated subject lacks the power to speak, so that the woman occupying this position in courtly lyric is characterized by passivity and silence. Since she is not a speaking subject, nor even a woman "echoing" a man speaking, she is stripped of all decision making. The challenge for the female lyric poet is to create a new site and a new subject of enunciation or speaker. As a matter of literary historical comparison, one might recall that in the third book of the *Metamorphoses*, Ovid portrays the helplessness of Echo as woman to enunciate her love for Narcissus: the woman who cannot initiate a dialogue with her beloved is reduced to repeating fragments of his statements. In other words, in courtly lyric before Christine the beloved woman responds to the lover with his own narcissism with his own speech.

With the help of linguistic models developed by Benveniste and Roman Jakobson, it is possible to show that the portrayal of women in courtly poetry marks a regression from Ovid's presentation of Echo and that Christine reacted against the linguistic conventions of courtly poetry in order to create a voice for women in lyric. Benveniste defines the term "enunciation" ("utterance," or "statement," *énonciation*) as a process of speech appropriation: "As an individual, realized event, a statement can be defined with regard to language as a process of appropriation. The speaker appropriates for himself the formal apparatus of a language and he enunciates his position as speaker with specific markers, on the one hand, and with accessory procedures, on the other" [En tant que réalisation individuelle, l'énonciation peut se définir, par rapport à la langue, comme un procès d'appropriation. Le locuteur s'approprie l'appareil formel de la langue et il énonce sa position de locuteur par des indices spécifiques, d'une part, et au moyen de procédés accessoires, de l'autre] (p. 82). The "I" of the speaker is thus the *sujet de l'énonciation*. The distinction between a statement, or *énonciation*, and the content of this statement, or *énoncé*, lies in the fact that the first is the act of utterance itself whereas the latter is its product. As Benveniste specifies: "One must pay attention to the specific condition of the statement: it is the very act of producing an utterance and not the text of the utterance" [Il faut prendre garde à la condition spécifique de l'énonciation: c'est l'acte même de produire un énoncé et non le texte de l'énoncé] (p. 80). The *sujet de l'énoncé* represents therefore the content of the utterance.

One might ask how the courtly paradigm is transformed when a female poet assumes the male poet's role, that is, when a woman becomes the "enunciating subject," as in Christine's love ballades, grouped together under the title *Cent ballades d'Amant et de Dame* (composed in 1410).[4] Christine, in championing *la cause des femmes* [the cause of women] (her term for feminism), modifies the masculinist courtly discourse not only by creating a female *sujet de l'énonciation* but also by establishing a dialogue between the lady and her knight. By modifying courtly lyric to refer to the historical situation of the woman as enunciating subject, she subverts the original patriarchal character of the genre.

Like Froissart and all her male courtly predecessors, Christine exploits courtly commonplaces in the *Cent ballades d'Amant et de Dame* initially in order to situate her work within the literary conventions of the time: the knight woos a married woman and the personae of the jealous husband and of the slanderers inevitably succeed in destroying the love relationship. The lady also calls upon Amour who both protects and persuades her to love the knight. Furthermore, the lover expresses his suffering and his loyal service to his lady. Christine borrows from the range of flattering and eulogistic expressions in courtly terminology to make her work fit within the framework of the contemporary lyric tradition.[5] Thus, not surprisingly, on the most fundamental level of language, Christine's ballades simultaneously follow and recast lyrical conventions.

In Froissart's *Ballades et rondeaux*, Ballades 19 and 22 are constructed around a speaker identified as female. In Ballade 19, the lady manifests her fear of losing her honor if her lover is not more careful: "Selonc le tamps se couvient ordener / Et mettre en li raison, sens et mesure, / Car on puet trop perdre par soi haster. / Lasse! j'en voi en tres grant aventure / Celi qui m'aimme et jou li" [It must be arranged according to time, and imbued with reason, sense and balance, for one can lose too much by haste. Alas! I see him who loves me and I him in great peril] (vv. 1–5). Ballade 22, however, depicts a contrary motive. Whereas in the earlier ballade, the lady refuses the knight's advances in favor of her virtue, she now feels obliged to give in to the wooing and courtship of her knight, providing he is discreet: "Secré, discré et joli, / Plain de toute courtoisie, / De sens et d'onneur garni, / Digne d'avoir belle amie: / A tel amer ne fail mie, / Et mon coer me juge, voir, / Que j'en doi pité avoir" [Secret, discreet and gay, full of every courtly virtue, outfitted with sense and honor, worthy of having a beautiful beloved: May he not fail in such love, and may my heart judge me, in truth, that I must take pity on him] (vv. 1–7). In the lady's eyes, her knight has lived up to the requirements of the courtly value system. He has, therefore, earned the lady's love and she will render it to him.

The lady in Christine's lyric faces the same conventional dilemma. She refuses her knight's courtship, fearing for her honor and reputation. Yet she also is prepared to share her lover's passion: "M'amour vous est accordée / Sí a ce vous accordez, / Mais qu'honneur y soit gardée, / Autrement ne l'entendez" [My love is granted to you, just as you agree to this, provided that honor be maintained, do not understand this otherwise] (XXIV.28–31). Both ladies seem to be confronted with the same difficulties concerning their reputation and honor.

The similarities between Froissart's two ballades and Christine's, which are placed in the mouth of a female speaker, show the importance of what Jakobson called the "site of utterance" or *scène de l'énonciation*, a fundamental concept in his theory of communication.⁶ Every utterance implies a context, contact, and code involving a transmitter, message, and receiver. These six aspects imply, according to Jakobson, six functions: referential, emotive, poetic, conative, phatic, and metalinguistic. The following diagram visualizes, following Jakobson's model, the structure of the lady's speech in Froissart's Ballade 19.

                        Context
                  (referential function)
            love discourse = androcentric

Transmitter←————Message————→Receiver
(emotive function)   (poetic function)   (conative function)
"je" = lady   1) Lover has to be   "je" = lady
lady = lover   more careful   lady = lover
                        2) Lady is seduced
                        by his flatteries
                        Contact
                        (phatic function)
                        Lady talks to herself
                        Code
                        (metalinguistic function)
                        courtly code (Jakobson 213–15)⁷

Jakobson's speaking subject is the transmitter sending his message to the receiver. In Froissart's poem, the role of the transmitter is assumed by the "I" or "je" of the lady, "Lasse! j'en voi en tres grant aventure" (v. 4). The "je" or speaker here (*sujet de l'énonciation*) evokes inevitably a "tu," the receiver, as Catherine Kerbrat-Orecchioni states: "The 'je' in fact unilaterally constitutes the 'tu'" [c'est en effet le "je" qui constitue unilatéralement, le "tu"] (p. 43). The receiver is by definition addressed by the pronoun of the second person (*tu, vous*). In Ballade 19, however, there is neither a "tu" nor a "vous." Consequently, the lady addresses herself (she is henceforth transmitter and receiver in one). The speech stemming from the lady's mouth reverberates back to her. The lover, on the other hand, is referred to in the third person "il," a pronoun which according to Benveniste signifies a "nonperson"[8] who plays the role of the object. The lover, himself, becomes henceforth part of the context and thus has no speaking power. As Benveniste explains: "The 'I' is a unique person, 'you' is a unique person, but 'he' represents whatever subject might be compatible with its gender and number, and can, repeated in the same utterance, refer to different subjects" ["Je" est une personne unique; "tu" est une personne unique, mais "il" représente n'importe quel sujet compatible avec ses genre et nombre et peut, répété dans le même énoncé, renvoyer à des sujets différents] (II.202). Thus, the lover is positioned outside the communicative chain of transmitter and receiver.

The lady, on the other hand, describes, within the metalinguistic function of the code she uses, a love relationship that follows the conventional rules of courtly love: the lover courts her, she is afraid of the slanderers, and she wants to keep her honor at all cost: "Perdre me poet, car il n'i voit point cler, / Car je crieng trop des gengleurs le pointure. / Qu'on le remonstre au doi pour mon ami; / Dont, se j'en di aucuns mos mal courtois, / J'ai a garder [men honneur, c'est bien drois]" [He could destroy me, since he does not see clearly, for I fear too much the wound of slanderers, that they will point out my love; therefore, if I speak discourteous words, I must take care for my honor, as is most right] (vv. 17–24).

Because, as Laurie Finke noted, "the social dynamics of gender and class . . . remain unspoken in the troubadour lyric but . . . are always lurking just beneath the surface" (p. 50), courtly lyric was firmly rooted in a masculinist language system: women's experiences depicted there are conventional, not historical. The lady in Froissart's ballade adheres strictly to that code. Her choice of vocabulary reveals the fact that she does not express her own desire, much less her own experience. In conformity with male courtly conventions, she places herself within a value system of obligation and fear: "couvient ordener" [it is necessary to order] (19.1); "j'ai a garder" [I must take care] (vv. 8, 16, 24); "c'est bien drois" [it is most right] (vv. 8, 16, 24); "crieng" [I fear] (v. 18). Consequently, her speech echoes in fact the man's utterance. It is merely pronounced by a woman.

Therefore, the man becomes the transmitter, talking to himself in the disguise of a female subject, an image that calls to mind Narcissus's mirror. Froissart places the self-admiring lover at the same time in the role of the transmitter and the receiver. Jane Burns explains: "the troubadour Narcissus falls in love not with a specific lady but with an idealized image of himself" (p. 259). Imprisoned in a masculinist language system, the female "je" acts as a ventriloquist, an empty box filled with speech that expresses her lover's will. Her status as speaker is thus eliminated. The "je" associated with the emotive function, according to Jakobson, implies the expression of feelings. However, here the female subject is barred from initiating discourse (the situation of Echo in Ovid) and is forced to echo a masculinist language.

Christine also uses the theme of the lady's fear to endanger her honor and virtue. Yet, the lady in the *Cent ballades d'Amant et de Dame* communicates her intention to refuse her lover in an assertive way, demonstrating her own will power. She responds to the courtship of the knight: "Je le vous dy, ostés en vo pensée, / Car ne m'en tient / Ne telle amour a dame n'appartient / Qui ayme honneur, si ne vous en soit grief, / Car vous ne autre je ne vueil amer brief" [I tell you this, strike it from your thoughts, for it repels me, nor is such love appropriate for a lady who loves honor, so may it not cause you pain, for I do not want to love you, nor any other, even briefly] (II.4–8). The content of this strophe transposed on the Jakobson diagram shows the following paradigm:

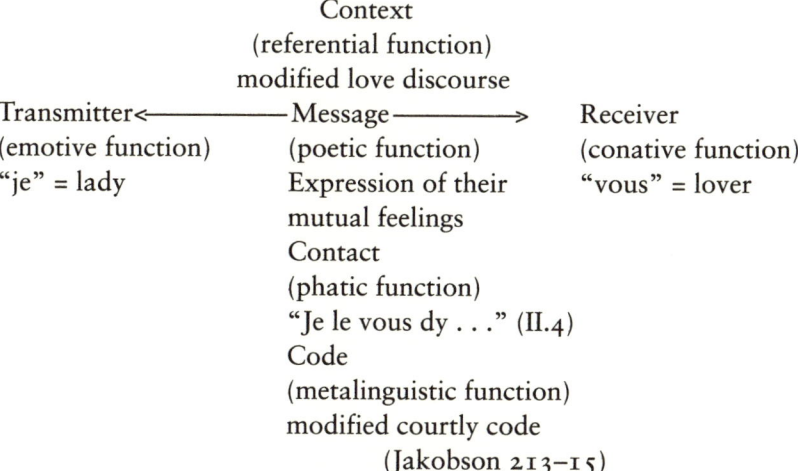

Context
(referential function)
modified love discourse

Transmitter<—————Message—————> Receiver
(emotive function)   (poetic function)   (conative function)
"je" = lady   Expression of their   "vous" = lover
                      mutual feelings
                      Contact
                      (phatic function)
                      "Je le vous dy . . ." (II.4)
                      Code
                      (metalinguistic function)
                      modified courtly code
                            (Jakobson 213–15)

Here we find a transmitter, which is the "je" of the lady, and a receiver, "vous," the lover. The content of the poetic utterance here, or *sujet de l'énonciation,* associated with the emotive function, is complete: "Car vous ne autre je ne vueil amer brief" (v. 8), and in the third stanza: "Plus n'en parlez, et desja suis lassée / De l'escouter" [Speak no more of it, for I am already weary of hearing it] (II.18–19). Distinctly unlike the female speaker in Froissart's Ballade 19, and unlike conventional courtly expectations, the lady in the *Cent ballades d'Amant et de Dame* chooses expressions of will rather than of obligation.

The contact is established through the phatic function, "Je le vous dy" [I tell you this] (II.4), which reinforces the dialogic setting that is absent in

Froissart's poem since there is no "vous" or "tu," leaving Froissart's poem in a vacuum. The intention is therefore clearly communicated from transmitter to receiver. Here, the reader can easily picture the dialogue with the lady as speaker and the lover as listener. The fact that the lover/receiver recognizes rather explicitly the refusal by the lady strengthens the communicative link and the comprehension between the two interlocutors. In the twenty ballades that follow, the lover tries to persuade the lady to submit to his wooing. Only after Amour's intervention and considerable reflection by the lady herself is she persuaded to grant him her love and to express it openly; yet she still demands a promise of fidelity and loyalty from her lover:

> Se vous me voulez promettre,
> Loyaument jurer sur sains
> Que m'amerés sans remettre,
> Si que vous dictes, ne fains
> N'estes en voz durs complains,
> L'amour qu'avez demandée
> J'acorde, et que demandez,
> Mais qu'honneur y soit gardée,
> Autrement ne l'entendez.

[If you agree to promise me, to swear faithfully upon the saints, that you will love me without fail, just as you say, nor be false in your harsh complaints, I grant the love that you have requested, and what you ask provided that honor be maintained. Do not understand this any other way.] (XXIV.1–9)

It is thus the lady who stipulates the conditions of their love relationship. In contrast to Froissart's passive lady, she situates herself in an active position within the *scène de l'énonciation*.

As Benveniste concludes in his discussion of the subjectivity of language: "Language proposes in some way 'empty' forms that each speaker, in the act of discourse, appropriates to himself and that he refers to his own 'person,' defining at the same time himself as 'I' and a partner as 'you.' The moment of discourse thus constitutes all the coordinates defining the subject" [Le langage propose en quelque sorte des formes "vides" que chaque locuteur en exercice de discours s'approprie et qu'il rapporte à sa "personne," définissant en même temps lui-même comme je et un partenaire comme tu. L'instance de discours est ainsi constitutive de toutes les coordonnées qui définissent le sujet] (1.263). The emptiness of the female "je" is filled with the persona of the lady, whereas the feminine "je" in Froissart's poem enunciates the will of the male lover's persona.

The second ballade uttered by a woman in Froissart's works, Ballade 22, appears for the first time in his *Prison amoureuse* (1372–3), a text which is structured as a fictional correspondence between Froissart and another male poet. The latter sends him Ballade 22 as a means of praising himself for the success he has achieved with regard to his lady, so that the one male poet only quotes a woman while speaking to another man for the sake of self-aggrandizement. In this poem, the woman could hardly be more full of praise for her lover, at least according to the lover, of course: "Je ne voi ne troeve en li / Cose pour quoi je l'oublie, / Car, quant il vient deviers mi, / De m'amour si bel me prie, / Et de maniere se lie, / A verité conchevoir, / Que j'en doi [pité avoir]" [I neither see nor find in him anything for which I would forget him, since, when he comes to me, so beautifully and joyfully does he beg for my love, to tell the truth, I must take pity on him] (vv. 8–14). The lady recognizes the noble qualities of her knight after all.

In Ballade 19, Froissart establishes a context, or *scène de l'énonciation*, in order to create an ostensibly female discourse. Once again in Ballade 22, Froissart relies on a female subject as speaker or *sujet de l'énonciation*. The knight is "digne d'avoir belle amie" [worthy of having a beautiful beloved] (v. 4) because he conforms to courtly values. Froissart has the lady outline all of the virtuous qualities that make him a noble knight. The lady, consistent with the conventional program of courtly lyric, has no choice but to acknowledge his courtship, regardless of her feelings. The knight adheres to the rules of the courtly code which demands that the lady love and accept him as her lover if he prove "worthy." The refrain "Que j'en doi pité avoir" [That I must take pity on him] (v. 14) hardly bespeaks the love felt by the lady, especially because the modal verb *devoir* places the emphasis on the lady's obligations. As in Ballade 19, where the lady finds herself obliged to resist her feelings of love, she is now forced by the same conventions to surrender to the wooing of her knight. She acts according to the values which the patriarchal system imposes on her and which are enshrined as conventions in courtly lyric. At no point are the male-centered conventions of courtly lyric called into question.

When the lady in the *Cent ballades d'Amant et de Dame* consents to love the knight who courts her, she does so out of free will and affection for her lover: "Doulz ami, mon cuer se pasme / En tes bras; t'alaine entiere / Me flaire plus doulz que basme, / Baisiez moy, doulce amour chiere" [Sweet lover, my heart faints in your arms, all your breath smells sweeter to me than balm, kiss me, sweet dear love] (XXXIX.28–31). In this ballade, the lady chooses the personal pronoun "tu" instead of the more formal (and, in courtly lyric, more usual) "vous," expressing a certain "experiential" intimacy between herself and her knight. The choice of "tu" is all the more striking choice in light of Christine's use of the humanist "tu" in the letters she wrote during the Quarrel of the *Rose*, and her use of asymmetric address in *Le Livre de la Cité des Dames* (she uses the "vous" form with the Virtues who in turn address her with "tu"): Christine attempts to make the dynamics of power and experience more transparent in her works. The reader can easily trace the development of their love relationship, which arises from decisions taken by both partners and not only by the man.

Separation prompts the woman to pray for "her sweet lover": "Ainsi l'octroit Dieux com je le desire / Et qu'a joye mon doulz ami remecte / En ce pas, mais de paour souspire / Qu'ainsi ne soit quant par moy suis seulecte" [Thus may God grant what I desire, and may my sweet lover be restored to joy in this way, but when I am alone by myself I sigh with fear that it not be so] (LXI.8–11). The sensual tone of her speech sets this poem apart from the rational discourse of Froissart's female subject. By actually saying "I desire" [je desire], the lady implies that she has a desire of her own and not an imposed one, a statement which explicitly fulfills the emotive function of Jakobson's transmitter. Deborah Hubbard Nelson even claims that the expression of emotions is, in fact, the theme of Christine's ballades: "The obvious subject of the ballades is the series of emotions experienced by the lovers at the hand of Amours" (p. 282). The lover uses the same vocabulary as the lady: "Prince, priez ma dame qu'adoulcir / Vueille le mal dont je tremble et fremy, / Et que l'octroy me doint que je desir: / Il me souffit qu'aye le nom d'amy" [Prince, pray to my Lady that she soften the pain with which I tremble and shake, and that she grant me the request that I desire. It is enough for me that I have the name of "lover"] (XXV.28–31). On the level of language, Christine succeeds in constructing a dialogue that posits the equality of the two speakers, the lady and the lover. The two are positioned on the same level of communication or *énonciation* with a female and male "je."

Unfortunately, the harmonious tone of the ballades does not persist. At the end of the work the two lovers succumb to jealousy and the relationship ends. The lady laments having been deceived by her lover and says: "Or sçay toute l'encloeure / Et la faulseté prouvée / De cil qui en paine dure / M'a mis, dont je suis grevée. / Tant ay quis que j'ay trouvée / Celle pour qui m'a laissié[e], / Dont durement suis blecié[e]" [Now I know the whole hidden meaning and manifest falseness of him who has caused me the harsh pain which afflicts me. I have searched enough until I found the woman for whom he left me and by which I am so deeply wounded] (XCVIII.1–7). Christine's choice of the word *encloeure* [hidden meaning, content] is striking: in her grief the woman has learned the true and hidden meaning of "courtly love." The end of the story is characterized by the disillusioned discourse of the lady. Christine adds a lai enunciated by the lady who expresses her pain and disappointment in a failed love:

> O Amours dure et sauvage,
> Certes, qui te fait hommage
> Se met en divers servage,
> Et si se puet bien attendre
> Que, par ce, deuil et dommage
> Lui vendra; c'est l'avantage
> Que tu fais au las courage
> Qui se laisse a toy surprendre.

[O Love, harsh and wild, certainly those who pay homage to you place themselves in cruel servitude, and so they can well expect that, for this reason, sorrow and hurt will overtake them, it is the advance that you pay to the unhappy heart that lets itself be taken by you.] (*Lay de Dame*, vv. 1–8)

Abandoned by her lover she turns back to Amour. The last pages express the lady's emotions and experience, neglecting those of the lover. The work ends with the death of the lady, provoked by her sadness and affliction. While, beginning with the popularity of the story of Tristan, the linguistic and thematic connection between love and death (*amor/mort*) had been a longstanding cliché of courtly love, Christine sees death not as the supreme and final obstacle for love to overcome but as the inevitable outcome of love itself. Christine's version of the love ballade thus displays a conclusion contrary to that of the traditional courtly code, a code that ignores the outcome of the love relationship for the woman.

Christine's ballades, enunciated by a female "je," reveal a woman's point of view and the final ballade, the *Lay de Dame*, places the emphasis on the woman's feelings: "Le mal que j'ay, et tu le scez, Amours, / Me vient d'amer un desloyal ami / Qui me promist qu'il seroit a tousjours / Mon vray amant" [The ill that I suffer, and you know it, Love, comes to me from loving a disloyal lover, who promised me that he would always be my true lover] (vv. 142–45). The lady manifests her sorrow at having fallen into the trap of loving a disloyal man. By paying heed to the feminine perspective on the love relationship, Christine constructs a woman-centered discourse, which distances her text from the androcentrism of traditional courtly poetry, as illustrated in Froissart's poems.

In the *Cent ballades d'Amant et de Dame*, the female persona enters into complicity with all women through her experiences and suffering: "Moy qui suis simple creature, / Quant mainte dame non pareille / Fault qu'elle en cueille / Dueil, et recueille / Pleur qui la meuille, / Par mainte diverse aventure, / Qui amerement la resveille" [Simple creature, I, whereas many an incomparable lady has been forced to reap sorrow and harvest a tear that wets her through many a cruel adventure that awakens her bitterly] (*Lay de Dame*, vv. 115–21). The lady not only refers in her suffering to contemporary women but also evokes the destiny of women in mythology (Proserpine, Medea, and Dido). Christine thus extends her message to all women, those of the present and the past. She provides a moral for her public but foremost for her women readers: Do not succumb to the seduction of men. Resist and act according to your own worthy judgment.

In a larger context, the conclusion of the *Cent ballades d'Amant et de Dame* is consistent with Christine's critique of courtly values. She provides her readers with a realistic image of courtly love, and while not neglecting the pleasure of love, she emphasizes its ultimately destructive impact on women. In presenting the ballades in dialogue form instead of using the conventional monologue, she places the speakers on an equal level of communication or *énonciation* and thus veers away from the male-centered communication characteristic of courtly lyric. Christine presents both lovers with their own emotions stripped of literary convention.

Although Christine adheres to the lyric conventions of the courtly love code promulgated by her male colleagues, she explodes and refashions these conventions in the name of women's experience in love. Thus the message that her poems convey is radically different from the one transmitted by earlier lyrical poets: "The importance of Christine's lyric work does not lie in her alleged 'sincerity' or in the fact that she was a feminist in her everyday life, but rather that she lent the women of her time a convincing voice to express their feelings and that she was able to bring the female perspective into the realm of the poetics of courtly love, traditionally reserved for male writers."[9] In rewriting courtly poetry from a female perspective, with a female speaker, Christine succeeds in deconstructing traditional courtly language and in undermining its androcentric base. At the same time, she infuses the female subject with her very own voice.

Notes

1. Nancy Freeman Regalado, *Poetic Patterns in Rutebeuf*, p. 256.
2. Marianne Shapiro, "The Provençal Trobairitz and the Limits of Courtly Love," and Laurie Finke, *Feminist Theory, Women's Writing*, pp. 29–74, especially pp. 49–50. Given the limited geographic transmission of Provençal lyrics in the late Middle Ages, it is unlikely that Christine knew these works directly.
3. The term "masculinist" is used, following Laurie A. Finke, among others, to underline male supremacy in the courtly tradition. Kamarae and Treichler give the following example of its usage in *A Feminist Dictionary*, p. 258: "Used as early as 1912: 'Mr. Edgar takes the usual masculinist standpoint of regarding women as incompetent weaklings except for their maternal functions.' (Rebecca West, *Manchester Daily Dispatch*, November 26, 1912)."
4. The *Cent ballades d'Amant et de Dame* are found in only one manuscript, British Library Harley 4431, ff. 376r-98r. There is some evidence that they may have also been included in what is called the Leiden Fragment, presumably all that remains of what was a presentation copy for the Dukes of Burgundy. The point, as made by both James Laidlaw and Barbara Altmann in this volume, is that the *Cent ballades d'Amant et de Dame* is Christine's last lyrical composition.
5. Hubbard Nelson lists numerous examples of traditional courtly expressions in her article "Christine de Pizan and Courtly Love": "Belle, plaisant, plus que autre creature" (5.22), "bon, bel, et gracieux" (49.3), "la blanche et blonde" (78.1–2) (p. 283).
6. Jakobson's theory of communication has been revised several times, particularly by Catherine Kerbrat-Orecchioni in *L'Énonciation, De la subjectivité dans le langage*. The most pertinent criticism of his theory seems to be of his representation of communication as a static process and his insufficient emphasis on the fluidity of language (the term *code*, for instance, is rather limited and does not demonstrate the existence of idiolects and variability in situations of discourse). Kerbrat-Orecchioni revises Jakobson's theory, pointing out both its flaws and its merits. However, these considerations are not pertinent to the study of the concept of the *scène de l'énonciation*. Jakobson's theory proves itself valid for my argument, since I apply it to a dialogue situation in which linguistic variability plays no role.
7. Bhatt Baligand and P. Léon, *Structure du français moderne*, pp. 9–10:

context: linguistic content of the message
referential function: indicates that the code refers to a linguistic or an extralinguistic context
transmitter: the person who speaks
emotive function: refers to the emotive state of the transmitter
receiver: the person receiving and listening to the message
conative function: refers to the linguistic means used to convince the other person
message: the particular form used to express certain information
poetic function: choice of vocabulary made by transmitter

contact: physical and physiological link between transmitter and receiver, permitting the transmission of a message
phatic function: verifies whether the contact is maintained
code: rules used to understand one another
metalinguistic function: verifies whether there is an understanding between transmitter and receiver

8. Benveniste uses this term to point out the difference between the opposition "I/you" on the one hand and the opposition between "I/you" and "he, she, it" on the other: "The [second] opposition, that of 'I-you/him,' opposing a specified person to a nonperson, effectuates reference and founds the possibility of discourse on something, on the world, on what does not belong to the speech act" [La (seconde) opposition, celle de "moi-toi"/"lui," opposant la personne à la non-personne, effectue l'opération de la référence et fonde la possibilité du discours sur quelque chose, sur le monde, sur ce qui n'est pas l'allocution] (p. 99).

9. Paola Malpezzie-Price, "The Love Poetry of Christine de Pisan," p. 51.

Works Cited

Baligand, Bhatt P., and P. Léon. *Structure du français moderne.* Toronto: Canadian Scholars' Press, 1992.

Benveniste, Émile. *Problèmes de linguistique générale.* 2 vols. Paris: Éditions Gallimard, 1966–74.

Burns, E. Jane. "The Man behind the Lady in Troubadour Lyric." *Romance Notes* 25 (1985): 254–70.

Christine de Pizan. *Cent ballades d'Amant et de Dame.* Ed. Jacqueline Cerquiglini. Paris: Union Générale d'Édition, 1982.

Finke, Laurie A. *Feminist Theory, Women's Writing.* Ithaca: Cornell University Press, 1992.

Froissart, Jean. *Ballades et rondeaux.* Ed. Rae S. Baudouin. Geneva: Librairie Droz, 1978.

Gottlieb, Beatrice. "The Problem of Feminism in the Fifteenth Century." In *Women of the Medieval World: Essays in Honor of John H. Mundy,* ed. Julius Kirshner and Susanne F. Wemple, pp. 337–64. Oxford: Blackwell, 1985.

Hubbard Nelson, Deborah. "Christine de Pizan and Courtly Love." *Fifteenth-Century Studies* 17 (1990): 281–89.

Jakobson, Roman. *Essai de linguistique générale.* Paris: Éditions du Nouveau Seuil, 1963.

Kamarae, Cheris, and Paula A. Treichler. *A Feminist Dictionary.* Boston: Pandora Press, 1985.

Kerbrat-Orecchioni, Catherine. *L'Énonciation, De la subjectivité dans le langage.* Paris: Librairie Armand Colin, 1987.

Köhler, Erich. "Observations historiques et sociologiques sur la poésie des troubadours." *Cahiers de civilisation médiévale* (1964): 27–51.

Malpezzie-Price, Paola. "The Love Poetry of Christine de Pisan." *Gender and Literary Voice* (1980): 37–53.

Regalado, Nancy Freeman. *Poetic Patterns in Rutebeuf: A Study in Noncourtly Poetic Modes of the Thirteenth Century.* New Haven: Yale University Press, 1970.

Shapiro, Marianne. "The Provençal Trobairitz and the Limits of Courtly Love." *Signs* 3 (1978): 560–71.

Willard, Charity Cannon. "Christine de Pizan's *Cent ballades d'Amant et de Dame*: Criticism of Courtly Love." In *Court and Poet: Selected Proceedings of the Third Congress of the International Courtly Literature Society,* ed. Glynn S. Burgess et al., pp. 357–64. Liverpool: Cairns, 1981.

———. "Lovers' Dialogues in Christine de Pizan's Lyric Poetry from the *Cent balades* to the *Cent ballades d'Amant et de Dame.*" *Fifteenth-Century Studies* 4 (1981): 167–80.

❧ *The Critique of Courtliness and
Expanding the Boundaries of Lyric*

∾ CHAPTER 8

Christine de Pizan's Phenomenology of Beauty in the Lyric and the Dream Vision

BENJAMIN SEMPLE

When Christine de Pizan took part in the debate on the *Roman de la Rose* in 1401–2, she had already earned a reputation as a skilled courtly poet. The descriptions of Christine furnished by her opponents in the debate indicate that they saw her as a woman of lofty understanding, but the principal basis of her fame was a body of courtly works comprising both short lyric pieces and narratives composed in verse. The *Rose* debate, however, would alter her authorial persona. In its wake she would practice genres other than those associated with the courtly poet's stock-in-trade. While many of her works continue to have a significant autobiographical component, the predominant form in which she relates her life experiences is no longer lyric, but narrative.[1]

In this progression from courtly poetry to the *Rose* debate and finally to the works she produced in the years immediately afterward, we can sense that Christine's strong reaction against the *Roman de la Rose* is tied to significant shifts in her conception of authorship, in the type of authorial persona she presented to her public, and in the literary genres she practiced, but these changes are so dramatic and cover such a wide range of formal, intertextual, and thematic issues that they raise a serious challenge when we try to gain any synthetic overview of her development. One thread that runs throughout this transformation of Christine de Pizan's life and works, and that can provide a stable vantage point from which to study her evolution as a writer during this period, is her meditation on beauty. Although Christine's thoughts on beauty change in the different formal contexts of the lyric and the dream vision, her concern with the topic is always phenomenological, in the sense that she investigates beauty not only as an objective reality but from the perspective of its effects on a sentient subject who perceives beauty with the senses, imagination, and intellect, contemplates its nature, and delights in the pleasure it produces.

The medieval world was extremely sensitive to aesthetic experience of all types, reveling not only in the beauty perceived by the senses (as in the eye's appreciation of colors, or the ear's love of sweet sounds) but also in transcendent beauty, the splendor of immaterial things, such as angels, or the human soul, or God. Christine was not a theoretician of beauty in the strict sense: she did not write treatises on aesthetics. But her works contain implicit attitudes toward beauty. With many of her contemporaries, she shared the idea that a work of art could not be admired for its aesthetic value alone, without any reference to its moral impact on the audience. This overlap of aesthetic and moral categories has led Umberto Eco to designate the medieval world as an "integrated culture . . . whose value systems are related to one another . . . by mutual implication" (p. 15). The interconnectedness of the beautiful and the good is striking in Christine de Pizan, for whom the words *beau* and *laid* often have a moral connotation. Beauty has a persuasive capacity: in revealing the beauty of the good, the poet inflames the reader with a desire for righteousness. Traditionally, Christian psychology and spirituality divided the powers of the soul into intellectual and affective capacities. The impact of beauty is that, when the intellect grasps something good, a corresponding experience of pleasure occurs.

The study of beauty in Christine's works also furnishes valuable insights into her concept of reader reception, which she saw not only as a cognitive process but as a response implicating the affective powers of the soul, the capacity to delight, to rejoice. We tend to conceive of reading today in more intellectual terms, using words such as "to interpret," "to understand," "to see," "to figure out." Although modern readers certainly can delight in the text, this experience tends to remain tacit: we feel it and presume others do as well, without necessarily articulating it. Indeed, modern literary studies have for quite some time now tended to move away from aesthetic "appreciation" and toward elucidation of structures, of narrative techniques, of hermeneutic strategies. For Christine, the reader's capacity to derive pleasure from the text is a result of the perception of its beauty. But beauty existed in a wide range of realities in the Middle Ages, both material and immaterial: as Christine began to forsake courtly poetry, she increasingly turned toward an intelligible beauty not to be found in the delights of this world, even as she began to describe that beauty through analogies with sense experience. We can trace her understanding of beauty through three stages: her courtly aesthetic, as represented in her *Cent balades*; her new understanding of reader reception formed in reaction to the *Roman de la Rose*; and finally the appearance of a new conception of beauty in the work she produced immediately after the *Rose* debate, her *Chemin de long estude*.

Christine's Courtly Aesthetic: The Concession to Pleasure

Through her practice in the courtly lyric genres of the ballade, rondeau, and virelai, Christine had of necessity developed a repertory of themes that she expanded to include didactic topics but that still concentrated heavily on erotic love. Love appears to be a subject matter almost required of the courtly poet, for the audience demands it. In her treatment of this sentiment, Christine will indicate its connections with poetic beauty. The poems in which Christine speaks as author of the collection reveal that perceptions of the beauty of a courtly piece did not stem entirely from an appreciation of the poet's craft (arrangement of words, effect of rhymes, sense of rhythm), as we might expect. Just as important were the emotions and sentiments awakened in the audience, with a heavy emphasis on feelings described as "sweet," "gracious," and "pleasurable."

In looking at the ballades, then, it is useful to keep in mind that Christine establishes two levels at which the successful poet must operate. One is technical in the etymological sense: poetry is an art, a gift, perhaps honed through practice, for making or producing artifacts. The verb *faire* [to make] occurs frequently in references to the poet's talent for composition. Just as important, however, is the second level, of the emotional resources upon which the poet draws, to which Christine usually gives the designation *sentement* [feeling]. In the integration of art and feeling, the poem is born.

In the first fifty of Christine's *Cent balades*, a tide of sentimental fluctuations inspires Christine. Most of the emotions we can identify with her own persona are, however, negative: pain, sorrow, mourning, devastation, and loneliness. But not all of these ballades are uttered in the poet's own voice; in fact, in the love poems that occur in Ballades 21–49, various courtly characters speak, usually in alternation between a female and a male voice.

Here we can find examples of the courtly sentiments: admiration of the beloved, hope in the future, satisfaction in the pleasure of love. Yet it is impossible to attribute these poems to Christine's own life experience, or to her voice, since on several occasions she specifies that she herself is not in love. Quite to the contrary, she is still in deep mourning for the husband she lost in her youth. The arrangement of the *Cent balades* also helps detach the voice of the author from the voices of lovers in her poems, for the love ballades of this series are framed by interventions of the poet in Ballades 20 and 50, where she affirms that in her own *sentement* such passions no longer exist. Together with the first ballade, which serves as a prologue to the entire collection, Ballades 20 and 50 constitute a treatise on courtly aesthetics and provide valuable evidence of how Christine viewed the effect of courtly poems on an audience.[2]

Ballade 1 conforms to a conception of poetry that integrates two types of resources: skill in construction of verbal patterns, and access to sentiments likely to produce pleasure in an audience. The verb *faire* will occur four times in this ballade, in lines 1, 5, 10, and 25. In each instance it is a question of making *diz* [poetic compositions]. The audience request that gives rise to this act of rhetorical invention specifies that they be *beaulz diz*, "beautiful poems." Christine has two doubts about her capacity to meet this demand for poetry; not only does she profess her lack of skill (the profession of humility is incumbent on the medieval artist who does not wish to suffer from charges of excessive pride), but she lacks the emotional resources to fashion poems inspiring joy or soothing the audience: "Mais je n'ay pas sentement ne espace / De faire diz de soulas ne de joye; / Car ma douleur, qui toutes autres passe, / Mon sentement joyeux du tout desvoye" [But I do not have feelings or space to make soothing or joyous poems; for my pain, which exceeds all others, completely drives out my joyous feelings] (vv. 9–12).[3] Here Christine establishes a causal relation between authenticity of feeling and poetic inspiration. Lacking pleasurable emotions, she can promise no poems to console or delight her audience. On the other hand, her pain makes her voluble on topics inspired by it, so that she can promise her audience numerous poems from this particular vein of feeling: "Mais du grant dueil qui me tient morne et coye / Puis bien parler assez et a plenté" [But of the great mourning that keeps me sad and quiet I can speak a lot, and in abundance] (vv. 13–14).

Given her declaration that she will treat her own emotional distress, it is not surprising that the majority of Ballades 2–19 can be related to Christine's widowhood. But in Ballade 20, the problem of poetic inspiration and creation arises once again, in connection with a reflection on beauty:

"Comment feroye mes dis / Beaulx, ne bons, ne gracieux / Quant des ans a prés de dix / Que mon cuer ne fu joyeux" [How will I make my poems beautiful, or good, or gracious, when it has been almost ten years since my heart was joyous?] (vv. 1–4). The second line of verse contains an accumulation of aesthetic terms—beautiful, good, gracious—but Christine proclaims that she lacks the proper emotional disposition necessary for poems in conformity with these ideals. Here again we find the two levels of fabrication of artifacts and emotion—of the artist's activity, linked to the verb *faire* (v. 1)—and the source of poetry in sentimental life, here linked to the heart as the seat of feeling (v. 4). In the following stanza of this poem, Christine compares her affective state to the weather: "J'os des biens assez jadis; / Mais en yver temps pluieux / Si pesent, si enlaidis, / N'est, ne si trés anuieux, / Comme adés en trestous lieux / M'est le temps . . ." [I had many good things once; but now, even in a rainy winter, the weather is not so heavy, so ugly, so disturbing, as time is to me now in all places] (vv. 8–13).

The passage poses an almost unresolvable ambiguity for the translator because Christine plays on the identity of the French word for "weather" and "time": she compares winter weather [en yver temps pluieux] with "weather/time in every place" [en trestous lieux . . . le temps]. The translator's obstacle, however, only enriches the poem, multiplying the possible interpretations. Christine may mean that in any kind of weather, her mood remains the same; this stasis in spite of external stimuli would be in counterpoint to a traditional topos of courtly poetry, the poet's changing emotions that correspond to the succession of seasons. An especially prevalent convention is the theme of the *reverdie*, the rebirth of the poet's joy and desire with the coming of spring, as flowers and plants put forth new shoots, leaves, and blossoms. For Christine, the changing of seasons produces no such effect on the paralysis of feelings. The second stanza introduces the concept of ugliness through the term *enlaidis*. Like winter weather, Christine's emotions are ugly. Mixing emotional and aesthetic categories, she suggests that "ugly" feelings give rise to "ugly" poetry; but the word ugly does not imply a failure of poetic craft; it is rather a deficiency of the sentiments necessary to produce a parallel experience of joy in the audience.

The position of Ballade 20 lends it an increased significance when we consider its role in the collection as it unfolds. It serves as a conclusion to the set of poems on widowhood. Curiously, immediately after this ballade, Christine's collection launches into a long series of love poems. Ballades 21–49 treat love, even if in Ballade 20 Christine had seemed to indicate her incapacity to compose poems not in keeping with her inner *sentement*. In this succession of poems, it is not the poet herself who speaks, but courtly characters who express their love in their own voice. Only in Ballade 50 will the author's voice surface once again. Here we find an explanation for the puzzling love poems, so out of keeping with Christine's repeated allusion to her *douleur* and to the total absence of joy after the death of her husband. She explains that, although the feeling of love is totally alien to her now, she has written love poems as a concession to the courtly aesthetic, which she describes in the second stanza of the ballade:

> Car qui se veult de faire ditz chargier
> Biaulz et plaisans, soient ou longs ou cours,
> Le sentiment qui est le plus legier,
> Et qui mieux plaist a tous de commun cours,
>   C'est d'amours, ne autrement
> Ne seront fait ne bien ne doulcement,
> Ou, se ce n'est, d'aucunes belles meurs,
> Je m'en raport a tous sages ditteurs.

[For anyone who takes on the task of making beautiful and pleasant poems, whether they are long or short, the feeling that is the lightest, and that pleases all most commonly, is the feeling of love, nor will poems be well made or sweet (unless, perhaps, they take their inspiration from beautiful acts); as proof, I refer to the practice of all wise poets.] (vv. 9–16)

Christine's tortuous and elliptical syntax in this ballade has a number of grammatical discontinuities; she breaks the flow of syntax and thought between the dependent clause in lines 9–10, in which she furnishes an anticipated subject of the main clause ("anyone who..."); yet when the main clause begins in line 11, its subject is "the feeling." In line 14, she introduces yet another verb whose only logical subject is the "ditz" mentioned in the first line of the stanza. From an aesthetic point of view, let's note in particular the association between beauty and pleasure in her description of the audience's reaction to a ballade. Love is a sentiment that pleases the public: Christine twice alludes to this connection, speaking of poems that are "biaulz et *plaisans*" [beautiful and pleasing] and then declaring that love is the sentiment that "mieux *plaist* a tous" [best pleases everyone].

Aesthetic appreciation and pleasurable sentiments are mutually implicated; Christine links the concepts of poetic fabrication and sentimental gratification when, in the sixth line of this stanza, she states that poems have to treat love if they are to be "well-made" (she thus evokes the element of craft) and "sweetly made" (she thus alludes to the sentimental enjoyment they cause).

But this same stanza introduces, if only in passing, in a discrete and parenthetical manner, an additional reflection on beauty. The only other way of gratifying an audience through a poem is to relate *belles meurs* [beautiful acts]. Here we see Christine combining aesthetic and ethical categories: admirable acts or behaviors can also be "beautiful," provoking an admiration tinged with moral approval. The word *meurs* forms an important part of Christine's ethical vocabulary (she would later write on the *bonnes meurs* of Charles V). It may refer to individual acts but it also is heavily impregnated with the Aristotelian conception that an ethical life produces enduring patterns of behavior allowing people to act righteously and also to take pleasure in moral behavior. This belief that probity produces pleasure was a vital element in Aristotle's ethics (which Christine knew well); it stands in contrast with early Christian ethical thought, in which the subject grapples with an inner conflict between temptation to seize some forbidden object or to indulge in a prohibited behavior, on one hand, and obedience to divine law, on the other.[4] Christine and her contemporaries still believed, like Augustine, that the fall had engendered a weakness of will destined to plague man. But they coupled it with the more optimistic view that nature could be conditioned and the inner conflict between knowledge of the good and desire to sin could be gradually effaced, as the will and the intellect came to act in concert.

In Christine's ballades, we see an awareness of the capacity of beauty to produce pleasure. We have also seen that beauty is not primarily a sensible property (as in the sound and rhythm of language) but one linked to an emotional experience that is soothing, agreeable, and uplifting. However, Christine's reference to "beautiful acts" in Ballade 50 permits us to envisage, if only momentarily, her belief in another kind of beauty: the beauty of morality and righteousness. The use of the adjective *biau* in an ethical sense reveals to us the interchangeability of ethical and aesthetic terminologies during Christine's period; it recalls to mind Umberto Eco's observation concerning the "integration of values" which led to "the absence in medieval times of a distinction between beauty (*pulchrum, decorum*) and utility or goodness (*aptum, honestum*)" (p. 15). Christine's quiet insertion of the pleasure of *belles meurs* in Ballade 50 may even slyly undercut the very courtly aesthetic she is in the process of describing. Certainly she herself strongly rejects the sentiment of love in the third stanza of the ballade, where she declares that her sentiments are altogether different from those of the courtly audience and include neither the joys nor the pains of love.

The Debate on the *Roman de la Rose*: New Categories of Reader Psychology

Although the terms *beau* and *laid* occur in the *Rose* debate, we do not find in this work a full-blown theory of artistic inspiration or of the effect of beauty per se on the reader as in Christine's courtly poetry. Rather, Christine's texts from this quarrel reveal that she was exploring the nature of reader reception using a new set of psychological categories derived for the most part from theology. A brief investigation of Christine's position in the debate can serve as a preliminary step in approaching the topic of beauty in the last work to be studied in this essay, the *Chemin de long estude*.

We have seen that in Christine's courtly poetry, she described the way an audience communicates its desires to a poet and the difficulties of meeting those demands when the source of inspiration in the poet's sentimental life is wanting. Christine treated the relation between author and audience in terms of production and reception, without implying that courtly poetry has any profound or lasting consequences for the audience or that it poses any moral dangers. She even gratified her public by composing love poetry, with no indication that she sees this concession to the audience's pleasure as an abrogation of the author's duty.

Christine's critique of the *Rose*, however, led her to conceive of author-reader relations in different terms. Her responses to Jean de Meun's defenders are replete with terms and images alluding to temptation: she speaks of passages in the *Rose* as containing "aluchement de carnalité" [encouragements of carnality], as "atisans le feu" [kindling the fire], as "enflammans" [inflaming] the reader.[5] She also uses analogy to convey the same notion, comparing the *Rose* to a tempting morsel of fruit or a thirst-quenching liquid. There is a strong emphasis on sense experience in her attack on the *Rose*, with repeated allusions to the defeat of reason by the appetites.

Not only is the reader assaulted by temptation; Christine also views him as predisposed to give in to such seductions. The reader suffers from an infirmity of the soul that "inclines" him to evil. The verb "to incline" and the adjective "inclined" are key words in Christine's psychological terminology. She uses them with a strong awareness of their literal sense of bending or orientation in a specific direction. To indicate the reader's weakened condition, she compares him to a sick person and repeatedly evokes the image of the "limping" reader by referring to "le pied dont il cloche" [the foot on which he limps]. This metaphor is not of Christine's making. A long line of Christian exegetes and writers, from Augustine to Gregory the

Great, from Alain de Lille to Dante, had used the metaphor of the feet of the soul to describe the two dimensions of the soul's activity, one cognitive (the intellect), the other appetitive (the will).[6] While the precise terms associated with the two feet vary, the distinction between faculties of discernment and faculties of volition is constant, as befits the metaphor, which stresses duality through the coordinated efforts of two sets of powers. The core idea is that humanity moves—walks—toward God by coming to know God and by coming to desire God. Within this tradition of attributing feet to the soul, there is an additional convention, a sub-theme: this is the notion of humanity's "limp," resulting from the debility of one of the feet, generally the will. It is for this reason that Christine repeatedly refers to "le pied dont il cloche" in her dispute with Gontier and Pierre Col, in order to keep bringing the quarrel back to her concern for the effect of the *Rose* on the affective powers of the reader, on the will.

Christine develops her position not only through discursive argument but through analogies, of which the most developed is a depiction of a pregnant woman (or sick person) tempted by a piece of fruit; it occurs at a point when Christine is decrying the way Reason, in the *Roman de la Rose*, describes body parts in her dialogue with the Lover:

> Rayson fist a l'Amant ainssy come se je parloie a une femme grosse ou a ung malade, et je luy ramentevoye pommes aigres ou poires nouvelles ou autre fruit, que luy fut bien apetisant et contraire, et je luy disoie que se il en mengoit, ce luy nuirroit moult. Vraiement je tiens que mieulx li souvendroit et plus luy aroit penetré en son appetit les choses nommees que la defence faicte de non en mengier: et sert au propos que autrefois ay dit—et tu tant le repprens—que on ne doit ramentevoir a nature humainne le pié dont elle cloche.

> [Reason's treatment of the Lover can be compared to what I would do if I spoke to a pregnant woman or a sick person, and made her imagine sour apples or new pears or another fruit that was very appetizing to her in her condition, but harmful, and then told her that if she ate it, it would hurt her. I firmly maintain that the things named would remain in her memory longer, and penetrate further into her appetite, than the prohibition not to eat the fruit: and this illustrates again what I said earlier—even though you criticized it—that we must not remind human nature of the foot on which it limps.] (p. 125)

In her courtly aesthetic, Christine characterized audience response as taking place in the domain of sentiments. She did not mention the role of the senses in reception of texts. But this analogy signals a new tendency in Christine to formulate reader reception in terms of the impact of sense experience. Furthermore, Christine never seemed to consider her courtly poems in terms of the eventual actions of an audience. The pleasure of their sweetness is enjoyable, but transitory: she does not investigate whether that pleasure shapes character in such a way as to influence behavior. Whereas the effect of courtly poetry was ephemeral, Christine now insists on the long-lasting impact of verbal representation, which lingers in memory and in other faculties, such as the appetite.

The analogy produces a different model of reader reception in which sense experience, imagination, will, and understanding conspire to shape behavior. In her ballades, she did not speak of imagination, either as a faculty used by the poet to invent her works or as a power of the reader implicated in reception of works. But two times in this passage she employs the key word *ramentevoir,* signifying "to evoke," "remind," or "awaken." Christine is not concerned with the words "sour apples," or "green pears" as signifiers but with their capacity to conjure up mental images (I intend images in the large sense here, as relicts of sense perception that may be auditory, tactile, gustatory, or olfactory, as well as visual).

Finally, Christine's insistence on the limits of cognitive understanding without the complicity of the will appears in her attitude toward the precept given to the pregnant woman. Even after the prohibition not to eat fruit is forgotten, the awakened desire will persist. At the end of the analogy, Christine alludes to the theme of "limping man" inclined to sin. In the debate, when Christine discusses the volitional and intellectual capacities of the soul, she always asserts the primacy of the will both as a causal agent and as a focus of the author's responsibility. She argues that if the will is defective or weakened, the intellect tends to follow. The mind deceives itself, viewing evil under some pleasing and false exterior aspect, so that, perceiving it as a good, the will can continue to pursue it.[7]

The debate on the *Rose* thus signals not a transformation or alteration of Christine's courtly aesthetic but rather the creation of an entirely new conceptual framework in which reader response and the aesthetic impact of texts could be understood. The psychology of the reader no longer consists of *sentement* but of faculties of the body and soul, such as sense, imagination, understanding, and will. The text is now considered not as an appeal to feeling but as an object of potential delight to the senses. In addition, Christine raises the stakes of reading and of authorship, for she holds that the reader's eternal soul can be affected by reading, and the author can play the role of a diabolical instrument to tempt the reader. Conversely, if the author has the power to cause the reader's downfall, might it not follow that the writer also has the capacity to accomplish much more than simply provide an ephemeral pleasure, as Christine did in her ballades? Might she not be able to participate in the reader's redemption and in turning the reader away from the things of this world and toward God?

Implementing a New Aesthetic: The *Biau Lieu* of the *Chemin de long estude*

Since the late nineteenth-century publication of Christine's *Chemin de long estude*, scholars have remarked on her numerous allusions to Dante in the work and on her use of his *Commedia* as a model.[8] Christine does not ascribe exactly the same ontological status to the tale she relates as Dante does to his—she claims that her record of events transpired in a dream, while Dante says he traveled literally, in the body, to Hell, Purgatory, and Heaven. But in terms of structure the works are strikingly similar. Traditional Dante scholarship distinguishes between the "pilgrim"—that is, Dante who made the trip—and the "poet"—the figure who struggles to put what he experienced into writing. Similarly, the *Chemin* contains a division of the author's persona into two distinct categories. Like the pilgrim in the *Commedia*, Christine takes a voyage into many realms and sees things surpassing the normal range of human faculties; like the poet, she gropes for words to describe the vision to her reader.

Christine's recourse to the convention of the dream results in a representation of the creative act with a decided platonic quality. There is an exemplar of the original lodged in the writer's memory, the vestiges left by the dream. The writer will try to produce a "copy" of this "model." But language is insufficient: the original will always surpass the text in beauty, grandeur, and immensity. Christine as narrator will stress the failure of "saying" or "recounting" [*dire*], which is subordinate to the faculty of "seeing" and sensing in general operative not only during the dream but also in the powers of imagination and memory used by the poet as she writes. Thus a further aspect of the dream vision that we can relate to "literary Platonism" is the transcendent nature of what the poet contemplates in her mind, which remains unrepresentable. The only way for the reader to access what the poet knows is through a reconstruction of the dream in the reader's own mind, in which he or she also draws upon imagination and memory.

The *Chemin* thus encourages an act of reception in which the reader actively participates in the elaboration of a mental image using the intensifying virtues of memories of sense experience. Let us examine the first episode of this literary dream, where Christine relates how she enters into an extremely lush natural decor at the outset of her journey. She qualifies this spot not as a "garden," or "orchard," or "forest" but simply as a "biau lieu," literally a "beautiful place."[9] This name recalls the rhetorical tradition of the *locus amoenus* or pleasance so prevalent in classical and medieval literature. In working on the *Chemin* so soon after the *Rose* debate, it seems likely that Christine had another well-known *locus amoenus* in mind: the "vergier" or garden of the *Roman de la Rose*, in which the Lover first caught sight of the object of his desire, suffered a degradation of his character in pursuit of it, and finally succumbed to carnal delight at the conclusion of the narrative.[10] Beyond this specific subtext, she undoubtedly had traditional depictions of the Garden of Eden in mind.[11] Like the garden in the *Roman de la Rose*, Christine's *biau lieu* is a place where nature abounds: it has singing birds, running water, luxuriant greenery, sweet fruit, refreshing shade, and brilliant sunlight. Like the Garden of Eden, it is situated in an elevated place and is fed by a fountain. Its beauty is its most striking attribute: over the course of her description, Christine will repeatedly apply the word to the place and to its features.

In the *Rose*, the garden is the scene of the Lover's descent into moral turpitude (as Christine understood it), and imagination has its role to play in his corruption. By presenting things as other than they are, by suffusing them with beauty even when they are morally "ugly," the imagination can participate in the creation of false goods that allow the will to sin. The role of imagination is altogether different in the *Chemin*: entering into the *biau lieu*, the protagonist—or the reader—finds a world where the will has been restored to its pristine state, and imagination beautifies only objects of desire consistent with God's law.

Study was a spiritual act in the Middle Ages; contemplative reading was one of the primary means of devoting oneself to God. If we consider for a moment the layout of this *biau lieu*, we can see that Christine has constructed the allegory so as to convey the spiritual restoration brought by the pious pursuit of knowledge and virtue. Without walls or boundaries of any kind, the *biau lieu* bears no marks of human artifice and implies a return to a prelapsarian state before nature became hostile, obliging humans to use their technological ingenuity to secure their livelihood. Only the roads that traverse the place bear witness to a human presence; the figures who once inhabited the *biau lieu*, even if they are not physically present when Christine traverses it, have left traces of their passing, the "chemins" or paths by which they made their way through the garden. These trails, which we might compare to the impressions the *biau lieu* leaves in memory, lead toward a focal point, high on a mountain, the fountain of the Muses. These goddesses signify not only poetic but also philosophical studies, for Christine was well aware, from her study of Boethius, that both lyric poetry and philosophy have muses.[12] The point of the allegory is that the love of learning as a means of ascending to God is a perfectly safe haven for the soul in a world of temptations. The *biau lieu* has no restraints or prohibitions reminiscent of the Fall: there are no walls to keep man from returning, no serpent to tempt him again (vv. 1075 ff.), no restrictions on eating (vv. 769 ff.), no necessity for clothing (as the nakedness of the Muses makes clear in vv. 813 ff.).

The convergence of the paths on the fountain, as those devoted to contemplation forsake the terrestrial world and rise up the mountain toward God, reinforces the theme of the perfected will. Medieval thinkers often resorted to metaphors of movement to figure the action of the will. When a good is perceived, the will causes the subject to move toward it. The paths of the philosophers and poets lead toward this goal and indicate that their will was directed to a true good, or legitimate end.

Because study leads to spiritual perfection, Christine can be unrestrained in her attribution of beauty to the place representing it. In the *Rose* debate, she criticized the way Jean de Meun "inflames" the reader's desire for a goal incompatible with God's will, or the way Reason "evokes" body parts. Here, the poet's role is totally different: in commending a true and unadulterated good, the pleasure of beauty becomes an additional stimulus. Christine strives to activate the reader's imagination and memory by emphasizing the limits of language. At one point in her description, she declares to the reader:

> Mais je ne diroie la somme
> De la biauté des biaux sentiers
> Se vivoie cent ans entiers,
> Et je ne finasse d'escripre,
> Si ne pourroie tout descripre.
> Car toute biauté delitable,
> Ymaginee plus notable,
> Qui cuer humain puet resjoir,
> On peut la veoir et oir.

[But I could not say the sum total of the beauty of these beautiful paths; if I lived a hundred years, and did nothing but write, still I would not be able to describe all of it. For every delectable beauty, augmented by imagination, that can make the heart rejoice, can be seen and heard there.] (vv. 748–56)

The discrepancy between the poet's memory and her powers of verbal expression leads her to admit the limits of her art of recounting (indicated by the verb "dire" in the first line of this passage, followed by the verbs "escripre" and "descripre," both in rhyme position). In her lyric poetry, she usually represented her ingenuity and technical skill as up to the task of composition, even if her emotional resources ("sentement") were wanting; here, the writer's craft fails in comparison to the imaginative experience. Throughout the description of the *biau lieu*, Christine will use verbs referring to sense experience, as she does in this passage, where she speaks of what one can "see" and "hear" in this lovely place. But this is not normal sense experience: the reader will never physically observe a *biau lieu* comparable to this one. Such places exist only in the imagination. Vestiges of sense experience may inform mental representations, but the mind has already abstracted them from their material support, giving them a luminosity and vividness uncharacteristic of any sensible reality.

A convention of the medieval period is the relation of art to nature: various traditional sayings embroidered on this theme by presenting art as "aping" nature (*ars simia naturæ*) or "imitating" nature (*ars imitatur naturam*). As Umberto Eco notes, these formulas need not be understood negatively: "if art imitates nature, this does not mean a servile copying of natural objects. It is inventive, and requires ingenuity" (p. 93). In her depiction of the *biau lieu*, Christine imitates nature, but not in the sense that she describes things existing in nature. Rather, just as the natural world, as conceived by medieval thought, is a material expression of ideas present in the divine mind, so she creates a textual dynamic inviting the reader to enter back into his or her own mind, to begin the process of abstracting from the world of sense and using the relicts of perception so as to move back toward the intelligible realm of ideas from which God created the material cosmos.

Christine views the imagination in this work as an essential quality for both author and reader. If the reader is to reconstruct the *biau lieu*, in accordance with Christine's intent as I have characterized it, he or she must draw upon the capacity of imagination to augment beauty. We can compare her positive approval of imagination to the medieval mystical sensibility in which tangible symbols facilitate the mind's ascent toward God. Figurative language during this period served not only a literary but a spiritual purpose. Reflecting on the use of metaphor in Scripture and its role in contemplative pursuits, Richard of St. Victor declared that the beauty of the biblical image enables the reader to begin to desire Paradise; it is essential to use the senses and the imagination fully in picturing Paradise. The activity of reading Scripture's imagistic language "impresses the memories of visible forms on our mind through the beauty of their desirable exterior aspect."[13] For this reason, "Scripture speaks of a land of milk and honey, and of flowers and sweet smells, and of the songs of men and harmonious melodies of birds." This is why, if we read the Book of Revelations, we will find "Jerusalem described as ornamented with gold and silver and pearls and precious gems." Richard, like Christine, conceives of reading as a process leaving concrete traces in the mind, and the appeal that makes the mind cling to them is beauty. The text does not simply remain on the page: the things mentioned in Scripture are "imprinted" as images, and their sensible beauty becomes a sign or promise of a future life to come.

This internalization of objects of art when the soul undergoes the effects of beauty is a persistent theme in Christine's aesthetic thought, in the genres of both the lyric and the dream vision. At the beginning of this essay, I described Christine's interest in beauty as "phenomenological": she wonders about its impact on a thinking, feeling, desiring human being. Lyric poetry acts on the sentiments or passions of the audience; the dream vision affects the reader in the realm of the imagination, where the beauty of the sensible world is intensified. However, a significant development also occurs in the movement from the lyric to the dream vision, because in the *Chemin*, Christine portrays herself as sharing in the aesthetic experience of the audience; she delights in the *biau lieu* along with her readers. By contrast, in her lyric writings, she had referred to her own detachment from her artistic products, her inability to experience beauty as the courtly audience does. In Ballade 50 of the *Cent balades*, she says that she is immune to love because "ailleurs sont mes labours" [my labors lie elsewhere] (line 18). At the end of her letter to Pierre Col, her last word in the *Rose* debate, she renounces the quarrel by explaining that "mieulx me plaist excerciter en autre matiere mieulx a ma plaisance" [it pleases me more to work on other matters more pleasing to me] (*Le Débat sur le "Roman de la Rose,"* p. 150). These allusions leave the reader wondering: from what, precisely, does Christine derive her pleasure? What does she find beautiful? Intriguingly, the letter to Pierre Col is dated 2 October 1402 (p. 150); in the *Chemin de long estude*, Christine claims that her dream took place on 5 October 1402 (lines 186–88): only three days after she concluded this letter.[14] Perhaps the *Chemin* is one of these "other" more pleasurable matters of which Christine spoke. Certainly, in her description of the beautiful place where scholarly contemplation occurs, she gives us a glimpse of the beauty that she herself sought in a life devoted to study in pursuit of intellectual, moral, and spiritual perfection.

Notes

1. For a discussion of perceptions of Christine at the time of the debate, see Eric Hicks, ed., *Le Débat sur le Roman de la rose* (Paris: Champion, 1977), xli-xlii.

2. For a study of the ballades that in many ways parallels mine (in particular concerning the importance of Ballades 20 and 50), see James Laidlaw, "L'unité des *Cent balades*."

3. Christine de Pizan, *Cent balades*, in *Œuvres poétiques de Christine de Pizan*. All translations are mine. References are to the line numbers of the ballade.

4. Bonnie Kent formulates this idea compellingly in her study *Virtues of the Will,* p. 204: "The vision of the moral hero prevailing again and again in the perpetual struggle with his lower appetites, a vision that gained considerable appeal among Christian writers, would be for Aristotle thoroughly distasteful. In Aristotle's ethics, internal division is a condition human beings can and should overcome."

5. All citations of the *Rose* debate are from the Hicks edition (see above, note 1). Translations are mine. The terms indicated here can be found on pages 16 and 122. In further citations of this edition, the page reference will be indicated in parentheses in the text.

6. For an overview of the tradition, with references to the writers I mention, see John Freccero's article on Dante's use of the motif, "The Firm Foot on a Journey without a Guide." For Alain de Lille's use of the image (not cited in Freccero), see *De planctu naturæ liber*, p. 465 (in the edition of the *Patrologia Latina*, vol. 210, col. 451), where the dreamer alludes to the "pagan gods who limped on the foot of deviance" [exorbitationis pede deos claudicasse].

7. Christine thus presents an interesting comparison with Boethius. In *The Consolation of Philosophy*, Boethius represents humans as straying away from the good because of a cognitive defect: they do not know the good. See the *Consolation of Philosophy*, especially Book III, Prose III, lines 1–6. Christine, on the other hand, stresses the complicity of the will in maintaining this self-deception.

8. There are a considerable number of studies on the relation between Christine's *Chemin* and Dante's *Commedia*. See in particular Kevin Brownlee, "Literary Genealogy and the Problem of the Father"; Earl Jeffrey Richards, "Christine de Pizan and Dante"; Dina De Rentiis, "*Sequere me.*" For an early study of Christine de Pizan's relationship to Dante, see Arturo Farinelli, *Dante et la Francia*, I, pp. 158–72. For other early works on Christine and Dante, see the bibliographical references given in the articles of Brownlee and Richards.

9. *Le Livre du Chemin de long estude*. In the references that follow, numbers in parentheses after quotations identify the verse numbers. Translations are mine.

10. As Earl Jeffrey Richards points out, thirteenth- and fourteenth-century Italian works such as Brunetto Latini's *Tesoretto*, the *Intelligenza*, and the *Commedia* itself use the motif of the *locus amoenus* as a way of alluding to the *Rose*; see Richards, *Dante and the "Roman de la Rose,"* pp. 24–27, 30–31, 85–88. French authors of the same period do likewise (as in Guillaume de Machaut's *Dit dou vergier*). Thus, Franco-Italian writers provide a precedent for Christine's use of the *locus amoenus* to evoke the *Rose*.

11. On the similarity between Christine's *biau lieu* and Eden, compare the following description of Eden in Peter Lombard, *Sententiæ*, *Patrologia Latina*, vol. 192, col. 686: "ad litteram intelligendum est [paradisum] esse locum amoenissimum fructuosis arboribus, magnum et magno fonte foecundum . . . et in alto situm . . . unde nec aquæ diluvii illuc pervenerunt" [paradise is to be understood as a very beautiful place with fruit-bearing trees, a large place fed by a great fountain . . . and situated up high . . . which is why the waters of the flood did not reach it]. For this *biau lieu* as a reminiscence of Dante's Limbo, see Brownlee, "Literary Genealogy," pp. 375–76. Brownlee notes that Christine borrows most of the names of philosophers and poets from *Inferno* 4.

12. Boethius mentions the Muses of Philosophy when Philosophia speaks of "my Muses" (*Consolation of Philosophy*, Book I, Prose I, line 40). On Christine's assimilation of wisdom (the object of philosophers, who are "lovers of wisdom") and poetry in this fountain, see Shigemi Sasaki, "Le poète et Pallas dans le *Chemin de long estude*."

13. Richard of St. Victor, *De præparatione animi ad contemplationem*, *Patrologia Latina*, vol. 196, cols. 10–11:

> Sed nec hoc prætereundum, quomodo Scripturæ divinæ huic speculationi alludent et humanæ infirmitati condescendent. Res enim invisibiles, per rerum visibilium formas describunt, et earum memoriæ per quarumdam concupiscibilium specierum pulchritudinem mentibus nostris imprimunt. Hinc est quod nunc terram lacte et melle manantem promittunt; nunc flores, nunc odores nominant; nunc per cantus hominum, nunc per concentus avium coelestium gaudiorum harmoniam designant. Legite Apocalypsim Joannis et invenietis coelestem Hierusalem ornatum per aurum, et argentum, per margaritas vel alias quaslibet gemmas pretiosas multipliciter descriptum.

[But neither should this be overlooked: how divine scriptures allude to this vision and condescend to human frailty. For they describe invisible things through the beauties of visible ones and the memories of them are imprinted on our minds through the beauty of various sensual likenesses. It is here that they now promise the land flowing with milk and honey; now they speak of flowers and now of sweet scents; they designate the harmony of celestial joys now with the singing of men, now with the song of birds. Read the *Revelations* of John and you will find the celestial Jerusalem decorated with gold and silver, with pearls and all other precious gems, and described in many ways.]

14. I would like to thank Earl Jeffrey Richards for pointing out to me the closeness in time between the date of the letter to Pierre Col and the date on which Christine says her dream occurred.

Works Cited

Alain de Lille. *Alani liber de planctu naturae.* In *The Anglo-Latin Satirical Poets and Epigrammatists of the Twelfth Century.* Ed. Thomas Wright. London: Longman, 1872. Rerum Britannicarum Medii Aevi Scriptores, no. 59, vol. 2, 429–522; also in *Patrologia Latina*, vol. 210, col. 429–82. Paris, 1855.

Boethius. *The Consolation of Philosophy.* Ed. and trans. S. J. Tester. Loeb Classical Library. Cambridge, Mass.: Harvard University Press, 1973.

Brownlee, Kevin. "Literary Genealogy and the Problem of the Father: Christine de Pizan and Dante." *Journal of Medieval and Renaissance Studies* 23 (1993): 365–87.

Christine de Pizan. "Cent balades." In *Œuvres poétiques de Christine de Pizan.* Ed. Maurice Roy. Vol. 1. Paris: Firmin Didot, 1886.

———. *Le Livre du chemin de long estude.* Ed. Robert Püschel. Geneva: Slatkine Reprints, 1974.

Christine de Pizan et al. *Le Débat sur le "Roman de la rose."* Ed. Eric Hicks. Paris: Champion, 1977.

De Rentiis, Dina. "'*Sequere me*': *Imitatio* dans la *Divine Comédie* et dans le *Livre du chemin de long estude.*" In *The City of Scholars: New Approaches to Christine de Pizan*, ed. Margarete Zimmermann and Dina De Rentiis, pp. 31–42. Berlin: De Gruyter, 1994.

Eco, Umberto. *Art and Beauty in the Middle Ages.* Trans. Hugh Bredin. New Haven: Yale University Press, 1986.

Farinelli, Arturo. *Dante et la Francia.* 2 vols. Milan: Ulrico Hoepli, 1908.

Freccero, John. "The Firm Foot on a Journey without a Guide." In *Dante: The Poetics of Conversion*, ed. Rachel Jacoff, pp. 29–54. Cambridge, Mass.: Harvard University Press, 1986.

Kent, Bonnie. *Virtues of the Will: The Transformation of Ethics in the Late Thirteenth Century.* Washington, D.C.: Catholic University of America Press, 1995.

Laidlaw, James C. "L'unité des *Cent balades.*" In *The City of Scholars: New Approaches to Christine de Pizan*, ed. Margarete Zimmermann and Dina De Rentiis, pp. 97–106. Berlin: De Gruyter, 1994.

Peter Lombard. *Sententiarum libri quatuor.* In *Patrologia Latina*, vol. 192, col. 519–964. Paris, 1855.

Richard of St. Victor. *De præparatione animi ad contemplationem liber dictus Benjamin minor.* In *Patrologia Latina.* Vol. 196, col. 1–64. Paris, 1855.

Richards, Earl Jeffrey. "Christine de Pizan and Dante: A Reexamination." *Archiv für das Studium der neueren Sprachen und Literaturen* 222 (1985): 100–111.

———. "Christine de Pizan, Courtly Diction, and Italian Humanism." In *Reinterpreting Christine de Pizan*, ed. Earl Jeffrey Richards with Joan Williamson, Nadia Margolis, and Christine Reno, pp. 250–71. Athens: University of Georgia Press, 1992.

———. *Dante and the "Roman de la Rose": An Investigation into the Vernacular Narrative Context of the "Commedia."* Tübingen: Niemeyer, 1981.

Sasaki, Shigemi. "Le poète et Pallas dans le *Chemin de long estude* (vers 737–1170 et 1569–1780)." *Revue des Langues Romanes* 92 (1988): 369–77.

∾ CHAPTER 9

Poems of Water without Salt
and Ballades without Feeling,
or Reintroducing History into
the Text: Prose and Verse in the
Works of Christine de Pizan

EARL JEFFREY RICHARDS

End of song—beginning of story.
Louis Armstrong

Tucked away near the beginning of the *Livre de la Cité des Dames*, 1.8.10, Christine presents one of the severest—and hitherto as best I know, completely overlooked—criticisms of "courtly poetry" as practiced in her day. Her reproach of courtly lyric focuses on its vapidity, on the fact that it reduced poetry to a verbal shell disconnected from morality and politics:

> Et si comme il n'est si digne ouvrage tant soit fait de bon maistre que aucuns n'ayent voulu et veulent contrefaire, sont maint qui se veulent mesler de dicter leur semble que ilz ne pevent mesprendre, puisque autres ont dit en livres ce qu'ilz veulent dire, et come ce, medire—j'en scay. Aucuns d'yceulx se veulent entremettre de parler en faisant dictiez de eaue sans sel, tieulx comme quieulx, ou balades sans sentement, parlant des meurs des femmes ou des princes ou d'autre gent, et eulx mesmes ne se scevent pas congnoistre ne corriger leurs chetifs meurs et inclinaisons. Mais les simples gens qui sont ignorens comme eulx dient que c'est le mieulx fait du monde. (p. 72)

[And just as there has never been any work so worthy, so skilled is the craftsman who made it, that there were not people who wanted, and want, to counterfeit it, there are many who wish to get involved in writing poetry. They believe they cannot go wrong, since others have written in books what they take the situation to be, or rather *mis*-take the situation—as I well know! Some of them undertake to express themselves by writing poems of water without salt, such as these, or ballads without feeling, discussing the behavior of women or of princes or of other people, while they themselves do not know how to recognize or to correct their own servile conduct and inclinations. But simple people, as ignorant as they are, declare that such writing is the best in the world.] (p. 20)

Christine's aesthetics are contained in a nutshell in these remarks: the recycling of received sources, the divorce between artistic creation and ethical conduct, the servile reproduction of tradition for its own sake. In her lyrical works she gave women a voice and made women's real-life experience the subject of lyric. A poem such as Christine's celebration of Joan of Arc, the *Ditié de Jeanne d'Arc* (1429), incorporates contemporary history into lyric in a manner absolutely unlike any previous lyrical work in medieval French literature and, with the exception of Dante, unlike any other medieval predecessor.

What Christine identifies as the malady of lyrical composition in her time recalls uncannily the retreat into textuality that literary criticism has promoted in recent decades, what Edward W. Said characterized as "the flight into method and system on the part of critics who wish to avoid the ideology of humanism" (p. 25). As Said noted, "It is not too much to say that American or even European literary theory now explicitly accepts the principle of noninterference, and that its peculiar mode of appropriating its subject matter (to use Althusser's formula) is not to appropriate anything that is worldly, circumstantial, or socially contaminated. 'Textuality' is the somewhat mystical and disinfected subject matter of literary theory. Textuality has therefore become the exact antithesis and displacement of what might be called history" (pp. 3–4). Christine's attitude toward her lyrical predecessors was to reintroduce experience and history into the disinfected courtly text. This attitude informs her entire renewal of the medieval French lyrical tradition and explains the perhaps unexpected affinities between her lyrical and prose works. Textuality and history merge in Christine in a way before unknown in French letters, and her use of prose and verse illustrates clearly this innovation.

Christine as a Test Case for the Modern Antithesis between Prose and Verse

The current critical distinction between prose and verse, dating back to Hegel's aesthetics but supported by the claims of Isidore of Seville, affords, surprisingly, little purchase on Christine's use of prose and verse. Christine's lyrical and prose works contradict virtually everything found in formalist criticism. For scholars in Christine studies, the classic locus on the relationship between prose and verse is found in the prose intercalation in the *Mutacion de Fortune* in which Christine recounts the history of the Jews. The first question that arises is thorny indeed: did Christine mean to assign greater veracity to this portion of the *Mutacion* or was she simply eager to finish the work?[1] The issue has been complicated by the additional fact that Christine's prose works, composed a century after the prosification—the *dérimages* or *mises en prose*—of the great chanson de geste cycles and Arthurian tales (whose diffusion Dante considered characteristic of the *langue d'oïl*), take their stylistic inspiration not from vernacular prosification but from the curial prose tradition,[2] and that they were also indebted to the growing body of didactic and scientific prose in medieval French.[3]

To begin with, Christine's prose works exhibit an enormous range of styles. It is this overriding fact that holds the key to understanding both the nature of her prose and the relationship between prose and lyric for her. The prose style that Christine chooses depends on subject matter, source, patron, and audience of the individual work, and it varies according to her changing needs, all of which, however, are consistent with her constant effort to reintroduce history—often exemplified by the concrete historical experiences and accomplishments of women—into literary composition, into textuality.[4] That Christine could deploy different prose styles was consistent with the fact that medieval writers, unlike Hegel, assumed the existence of numerous prose styles. For example, John of Garland was quick to observe that "the prose arts that schools and courts use are different" [alia est dictamen qua utitur schola et curia].[5] Somewhat later Dante distinguished between various constructions in prose in the *De vulgari eloquentia* [On vernacular eloquence] and thereby underscored further the heterogeneous nature of prose in medieval usage. Christine felt no inherent tension between prose and verse and assigned no inherent truthfulness to prose. Erudition and the love of study, as reflected in a work's content, guaranteed veracity for a literary work, whether composed in verse or in prose.

Christine's long unrecognized mastery of late medieval French lyrical forms and conventions went hand in hand with her equal mastery of prose. As William D. Paden has demonstrated, in lyrical compositions Christine was acutely sensitive to the conventions and requirements of the various *formes fixes*, to rhetorical topoi and to lexical registers, and she composed in as many verse styles as in prose styles. Similarly, in prose compositions, she could range from a careful curial style, as in the *Livre de la Cité des Dames* and the *Livre de la paix*, to a more direct narrative style as in her biography of Charles V.[6] She was as much a master of the verse epistle as the prose epistle, in which she followed the five-part division recommended by Italian dictaminal arts and Brunetto Latini.

Christine was acutely sensitive to the concrete historical content of her works, even when she allegorized history, and this specific concern for truth informed her various strategies for establishing her authority. The fact that she allegorized history, moreover, meant that she embraced its truth, rather than that she fled from it. However, when Christine calls attention to her deployment of curial style, erudition, and the authority topos, it is in a manner reminiscent of the Russian Formalist concern for literariness [*literaturnost'*], that is, how a text emphasizes or thematizes its formal qualities, especially through the technique of "estrangement" [*priëm ostranenija*], in which familiar situations are detached from everyday experience and recontextualized in the literary work (divorced from history, as it were). The crucial difference between Christine's literary values and those of Russian Formalism is that Christine uses form in order to make a truth-claim whereas Russian Formalism, consistent with its retreat from history (and sociology), claims a self-referentiality for literature utterly foreign to Christine but frequently present in medieval lyric prior to her time (the best example being the Provençal poet Guillaume IX's famous claim to make a poem out of or about nothing, *farei un vers de dreyt nien*). At the same time, Christine's rejection of the celebration of literary form for its own sake perhaps is rooted in her feminism as well.

While Christine's practice diverges from that in the *mises en prose* of contemporary vernacular romance, it is entirely consistent with contemporary international Latin practice, stemming from the *ars dictaminis* and *ars notaria*. The prose romances of the early fourteenth century attempted to reinforce "courtly" values and rituals which Christine herself criticized.[7] Therefore, the divergence between Christine and the prose romances was virtually programmatic especially given the humanist orientation underlying Christine's verse compositions.[8] Thus one can see how Christine's innovations in using prose parallel her lyrical innovations as well.

The Checkered History of the Rise of Prose

The modern effort to see prose as the opposite of verse posits an antithesis that did not exist in medieval rhetoric. Formalist criticism uses this opposition to explain the meaning of literature exclusively as a function of its form rather than of its content, as though artistic form as such were a form of knowledge, emotive rather than cognitive, ineffable and ultimately irrational, to be sure, but a form of knowledge all the same. For Christine, such purely formal concerns were embodied in the sophistry of Jean de Meun, whose continual *mise en abyme* of linguistic referentiality was connected in Christine's mind to his fundamental misogyny. When is a rape not a rape? When it is "artistically" presented, of course, as in the *Roman de la Rose*.[9]

Formalist analyses of the prosification movement in fourteenth-century France have produced tempting but often inaccurate results. Following the classic work of Georges Doutrepont on the prosification of the medieval French epic and romance, some scholars would like to posit that late medieval French writers—or all writers in general—suspected that verse composition was inherently mendacious, a claim that dovetails with the formalist belief that verse per se did not lay claim to truthfulness. Doutrepont listed the various intentions given by prosifiers for their works: the desire to lend greater credibility to the now outdated *chansons de geste*, the care for introducing narrative proportion, the need for realism in response to the changing tastes of the public, and the nostalgia felt by noble and bourgeois (that is, would-be noble) patrons for the chivalric deeds of the past.[10]

Did Christine (like the Russian Formalists) perceive an opposition or competition between prose and verse? In a crucial passage in *L'Avision-Christine*, she explains how she turned away from "pretty things" [choses jolies] in order to dedicate herself to "more subtle and loftier subjects" [plus grant soubtilleté et plus haulte matiere], and here one might see support for the modern antithesis: "Adonc me pris a forgier choses jolies, a mon commencement plus legieres, et tout ainsi comme l'ouvrier qui de plus en plus son oeuvre s'asoubtille comme plus il la frequente, ainsi tousjours estudiant diverses matieres, mon sens de plus en plus s'imbuoit de choses estranges, amendant mon stile en plus grant soubtilleté et plus haulte matiere" [Then I began to compose pretty pieces, at first lighter ones, and just like the artisan who makes his work more subtle the more he devotes himself to it, so too my mind, always studying different topics, became more and more imbued with alien matters, modifying my style to be much subtler and loftier.][11] By the same token, at the beginning of the *Cité des Dames* Christine draws a pointed contrast between the weighty study of the *auctores* and the light, happy ditties of the poets.

Selon la maniere que j'ay en usage et a quoy est disposé le excercice de ma vie, c'est assavoir en la frequentacion d'estude de lettres, un jour comme je feusse seant en ma cele, anvironnee de plusieurs volumes de diverses matieres, mon entendement a celle heure auques traveillié de recueillir la pesanteur des sentences de divers aucteurs par moy longue piece estudiez, dreçay mon visage ensus du livre, deliberant pour celle foiz laisser en paix choses soubtilles et m'esbatre et regarder aucune joyeuseté des diz des poetes. (p. 40)

[One day as I was sitting alone in my study, surrounded by books on all kinds of subjects, devoting myself to literary studies, my usual habit, my mind dwelt at length on the weighty opinions of various authors whom I had studied for a long time. I looked up from my book, having decided to leave such subtle questions in peace and to relax by reading some light poetry.] (p. 3)

In these passages, both written in 1405, Christine contrasts the delicacy of verse with the gravity of serious literature, a dissimilarity based here on content rather than form. Christine recognized that verse could also take on weighty issues when it sought to present the truth. When she excused herself for using prose in the *Mutacion de Fortune*, she noted: "Et qui de bien rimer se charge, / Ce n'est mie petite charge, / Et par especial histoires / Abriger en parolles voires" [It is hardly a small task whenever one undertakes to rhyme well, and especially to abbreviate historical narratives into true words] (vv. 8745–48). In these three examples, Christine's analysis of the differences between prose and verse inverts the terms of formalist analysis: prose and verse for Christine are not antithetical, and their literary value derives from their veracity and from the author's formal talents in presenting the truth of history.

Formalism, in one sense, searches not only for the procedures used by literary artists but also for potential essential qualities inhering in language which manifest the nature of poetic language and meaning. Victor Erlich's now classic *Russian Formalism, History—Doctrine* summarizes the central concerns of Russian Formalism and sheds light on the defining features of Christine's poetics. Christine, for example, objected to the use of the word *coilles* [balls, testicles] in the *Roman de la Rose* because she rejected the belief, as best formulated by Roman Jakobson, that "the distinctive feature of poetry lies in the fact that a word is perceived as a word and not merely a proxy for the denoted object or an outburst of an emotion, that words and their arrangement, their meaning, their outward and inward form acquire weight and value of their own."[12] She saw in Jean de Meun's endeavor to separate word and reference—even for the sake of underscoring the artificiality of poetic language—a pivotal aspect of literary misogyny.

The other overruling aspect of Russian Formalist analysis is to assign poetic language its own distinct epistemological character. As Erlich puts it, "Verse, claimed the Formalists, is not merely a matter of external embellishments such as meter, rhyme, or alliteration, superimposed upon ordinary speech. It is an integrated type of discourse, qualitatively different from prose, with a distinctive hierarchy of elements and internal laws of its own—'speech organized in its entire phonic texture'" (p. 211). This proposition is subject neither to verification nor to falsification, and as such brings no methodological purchase on the study of the relationship between verse and prose. How can one verify the qualitative differences between prose and poetry without resorting to metaphysical arguments that merely compound the problem?[13] A form of discourse that is subject to its own internal laws simply means that poetic language is circular and nonreferential, but all this conclusion does is restate the original assumptions. But, given Christine's sensitivity to what she later called in the *Fais d'armes et de chevalerie* the "subtilités de paroles polies" [the subtleties of polished words], she was keen to reconcile words and meaning, textuality and history.

Since Russian Formalist theory focuses on the distinction between poetic and nonpoetic language, it must address the question of the nature of prose in order to establish the qualitative differences between verse and prose. Russian Formalists tended to consider imaginative prose as an imitation of an oral monologue so that the artistic qualities of prose would then derive from the techniques employed to imitate orality. Erlich summarized the position in the following terms: "With the exception of drama and works of narrative fiction which employ what Henry James calls the 'scenic method,' the monologue is the predominant type of utterance in imaginative literature.... A further subdivision may be in order here. If the bulk of expository prose ... is couched in polished, highly literary monologue, there are works of literature which exhibit a tendency toward what might be called 'oral' monologue. Not infrequently, especially in cases where we have to do with a 'narrator' mediating between the author and the audience, the story is told in such a manner as to emulate the phonetic, grammatical and lexical patterns of actual speech and produce the 'illusion of oral narration'" (237–38).[14] The parallels between this analysis of prose and the claims raised for prose over verse in fourteenth-century *mises en prose* are striking. The prosifications rely on a series of techniques designed to enhance the work's veracity and existential immediacy—the illusion of oral narration—and in this regard the techniques, well described by Emmanuèle Baumgartner,[15] are reminiscent of the Russian Formalist approach to prose. The illusion of orality in the prosifications, however, serves the praises of an irretrievable age of chivalric prowess, a kind of flight from history in the name of nostalgia, all the more paradoxical in light of the sense of immediacy that the prosifications try to create. (The obvious modern parallel is found in boulevard television journalism, in which quotidian crimes and passions, presented with a breathtaking immediacy and an incomparable orality, suffocate any sense of history and reinforce the self-containment of the media's world.)

Writing in their provocative study *The Emergence of Prose*, Jeffrey Kittay and Wlad Godzich argue that verse, given its link to the oral performance of the jongleur, possessed for late medieval audiences a greater veracity than prose. The theoretical affinities between Kittay and Godzich and Russian Formalism are undoubtedly close, though Kittay and Godzich, in examining how late medieval French prose creates "the illusion of oral performance" considerably refine the Russian Formalist analysis of prose. Depending on the particular situation, prose may either rely on a variety of devices, in order to compensate for the loss of the immediacy and deixis of verse, or exploit its deictic autonomy in order to problematize the subject, creating subjectivity in order to contain the disorientation that accompanies the loss of verse. Kittay and Godzich, citing Curtius, take care to recall that in medieval Latin usage there was no opposition as such between prose and verse. The issue boils down to what extent Latin (both in oral usage in the universities, churches, monasteries, and diplomatic councils and curiae, and written composition) impinged on the vernacular and its oral traditions. The early fourteenth-century prosification movement in France, while immensely influential in transmitting and adapting earlier verse romances for the rest of Europe, has little in common with the far more widespread use of prose in ecclesiastical, university, and curial circles.

In a pan-European context, the simultaneous existence of curial, patristic, and scientific prose styles in Latin was anything but destabilizing. Since, as Bernard Ribémont has demonstrated, Christine was heavily indebted to scientific prose both in Latin and Old French, she used prose to demonstrate her authority and erudition, and while she perhaps destabilized the male-dominated tradition in so doing, this effect stemmed not from the form that she had chosen per se but from the manner in which she exploited it as a woman, in which she as a learned woman, a *clergece* (a term she uses three times in the *Cité des Dames*),[16] mastered a body of learning whose content had hitherto been denied to women. (One must recall here Gayatri Chakravorty Spivak's penetrating observation that humanism, when put in the service of the dispossessed, can be disruptive.)[17] For Christine as an outsider to the clerkly male culture of her time, courtly discourse must have seemed an elaborate self-absorbed masquerade used by male poets and male listeners to exclude women.

The most serious reservation that must be raised against all formalist approaches to prose is that they assign epistemological qualities to language, or more precisely to metrical and prosaic forms of language. This method is consistent with the Sapir-Whorf hypothesis that consciousness is shaped by language and ultimately leads to the Heideggerian position on language as the house of being (summed up in the formula *Die Sprache ist das Haus des Seins*).[18] The question, and here the relationship between verse and prose affords a particularly productive angle, is how the formal qualities of literary texts may change the meaning of words.

Many of the conclusions reached by Kittay and Godzich reflect developments peculiar to the fourteenth-century developments of prose in France. It would be a serious mistake, however, to consider that the history of French prose should take its cue from the *mises en prose* of the early fourteenth century or that developments peculiar to French represent the epitome for the development of prose for all other languages. Here the example of medieval English curial prose and its relationship to contemporary French curial prose is noteworthy. In 1986 J. D. Burnley published a remarkable essay in which he examined the ease with which one could pass from curial English into curial French. He presents a passage in perfectly good Middle English which, it turns out, was Burnley's own translation from a French original. The style in English was a perfect calque of the style in French, itself imitated from Latin curial models. This linguistic interchangeability has important ramifications for the consideration of the nature of prose in Christine's works. Burnley concludes: "Before the middle of the fourteenth century, when Chaucer was still a child, Englishmen in an administrative milieu using Anglo-French could write prose which in its essential structures was hardly distinguishable from late-fifteenth-century English curial prose. The major difference is in lexical choice: French vocabulary or English. For men bilingual in this specialist field, the transition from one language to the other must have been an easily bridgeable divide. The essentials of the style transcended the language barrier" (p. 594). While Burnley has elsewhere tried to bring precision to Christine's use of the *style clergial* and would reject the claim that Christine used the curial style in her letters from the Quarrel on the *Rose*, the analysis he offers of English curial prose helps explain what has otherwise been called Christine's notarial or legal style.[19] Curial style and curial prose, as Burnley notes, constitute "a set of formal features used in legal and diplomatic documents with the functional purposes of precision in reference and ceremony of tone" (p. 595). These features include "Latinate constructions, extensive clausal qualifiers, lexical doublets and triplets, and anaphoric cohesive devices"—stylistic devices omnipresent in varying degrees in Christine's prose, often to the chagrin of modern readers.

The stylistic affinities between medieval French and Middle English prose stem from common rhetorical models and the presence of a supranational administrative language, Latin, which facilitated the transfer between the three languages. In his examples of curial prose Burnley has provided stunning counterexamples to the Sapir-Whorf hypothesis: in the logocentric world of late medieval culture, not languages but supranational and supralinguistic stylistic models, transmitted by an erudite supranational tradition of rhetoric, influenced thought.[20]

Christine's Prose Styles

For Christine there was no inherent opposition between the truthfulness of verse and of prose, significant when one considers that she was writing a century after the first *mises en prose* had been composed in France precisely because prose was held to be more truthful than verse. Her position on prose styles has general parallels in earlier medieval usage. John of Garland had distinguished four prose styles ("stilus gregorianus, tullianus, hilarianus, ysidorianus"), whereas Dante, writing in *De vulgari eloquentia*, II.vi, gives five examples of stylistic hierarchy or *gradus constructionum*. Clearly there was no sense of the inherent unity of prose discourse. Curtius, following the lead of Eduard Norden's *Die antike Kunstprosa* (1892), demonstrated long ago that no opposition between prose and verse as such existed in the Middle Ages, that the divisions applied were those of various styles. Christine's explanation in *L'Avision* corresponds clearly to this larger medieval context:

> Puis me prist aux livres des pouetes, et comme de plus en plus, alast croiscent le bien de ma congnoiscence. Adonc fus je aise quant j'oz trouvé le stile a moy naturel, me delittant en leurs soubtilles covertures et belles matieres mucees soubz fictions delictables et morales, et le bel stile de leurs metres et proses deduittes par belle et polie rehtorique aournee de soubtil lenguage et proverbes estranges.

[Then I occupied myself with the books of the poets, and more and more the measure of my knowledge increased. Then I was content when I found their style natural for me, delighting in their subtle covers and fair subject matters hidden under delightful and moral fictions, and the beautiful style of their verse and prose works conveyed in beautiful and polished rhetoric, adorned with subtle language and unusual proverbs.]

Christine's phrase "le bel stile de leurs metres et proses" [the beautiful style of their verse and prose works] demonstrates that she sees style as a factor unifying verse and prose, an attitude in complete accord with the medieval belief in the primacy of style. The inquiry into the relationship between verse and prose turns on the contention that prose is somehow formless or more direct or unmediated when compared to verse and that verse form per se adds a credibility—an epistemological *je ne sais quoi*—that is otherwise not found in prose. The content of a work always brings us back to reality, and Christine knew that literary content was not a Cheshire cat that materialized and then vanished again in literary works. Excessive concern with form in lyric composition led to the writing, as Christine put it, of *balades sans sentement* and *dictiez de eaue sans sel*.

Let us look at five of Christine's works for evidence they might give us regarding her perception of the differing but not necessarily antithetical qualities of prose and verse: first, the *Epistre d'Othea* (1401); second, the *Chemin de long estude* (1402); third, *L'Avision-Christine* (1405); fourth, the *Mutacion de Fortune* (written between August 1400 and November 1403); and fifth, the *Fais et bonnes meurs du sage roy Charles V* (1404). The reason for looking at *L'Avision* and the *Mutacion de Fortune* out of chronological order here is that it helps confirm the pattern of Italian influence on Christine's use of prose and verse.

Of all of Christine's works, the most formally integrated or sophisticated combination of prose and verse is found in the *Epistre d'Othea*. Scholars of Christine have long puzzled over its form since it is a highly unique combination of text, gloss, and allegory. It is useful to quote Charity Cannon Willard's description of the earliest *Othea* manuscript, BNF 848. It consists of only the *Epistre d'Othea* with just four illustrations. "These are handsome black-and-white drawings, although they can scarcely be compared in splendor with the hundred colored illustrations to be found in three later copies. The Text is placed in the center of the page with the Glose in the margin on the left and the Allegory on the right, a format recalling legal texts and their commentaries from the University of Bologna, or Diogina da Borgo San Sepulcro's commentary on Valerius Maximus, or, indeed, Benvenuto da Imola's gloses on Dante's *Divine Comedy*. Such texts were undoubtedly familiar to Christine, and her use of a similar format suggests that she had in mind some sort of commentary on Ovid" (p. 95). What the Italianate form of the earliest *Othea* manuscript clearly shows is that Christine viewed prose and verse as complementary in the most fundamental sense.

While Christine supplies general dates to most of her works, in several cases she took special pains to date a work precisely. Her *Epistre a Eustache Morel* was dated 10 February 1403, the feast of Saint Scholastica, the patron saint of female intellectuals. As I have shown elsewhere, Christine used this date to establish a parallel between herself and the saint, since both sought out dialogue with male intellectuals.[21] In the *Chemin de long estude*, Christine attempts in verse to show herself as Dante's successor, and she dates this work 5 October 1402, or three days after her final letter to Pierre Col. In other words, she saw her poetic mission in the *Chemin* as a further answer to the defenders of the *Rose*, as an attempt to prove the superiority of Dante's *Commedia* and of its allegory to that found in the *Rose*. In the *Chemin*, Christine describes herself as sitting in her study, surrounded by books. The description in verse anticipates the famous opening of the *Cité des Dames* composed in prose three years later: "Un jour de joie remise / Je m'estoie a par moy mise / En une estude petite, / Ou souvent je me delite / A regarder escriptures / De diverses aventures" [One day, filled with joy, I betook myself to a small study where I often enjoyed looking at writings of various events] (vv. 171–76). The prose opening of the *Cité* paraphrases the verse of the *Chemin*: verse and prose may exhibit different styles but a single truth. For Christine, verse and prose were interchangeable, when united by a single truth, just as English and French curial prose were linguistically interchangeable since they were united by a common rhetorical tradition.

In other words, even if some of Christine's older French contemporaries posited an opposition between prose and verse, the mix of verse and prose in the *Othea* shows that Christine, perhaps taking her cue from Italian models, saw no conflict between the two modes of composition. By way of further comparison, she wrote both prose and verse letters, usually depending on her audience and purpose in writing. In the third part of the prose *L'Avision*, which is heavily dependent on Boethius's *Consolation of Philosophy*, the preeminent model of the *prosimetrum* for medieval writers, which she knew and used from a verse and prose translation, she included a ballade on widowhood—addressing the still current issue of the feminization of poverty—"Helas ou donc trouveront reconfort / pouvres vesves de leurs biens despouilliees" [Alas, where then will poor widows, robbed of their possessions, find comfort?]. If we examine the careful research of Glynnis M. Cropp, ("Boèce et Christine de Pisan"), it is apparent that sometimes, as in the *Mutacion de Fortune*, Christine versifies parts of Boethius that were in prose in the translation she used, and at other times, in *L'Avision*, she follows the prose of her source in prose as well. Verse is not the constituent element of a text's truth to begin with. Even scientific works exhibit a mixture of prose and verse, as Bernard Ribémont has demonstrated.[22]

Further confirmation that Christine saw no formal contradiction between prose and meter comes in the first sentence of *L'Avision* that renders and selectively comments on the opening of *Inferno*: "Ja passé avoye la moitié du chemin de mon pelerinage, comme un iour sus lavesprir me trouvasse pour la longue voye lassee et desireuse de heberge" [I had already passed the half of the path of my pilgrimage, when one day, toward evening, I found myself weary of the long road and eager to find shelter]; Dante's "il mezzo del cammin di nostra vita" [the middle (or half) of our life's journey] becomes "la moitié du chemin de mon pelerinage" [half of the path of my pilgrimage]. Now, by substituting "my pilgrimage" for Dante's "our life" Christine has made explicit the obvious interpretation of the opening of the *Commedia*, a fact that early commentators on Dante immediately mentioned—and we should not forget once again that the form of the earliest *Othea* manuscript looks like the manuscript of Benvenuto da Imola's commentary on Dante. And Christine incorporates Dante's sense of weariness at the beginning of *Inferno* 1 as well, since her phrase "me trouvasse pour la longue voye lassee" [I found myself weary from the long road] combines and abbreviates "mi ritrovai per una selva oscura/che la via diritta era smarrita" [I found myself in a dark forest because the direct way was lost] and "tant era pieno di sonno" [I was so filled with sleep]. In strict medieval rhetorical terms she has abbreviated Dante's opening into her prose work in order to set the key for the entire work. This single example of an *abbreviatio* of Dante's verse in her own prose shows that she held to a complementarity of prose and meter. This position also corresponds both to Dante's statement about the relationship of meter and prose at the beginning of *De vulgari eloquentia*, Book II, and to Dante's practice in the *Vita Nuova* and in *Convivio* combining verse and prose commentary.

It should be noted that Dante in fact further differentiates metrical writers into *poetæ* and *versificatores*, the former being metrical writers in serious subjects, the latter being more properly lyric poets treating love (never a serious subject . . .), so that even a clearly defined prose/meter dialectic as such did not exist in Dante's mind. Moreover, Dante's distinction between poet and versifier means that he was sensitive not only to the form or style of a literary work but also to its content.

At the opening of *De vulgari eloquentia*, Book II, Dante sums up his attitude on the differences between metrical and prosaic composition in the following terms: "First of all, we recognize that it is as fitting to employ the illustrious vernacular in prose as in verse. But since prose writers accept more from those writers who bind their words to verse with music [*avientibus* < AVIEO, a rare word that Dante comments on in *Convivio*, IV, vi, 4] and since what is bound in verse in music seems to stand as a model to prose writers, and not vice versa, [a model] which they seem to grant a certain first place, first we will distinguish what is metrical" [ante omnia confitemur latium vulgare illustre tam prosayce quam metrice decere proferri. Sed quia ipsum prosaycantes ab avientibus magia accipiunt, et quia quod avietum est prosaycantibus permanere videtur exemplar, et non e converso (que quendam videntur prebere primatum), primo secundum quod metricum est ipsum carminemus]. Dante's term *primatus* for the position of verse vis-à-vis prose seems to be echoed by Christine in the *Mutacion de Fortune*, when, after using prose to describe the history of the Jews, she resumes her verse narrative with the phrase, "Si remeray, com j'ay amors, suivant mon stile premerain" [And so I will resume, as it pleases me, following my initial style] (vv. 8752–53). Verse was, chronologically speaking, her first style, but it was not her only style, and that is the important distinction. However, whether or not Christine knew the *De vulgari eloquentia*—and, given its spotty manuscript transmission, she probably did not, unless she had information about it from her father—her use of the phrase *mon stile premerain* also shows that prose and verse for Christine were stylistic categories, not epistemological ones.

In Book III of *L'Avision*, she describes her own career as a writer specifically in terms of her devotion to study and of her choice of style and content—itself a Dantean tag, "vagliami 'l lungo studio" [may the long study avail me] is what Dante says to Vergil—and this characterization is a far cry from the contemporary critical debate on verse and prose. "Adonc me pris a forgier choses jolies a mon commencement plus legieres, et tout ainsi comme l'ouvrier qui de plus en plus en son oeuvre s'asoubtille comme plus il la frequente, ainsi tousjours estudiant diverses matieres mon sens de plus en plus s'imbuoit de choses estranges, amendant mon stile en plus grant soubtilleté et plus haulte matiere" [Then I began to forge beautiful things, lighter when I started. And just as the craftsman who refines his work the more he works at it, so too my mind, studying different subjects, became more imbued with strange matters, modifying my style in greater subtlety and more sublime topics] (Towner, ed., p.164, punctuation added). Study, style, and subject matter: these were the three most important attributes of literary creation for her.

If we pause for a while to consider the importance of the term *style* to distinguish between prose and verse, we will see that Christine may again be taking her cue from Dante when she talks about verse and prose as different styles. *Stile* occurs in two famous passages in the *Commedia*: in *Inferno* 1.85–87, to describe Dante's imitation of Vergil's style, "tu se' solo colui / da cu' io tolsi lo bello stilo che m'ha fatto honore" [you are the only one from whom I took the fair style that has done me honor], and in *Purgatorio* 24.57, to describe the new kind of lyric poetry as the *dolce stil novo* (cf. also, *soave stile* of the poets of love in *Convivio* IV.ii.11, *il piú alto stile* of scientific and philosophical poetry in *Convivio* I.iv.13) and, significantly, this passage from *Inferno* inspired the title of Christine's *Chemin de long estude*. Christine's understanding of style can thus be linked directly to Dante's. The important point remains that prose and meter were styles, not opposite forms, and that in any event, as styles they did not make any claims to special knowledge or truthfulness. Verse or prose must convey experience in order to be truthful, and here resided the challenge of literary composition.

If we examine Christine's reason for turning to prose in the *Mutacion*, we will find further evidence that Christine saw rhyme primarily as a style and that good rhyme, like good prose, told the truth. Note however, that the judgment of a work's veracity did not depend on its style or form per se:

> Or me couvient cy excuser
> Un petit, car ne puis muser
> A rimer, pour fievre soubdaine
> Qui m'a seurpris, dont suis en peine.
> Sus ce pas faut laisser ester;
> Mais, pour mon ouvrage haster,
> Mettray la prose en la maniere
> Que mot a mot l'escri plainiere,
> En la sale cy devant dicte
> Ou la Bible trouvay escripte;
> Si ne soit pas tenu a faute
> Pour ce qu'ay de santé deffaute,

Dont troublé mon entendement
Est a present aucunement;
Et qui de bien rimer se charge,
Ce n'est mie petite charge,
Et par especial histoires
Abriger en parolles voires.

[Now you must excuse me here a little, for I cannot waste my time in rhyming because of a sudden fever that has surprised me and from which I am suffering. At this point we must let things stand, but, to hasten my work, I will put into prose in the complete manner that I have written it word for word in the room described above where I found the Bible written. So it should not be held as a fault because I have faulty health so that my understanding is somewhat troubled at present. For whoever undertakes to rhyme well (knows that) it is hardly a light burden, especially shortening histories into true words.] (vv. 8731–48)

Now, Christine does not impugn the veracity of verse composition since she has been writing here in verse the whole time. Interestingly enough, she does associate lyric with a kind of literary leisure or *otium* when she says that she can no longer "waste her time in rhyming" [muser a rimer], since *muser* means both "to waste time" and "to amuse." She excuses herself for switching to prose, she wishes to hasten her work to its end. Christine's prose will be just as truthful as her verse, she explains, which means she knew that prose was also not automatically truthful. She then pointedly notes that the Bible is the source of her prose so that the truth of her work is not a matter of its form but again of the source of its content. And finally she comments on the nature of truth in verse: "Et qui de bien rimer se charge, / Ce n'est mie petite charge, / Et par especial histoires / Abriger en parolles voires." Rhyming well entails the abridgment of narrative into true words, but the truth of the language of poetry depends for Christine on its referentiality, on its ability to forge textuality and history together.

The passage on rhyme and prose in the *Mutacion* comes after a section in which Christine translates from Isidore of Seville's *Etymologiæ*, Books II and III, concerning astrology, the difference between rhetoric and dialectic, music (and its relevance to lyric poetry), and geometry. This knowledge of Isidore—and Solente prints the relevant passages in facing columns to show the proximity of the texts—may justify the assumption that Christine knew the classic passage from Isidore, near the end of Book I, chapter 38, on the difference between verse and prose. While Isidore observes that metrical composition historically precedes prose composition, Isidore does not claim that verse is superior to prose, only that it historically antedates it.

> Prosa est producta oratio et a lege metri soluta. Prosum enim antiqui productum dicebant et rectum. Unde ait Varro apud Plautum "prosis lectis" significari rectis; unde etiam quae non est perflexa numero, sed recta, prosa oratio dicitur, in rectum producendo. . . . Praeterea tam apud Graecos quam apud Latinos longe antiquiorem curam fuisse carminum quam prosae. Omnia enim prius versibus condebatur; prosae autem studium sero viguit.
>
> [Prose is speech produced and set free from the constraint of meter, for the ancients called something extended and straight "prose." Thus Varro says that in Plautus' phrase "prosis lectis," [prosis] means "direct," whence even that which is not rhythmically turned, is called direct speech, produced directly. . . . Moreover, among the Greeks as well as the Romans, the cultivation of verse was far older than of prose, for everything was first set in verse whereas the study of prose flourished late.]

Isidore then goes on to discuss meter and notes that the cultivation of verse, or *studium carminum*, was older among the Jews than the Gentiles. When he then discusses the difference between *fabula* and *historia*, the only remark he proffers on the truth value of either is to say that it is better for eyewitnesses to write history since what is seen is presented without lying, "quae enim videntur, sine mendacio proferuntur" (chapter 41). In her history of Charles V's life, Christine does in fact claim that she has seen a number of events that she is recording, and in *L'Avision* she recollects how her family had been received by the King in the Louvre.[23] Thus the approach that Dante took to prose and verse seems steeped in Isidore — and Christine surely took it from Isidore if not from Dante as well: both writers are careful not to view meter and prose as opposites. The tie between truth and personal experience and by extension to autobiography seems implicit in both Isidore and Dante as well, and this connection may explain why Christine couches so much of her writing in terms of allegorical visions in which she is a direct protagonist.

Christine's position that good verse constituted an *abbreviatio* that remained historically true contrasts with the contemporary practice of *dérimage*. Especially important among Christine's patrons were the Dukes of Burgundy, for whose court it must be remembered so many *mises en prose* were undertaken. Georges Doutrepont needs to be cited on this last point since it touches on Christine's use of chivalry as a theme and also demonstrates that Christine's use of prose in works for Philip the Bold and John the Fearless should not be viewed in light of the tastes of Philip the Good, Philip the Bold's grandson who commissioned a large number of *mises en prose*: "The concern for having the aristocracy intervene in the romances, or even the advantageous role assigned to it, similarly prompted the tendency for romance-writers to fill their works with the noise of military feats. It also explains the presence of so many prose versions of the grandiloquent couplet, the *bel canto*, placed at the opening of so many prose versions because of the necessity for supporting the cult of the knightly values of yore" [Le souci de faire intervenir l'aristocratie dans les romans, ou bien le rôle avantageux qu'on lui assure, motive, à son tour, le penchant qui pousse les romanciers à remplir leurs oeuvres du bruit des exploits guerriers. Il explique également la présence du couplet grandiloquent, du bel canto en tête de tant de mises en prose, sur la nécessité d'entretenir le culte des vertus chevaleresques de jadis] (p. 403). Christine's prose and lyrical treatments of chivalry diverge sharply from other earlier and later nostalgic evocations of past knights in prosified romances.

History and textuality are merged in Christine, but never in the name of nostalgia, and her verse practice reveals her consistent abhorrence of the kind of nostalgia rampant in much courtly lyric. Christine does not tell of past glories as an example of the topos of *laudatio temporis acti*, in order to invoke nostalgically the "good old days" (when men were men and women were grateful, since male writers largely seem to have construed the past this way). Instead, in the *Fais d'armes et de chevalerie* from 1410, she treats chivalry didactically in the most pragmatic terms of military tactics. In the *Fais d'armes et de chevalerie*, Christine reiterates the source of her authority in similar terms. Her truthfulness comes from diligence, intelligence—not from overly subtle polished words—and from her sincere and very pedagogical desire to communicate:

> Mais comme il affiert ceste matiere estre plus excecutee par fait de diligence et sens que par subtilités de parolles polies, et aussy consideré que les excerceans et expers en l'art de Cheualerie ne sont communement clercz ne instruis en science de langage, je n'entens a trattier ne mais au plus plain et entendible langaige que je pourray, a celle fin que la doctrine donnee par plusieurs aucteurs . . . puist estre cler et entendible.

[But as it is appropriate that this subject be expounded through the work of diligence and good sense than through the subtleties of polished words, and also considering that the practitioners and experts in the art of knighthood are not commonly clerics nor instructed in the science of language, I intend to treat it in the plainest and most understandable language possible, for the purpose that the learning given by several authors can be clear and understandable.] (pp. 6–7)

Her pragmatic approach to chivalry here contrasts with her use of chivalry in the *Othea* as an allegory of the human soul in which the knight is the "soldier of Christ" or *miles Christi*. In both cases, nevertheless, the celebration of chivalry for nostalgic purposes is utterly absent. In the *Lamentacion sur les maux de la guerre civile*, Christine's sense of the historical failings of *chevalerie* as responsible for the current plight of France could not be more clearly pronounced.[24]

When she waxes nostalgic, it is for a "good monarch," fully understandable in light of the chaos among contemporary French royals. She explains her moral didactic intentions in her prose history of Charles V in the following terms: "douée de don de Dieu et nature en tant comme desir se peut estendre en amour d'estude" [endowed with the gift from God and nature as far as desire can be extended into love of study] (p. 5). She notes that she is "following the style of the first [writers] and [her] predecessors" who were, she adds, "our advisers in worthy morals" [suivant le stille des premierains et devanciers, noz ediffieurs en meurs redevables] and, repeating the word *style* to describe prose, she calls her work a "nouvelle compliacion menée en stile prosal et hors le commun ordre de mes autres choses passées" [new compilation conducted in prosaic style outside of the common order of my former works]. No, she cannot claim to be an eyewitness to all events in her history, but she begins the entire prose narrative with a prayer, citing Psalm 50.17, "Sire Dieux, euvre mes levres" ("Domine, labia mea aperies") [O Lord, open thou my lips] in order to emphasize her sincerity and her desire to tell the truth as best she can. Christine explains that she will use prose chronicles and surviving eyewitnesses [survivans] as her sources, surely as a response to Isidore's claim that things that have been seen are presented without lies. Her truthfulness however ultimately derives, once again, from her devotion to study.

A quarter of a century separates Christine's biography in prose of Charles V and her tale in verse of Joan of Arc. The first work evokes an ideal monarch as a mirror for the current king, the second portrays a contemporary woman restoring French knighthood to its former triumphant status. Both works assimilate sacred history and the history of France and resist easy nostalgia for past glory. The political renewal envisioned by both works depends on a clear sense that a literary text must refer directly and immediately to history. The continuity between the works could not be clearer. Christine's practice shows that she does not attribute different signifying practices to prose and meter. She is not lost in the ineffabilities of either a prosaic world or a metric one.

Christine's foremost concern, regardless whether she chose to write in verse or in prose, was to tell the truth. Writing in Book III, chapter 58, of the *Livre des fais et bonnes meurs du sage roy Charles V*, Christine suggests that the ultimate purpose of poetry is to tell the truth: "plus proprement dire celle soit poesie, dont la fin est verité, et le proces doctrine revestue en paroles d'ornemens delictables et par propres couleurs" [one can more properly call that writing poetry whose end is truth and whose elaboration is doctrine clothed in words of delightful ornaments and fitting colors]. The marriage of form and content in Christine was a marriage made in, and supported by, the service rendered by literature to truth itself, a challenge which Christine gladly accepted and usually met.

Notes

1. Questions raised during the discussion of my paper "Christine and Sacred History" at the 1992 Berlin congress on Christine de Pizan turned on the famous passage on the history of the Jews in the *Mutacion de Fortune* where Christine claims that a fever prevented her from continuing her narrative in verse. Could it be, came the question, that in fact Christine wanted to assign greater truth and authority to her remarks on the Jews by consigning them to prose? My answer then was that we need to take Christine at her word and that she was not being coy in using prose but was rather a writer with a deadline. I was taking my cue from Nadia Margolis, whose judicious remarks bear repeating: "The fact of Christine's illness is corroborated, as Solente's notes indicate in referring us to the contemporaneous *Cent Balades*, 43, and to her autobiographical recollection in *L'Avision*. Furthermore, after the prose history that completes Part 4, Christine again laments having had to abandon her 'primary style' (v. 8753) and rejoices at regaining her strength and ability to rhyme. The timing of her recovery—that is just at the point where she could proceed to non-Jewish historical phases—does give us pause. Yet considering her apologies and their factual basis, it would still be difficult to assert that Christine intended to 'condemn' the Jews by prose, especially since, in her later section on the Assyrians and, more specifically, Holofernes's siege on the Jews (vv. 10031–48), she portrays them not only in verse but also sympathetically as pre-Christian monotheists threatened by a pagan adversary. . . . As she says in the cited passage, prose provides an abridgement fulfilling her criteria of truth and completeness (vv. 8740–48), while also enabling her to meet what must have been relentless deadlines

in this most fruitful period of her career (1403–1410) by keeping the ship of literary productivity afloat" ("Christine de Pizan and the Jews," p. 59).

2. Although J. D. Burnley notes "Christine de Pizan's use of the phrase *stille clergial* is embedded in the context of the learned use of *tutoiement*, and in an atmosphere of debate; there is no evidence for the association with elaborate prose style with which modern critical custom seeks to invest it" ("Christine de Pizan and the So-Called *style clergial*," p. 6), the observations on curial prose style that Burnley makes in "Curial Prose in England" would in fact apply to Christine's prose in the *Cité des dames*.

3. Liliane Dulac, "Authority in the Prose Treatises of Christine de Pizan"; Bernard Ribémont, "Christine et l'encyclopédisme scientifique."

4. Charity Cannon Willard noted in her edition of *Le Livre de la paix* (The Hague, 1958), pp. 49–50: "It would, indeed, be more accurate to speak of Christine's styles, for her more or less straightforward presentation of her material in the *Livre des Trois Vertus* is quite different from the 'stille clergial' which she considered more 'soubtill' and thus adopted for her political treatises such as the *Livre de la paix*."

5. Cited in Dante, *De vulgari eloquentia*, p. 205, n.

6. I prefer the term *curial* in English, taking my cue from Burnley's translation of the Middle French *clergial*. Dante in *De vulgari eloquentia* also uses the term *curialis*.

7. See Erich Köhler, "Zur Entstehung des altfranzösischen Prosaromans," p. 221; and the contributions in *Der altfranzösische Prosaroman*.

8. See my "Christine de Pizan, the Conventions of Courtly Diction, and Italian Humanism."

9. It is amazing to what extent Christine's arguments about language parallel Catharine MacKinnon's polemical *Only Words*. Regardless whether one agrees with either author, both are acutely aware of the power of language.

10. Georges Doutrepont, *Les mises en prose des épopées et des romans chevaleresques du XIVe au XVIe siècle*, p. 396.

11. *L'Avision-Christine*, p. 164.

12. Quoted by Erlich, p. 183. Husserl differentiated "between the 'object' (*Gegenstand*), the nonverbal phenomenon denoted by the word, and the 'meaning' (*Bedeutung*), i.e. the way in which the 'object' is presented," Erlich, p. 185. Roman Ingarden claimed in *Das literarische Kunstwerk* that a sentence found in a work of literature, as distinguished from an informative utterance, does not purport to be "true" or, in Ingarden's own words, lie in a claim to the truth [*Wahrheitsanspruch*] (p. 207).

13. The best example of how metaphysical categories have been used in formalist analysis to muddy the waters is André Jolles, *Die Einfachen Formen* (1930), which would situate the meaning of art in some transcendental, metahistorical realm. Jolles claimed that form endowed literary works with a new kind of power: "We have seen how ultimately the Simple Form can transfer its power to an object, how the object can be imbued with the power of the form"

[Wir haben gesehen . . . wie schließlich die Einfache Form ihre Macht auf einen Gegenstand übertragen, der Gegenstand mit der Macht der Form geladen werden kann], p. 262. His formalist approach fueled an aesthetic approach to literature that was based on ineffable, privileged, not to mention elitist, and indeed in its final metamorphosis biologically based, forms of subjectivity. His popularity among nonreconstructed Nazi literary theorists (after World War II) and the revival of interest in his works during the 1970s, was promoted (unwittingly?) by the group of critics associated with the journal *Poétique*.

14. See also Jurij Striedter, "Zur formalistischen Theorie der Prosa und der literarischen Evolution."

15. Emmanuèle Baumgartner, "Les techniques narratives dans le roman en prose." Baumgartner singles out the techniques of repetition, *entrelacement*, interpolation, and rhythm, among others.

16. This finding is based on the computer-generated concordance completed by James Laidlaw of my edition of the *Livre de la Cité des Dames*.

17. Gayatri Chakravorty Spivak, *Subaltern Studies*.

18. Heidegger repeats what Wilhelm von Humboldt had claimed in his *Einleitung über die Verschiedenheit des menschlichen Sprachbaus und ihren Einfluß auf die geistige Entwicklung des Menschengeschlechtes*: "Die Sprache ist das Organ des inneren Seins, dies Sein selbst, wie es nach und nach zur inneren Erkenntnis und zur Äußerung gelangt. Sie schlägt daher alle feinste Fibern ihrer Wurzeln in die nationale Geisteskraft, und je angemessener diese auf sie zurückwirkt, desto gesetz-mäßiger und reicher ist ihre Entwicklung" [Language is the organ of inner being, how this being itself, again and again, reaches inner knowledge and utterance. It plunges therefore all the finest fibers of its roots into the mental strength of the nation, and the more appropriately these roots influence it, the more regular and richer is its development], p. xvii. See also Wilhelm Luther, *Sprachphilosophie als Grundwissenschaft*.

19. Maureen Curnow, "'*La Pioche d'inquisicion*.'"

20. Jens Rasmussen had noted as early as 1958, "Il faut souligner le caractère intellectuelle de l'écriture du XVe siècle. En caractérisant le style de l'époque comme logocentrique, nous avons déjà relevé ce principe fondamental, mais l'orientation rationelle marque toutes les couches stylistiques. Elle est à l'origine des tendances 'curiales' et rhétoriciennes, elle se montre dans la technique narrative par l'impor-tance des procédés mécaniques et, dans la substance des oeuvres, par les descriptions systématiques qui s'appliquent à certains thèmes favoris" (*La prose narrative française du XVe siècle*, p. 163) [One must underscore the intellectual character of fifteenth-century writing. In characterizing the style of this period as logocentric, we have already drawn attention to this fundamental principle, but a rational orientation marks all stylistic levels. It is the origin of "curial" and rhetoricizing tendencies; in narrative technique it is evident in the importance of mechanical procedures and in the substance of works in systematic descriptions which were applied to certain favorite subjects.]

21. "The Lady Wants to Talk."

22. Ribémont, "Vers et prose dans l'écriture à caractère scientifique médiévale."
23. My thanks to Christine Reno for pointing this out to me.
24. As Margarete Zimmermann noted, "Christine's criticism of the estate of the *chevaliers* is particularly biting. She goes beyond the charge that they have neglected their duty to protect and undertakes a radical redefiniton of the concepts of *victoire, gloire* and *renommee*" ("Vox Feminæ, Vox Politica," p. 121).

Works Cited

Der altfranzösische Prosaroman. Ed. Ernstpeter Ruhe and Richard Schwaderer. Munich: Fink, 1979.

Baumgartner, Emmanuèle. "Les techniques narratives dans le roman en prose." In *The Legacy of Chrétien de Troyes*, ed. Norris Lacy, Douglas Kelly, and Keith Busby, pp. 167–90. Amsterdam: Rodopi, 1987.

Burnley, J. D. "Christine de Pizan and the So-Called *style clergial*." *Modern Language Review* 81 (1986): 1–6.

———. "Curial Prose in England." *Speculum* 61 (1986): 593–614.

Christine de Pizan. *L'Avision-Christine*. Ed. Mary Louis Towner. Washington, D.C.: Catholic University of America, 1932.

———. *Livre des fais d'armes et de chevalerie*. Quoted from *The Book of fayttes of ames and of chivalrye translated and printed by William Caxton*, ed. A. T. P. Byles. Early English Text Society, p. 189. London: Milford, 1932.

———. *La Città delle dame / Le Livre de la Cité des Dames*. Bilingual ed. Ed. Earl Jeffrey Richards. Trans. Patricia Caraffi. Milan: Luni Editrice, 1997.

———. *The Book of the City of Ladies*. Trans. Earl Jeffrey Richards. 2d ed. New York: Persea, 1998.

Cropp, Glynnis M. "Boèce et Christine de Pisan." *Moyen Age* 87 (1981): 387–417.

Curnow, Maureen. "'*La Pioche d'inquisicion*': Legal-Judicial Content in Style in Christine de Pizan's *Livre de la Cité des Dames*." In *Reinterpreting Christine de Pizan*, ed. Earl Jeffrey Richards with Joan Williamson, Nadia Margolis, and Christine Reno, pp. 157–72. Athens: University of Georgia Press, 1992.

Dante. *De vulgari eloquentia*. Ed. A. Marigo. 3d ed. Opere di Dante. Vol. 6, p. 205n. Florence: Felice Le Monnier, 1968.

Doutrepont, Georges. *Les mises en prose des épopées et des romans chevaleresques du XIVe au XVIe siècle*. Brussels: Palais des Académies, 1939.

Dulac, Liliane. "Authority in the Prose Treatises of Christine de Pizan." In *Politics, Gender and Genre*, ed. Margaret Brabant, pp. 129–40. Boulder, Col.: Westview, 1992.

Erlich, Victor. *Russian Formalism, History—Doctrine*. New Haven: Yale University Press, 1955, 1965.

Humboldt, Wilhelm von. *Einleitung über die Verschiedenheit des menschlichen Sprachbaus und ihren Einfluß auf die geistige Entwicklung des Menschengeschlechtes* (Introduction to the Differences of Human Linguistic Construction and

Its Influence on the Mental Development of the Human Race]. Berlin, 1836.
Isidore of Seville. *Etymologiæ sive Origines, Libri XX*. Ed. W. M. Lindsay. 2 vols. Oxford: Clarendon, 1911.
Kittay, Jeffrey, and Wlad Godzich. *The Emergence of Prose: An Essay in Prosaics*. Minneapolis: University of Minnesota Press, 1897.
Köhler, Erich. "Zur Entstehung des altfranzösischen Prosaromans." In Erich Köhler, *Troubadorlyrik und höfischer Roman*. Berlin, 1962.
Luther, Wilhelm. *Sprachphilosophie als Grundwissenschaft*. Heidelberg: Quelle & Meyer, 1970.
MacKinnon, Catharine. *Only Words*. Cambridge: Harvard University Press, 1993.
Margolis, Nadia. "Christine de Pizan and the Jews." In *Politics, Gender and Genre*, ed. Margaret Brabant, pp. 53–74. Boulder, Col.: Westview, 1992.
Rasmussen, Jens. *La prose narrative française du XVe siècle*. Copenhagen, 1958.
Ribémont, Bernard. "Christine et l'encyclopédisme scientifique." In *The City of Scholars*, ed. Margarete Zimmermann and Dina De Rentiis, pp. 174–85. Berlin: De Gruyter, 1994.
———. "Vers et prose dans l'écriture à caractère scientifique médiévale: L'exemple de l'encyclopédisme." In *L'art narratif aux XIIe et XIIIe siècles*, tome V, section VIII, XXe Congrès International de Linguistique et Philologie Romanes, pp. 341–52.
Richards, Earl Jeffrey. "Christine de Pizan, the Conventions of Courtly Diction, and Italian Humanism." In *Reinterpreting Christine de Pizan*, ed. Earl Jeffrey Richards with Joan Williamson, Nadia Margolis, and Christine Reno, pp. 250–71. Athens: University of Georgia Press, 1992.
———. "The Lady Wants to Talk: Christine de Pizan's *Epistre a Eustache Morel*." In *Deschamps and His World*, ed. Deborah Sinnreich-Levi (forthcoming).
Said, Edward W. *The World, the Text and the Critic*. Cambridge, Mass.: Harvard University Press, 1983.
Spivak, Gayatri Chakravorty. *Subaltern Studies* (1987): 202–7.
Striedter, Jurij. "Zur formalistischen Theorie der Prosa und der literarischen Evolution." *Texte der russischen Formalisten*, ed. Jurij Striedter (Munich, 1969): ix–lxxxiii.
Willard, Charity Cannon. *Christine de Pizan: Her Life and Works*. New York: Persea, 1984.
Zimmermann, Margarete. "Vox Feminæ, Vox Politica: *The Lamentacion sur les maux de la France*." In *Gender, Genre and Politics: The Political Thought of Christine de Pizan*, ed. Margaret Brabant, pp. 113–27. Boulder, Col.: Westview, 1992.

Contributors

Barbara K. Altmann received her Ph.D. from the University of Toronto in 1989 with a dissertation that presented a study and critical edition of Christine de Pizan's "Livre du Dit du Poissy." This edition will be published by the University Press of Florida. She teaches French at the University of Oregon and has published extensively on late medieval French lyric.

James C. Laidlaw received his Ph.D. in 1963 from Cambridge University, where he was a Fellow of Trinity Hall until 1974. Besides his numerous articles on Christine, he is well known as the editor of the works of Alain Chartier. He is preparing a database of all of Christine de Pizan's works and currently is a professor of French at the University of Edinburgh.

Judith Laird received her Ph.D. in English in 1997 from Southwest Texas State University, San Marcos, where she now teaches English. She has published on "Good Women and Bonnes Dames: Virtuous Females in Chaucer and Christine de Pizan" and will soon publish her English translation of Christine's biography of Charles V, *Le Livre des fais et bonnes moeurs de Charles V.*

Nadia Margolis received her Ph.D. from Stanford University in 1977 with a dissertation on Christine de Pizan's *Livre de la mutacion de Fortune.* A private scholar living in Amherst, Massachusetts, she edited and published the *Christine de Pizan Newsletter* (1991–96). Besides being the author of numerous articles on Christine and coeditor of *Reinterpreting Christine de Pizan* (1992) she is the author of *Joan of Arc in History, Literature and Film* (1990).

Christine McWebb is a graduate student in the Department of French at the University of Western Ontario, London, completing her dissertation on the concept of the didactic mirror in the works of Christine de Pizan, Elisabeth von Nassau-Saarbrücken, and Elenore von Österreich. She has published studies of revisionist mythology in Christine's works and on Christine's treatment of Joan of Arc.

William D. Paden received his Ph.D. in 1971 from Yale University with a dissertation on the medieval *pastourelle*. He is professor and chairman of the Department of French at Northwestern University. He has published numerous authoritative essays on medieval Provençal, Italian, and French lyric and is the editor of *The Voice of the Trobairitz: Perspectives on the Women Troubadours* (1989) and *The Future of the Middle Ages: Medieval Literature in the 1990's* (1994).

Earl Jeffrey Richards received his Ph.D. in comparative literature from Princeton in 1978 and is currently professor of Romance languages and literatures at the University of Wuppertal. He has published *Dante and the Roman de la Rose* (1981), the English translation of Christine de Pizan's *Book of the City of Ladies* (1982), and *Medievalism, Modernism and Humanism: A Research Bibliography on the Reception of the Works of Ernst Robert Curtius* (1983). He edited *Reinterpreting Christine de Pizan* (1992). His edition of the medieval French text of Christine de Pizan's *Livre de la Cité des Dames* was published in 1997 by Luni Editrice, Milan, Italy. His next book is *European Literature and the Labyrinth of National Images*.

Benjamin Semple is an assistant professor of French at Gonzaga University. He received his Ph.D. in Romance languages from the University of Pennsylvania in 1992. He is the author of articles on Christine de Pizan, Marie de France, and the *Roman de la Rose* and is preparing a monograph on allegory in late medieval French literature.

Lori Walters received her Ph.D. in Romance languages from Princeton in 1987 with a dissertation on Chrétien de Troyes and the *Romance of the Rose*. She has published extensively on Chrétien de Troyes, manuscript illumination, the *Romance of the Rose,* and Christine de Pizan. In 1995 she edited *Lancelot and Guinevere: A Casebook* (New York). She is professor of French at Florida State University and is currently writing a monograph on "Self and Autobiography in Christine de Pizan."

Index

Individual works of Christine are listed under Christine de Pizan, works.
abbreviatio, 222
Adonis, 75–76
Aeneas, 160
aesthetics: concession to pleasure, 189, 192–93; medieval, 3, 18–19, 188;Parnassian, 33; Romantic, 31
Alain Chartier, 136
Alain de Lille, 140, 195, 202n.6
Alexander von Roes, 164n.7
allegory, differences in, in *Cent balades* and *Epistre d'Othea*, 80n.24
Altmann, Barbara K., 10–12, 106, 115, 181n.4
Amor, Amour(s), 144, 172, 178, 179
amplificatio, 116, 119
Aristotle, 159, 193
audience, inscribed female, in Letter of Sebille in *Duc des vrais amans*, 122–23. *See also* reception, reader
Aue, Hartmann von, 17
Augustine, St., 193, 194
authenticity, 7, 21n.14
authority, 7, 10; for Christine, 105

Bagoly, Suzanne, 36, 54
balades de personnages, 69–70; alternation of male and female speakers in, 168; stanza form in, 72; use of ballade layée form in, 74. *See also prosopopoiea*; voice
balades notées, 79nn.10, 13
ballade, 29–30, 35–36, 38, 47n.33, 137; *ballades bonnes à tout faire* in Christine, 66; before Christine de Pizan, 54–57; formal properties of, 101n.27; increasing length in *Cent balades*, 62; isometric vs. heterometric, 57–58; late 14th-c. development, 55; as option in Middle French genre system, 44n.2; parts of (ouvert, clos, oultrepassé), 56, 83; stanza proportions of, 56; structures in *Cent balades*, 64–65; transformation of, from traditional monologue to dialogue in Christine, 180; tripartite structure of, 56
—in Machaut: in *ballades bonnes à tout faire*, 59; meter, 59; sequences, 62
ballade layée, 59; in Christine and Machaut, 66; form in *Cent balades*, Ballade 50, 62; specific use of, in *Cent balades*, 72–75
Banville, Théodore de, 31–33, 34, 36, 41, 44n.11
Baudelaire, Charles, 3, 8
Baudouin, Rae S., 169
Baumgartner, Emmanuèle, 213, 227n.15
beauty, moral and sapiential, 3; Christine's meditation on, 188–202. *See also* aesthetics, medieval
Bec, Pierre, 27, 44nn.1, 2
Beer, Jeanette, 114
belles meurs, 18, 77, 193; in *Cent balades*, Ballade 50, 71
Benveniste, Émile, 15, 16, 22n.22, 169–70, 182n.8

234 ~ Index

Benvenuto da Imola, 217
Bernard of Clairvaux, 19, 23n.29
Bernardo, Aldo, 158, 164n.11
Bersuire, Pierre, 158, 164n.14
Bertran de Born, 47n.36
biau lieu, 19, 197–202, 203n.11. See also *locus amoenus*
Blanchard, Joël, 164n.12
Boccaccio, 143
body, female, in trouvère lyric, 3
Boethius, 158, 199, 202n.7, 203n.12, 217–18
Brabant, Margaret, 161
Brownlee, Kevin, 112, 158–59, 165n.22, 202n.8, 203n.11
Brunetto Latini, 124, 129n.31, 203n.10, 209
Brutus, 160
Bumgardner, George H., Jr., 163n.3, 164n.12, 165n.21
Burnley, J. D., 214–15, 226n.2
Burns, Jane, 174
Byron, 8

Caliban, 13
Campbell, P. G. C., 1
Cerquiglini-Toulet, Jacqueline, 87, 152n.31
chanson royale (*chant royal*), 29, 30, 83, 95
Charles d'Orléans, 83–84
Charles V, 155, 193, 224. See also Christine de Pizan, works, *Le livre des fais et bonnes meurs de Charles V*
Charles VI, 63, 145, 157; sickness of thematized in *Cent balades*, Ballade 95, 75
Chaucer, 214
chevalerie, 135, 224
Chrétien de Troyes, 109, 135–37, 150n.7, 156, 162
Christine de Pizan: ballade as favorite lyrical genre, 35–36; ballade structure, 36; line numbers in lyric, 42–43
—manuscripts
　Burgundy Manuscript (lost), 97n.4, 145, 152n.26, 181n.4
　Duke's Manuscript (BNF 835, 606, 836, 605, 607), 11, 20n.1, 53, 72, 78n.1, 140
　ex-Phillipps 128, 97n.4
　Leiden Ltk. 1819, 97n.4, 181n.4
　Le Livre de Christine (Chantilly, Musée Condé 492–93; BNF 12779), 20n.1, 53, 65, 68–69, 75, 78, 80–81n.34, 140, 145–46, 150n.9
　Othea, BNF 848, 216
　Queen's Manuscript (BL Harley 4431), 4, 5, 11, 20n.1, 53, 78, 86, 97n.4, 98nn.6, 7, 99n.13, 140, 145–46, 150n.9, 181n.4
—works
　Autres balades, Ballade 37, 156, 159–60
　Cent balades, 4, 11, 38, 53–81, 145, 163, 189–93, 201; change of voice in, 69; critique of contemporary society in, 64; evolution of text in, 53–54; framing narrative in, 76–77; Ballade 1, 50, 100, 62; Ballade 2, 156–59; Ballade 3, 68; Ballade 6, 39–41; Ballade 7, 67; Ballade 11, 67, 79n.20, 84; Ballades 5–11, 63 ("Women's Stories" in, 63, 70; "Men's Stories" in, 63); Ballade 24, 72–74; Ballade 50, 13, 18; Ballades 54, 61, 65 and 92, 71–72; Ballade 90 as cautionary tale of Adonis, 75–76; Ballades 91–99 as narrative, 64, 75–76; Ballade 95, 63, 157
　Cent ballades d'Amant et de Dame, 11, 13, 16, 38, 84–85, 147, 169–80
　Chemin de long estude, 14, 18–19, 89, 109, 158–59, 161, 165n.24, 194, 197–202, 216–17
　Cité des Dames, 4, 10, 19, 89, 96, 110, 111, 117, 119–20, 137, 156, 160, 178, 206–7, 209, 210, 213, 217
　Complaintes, 13, 93, 138–49
　Debat de deux amans, 92
　Dit de Poissy, 115

Ditié de Jeanne d'Arc, 89, 207, 224–25
Duc des vrais amans, 2, 11, 12, 17–18, 92, 96, 137, 146–48, 152n.21; Christine's self-inscription in, 111; direct citations in, 108; direct discourse in, 106; formal divisions in, 108, 124–26; relationship of lyric to narrative in, 108
Epistre a Eustache Morel, 217
Epistre a la Reine, 163
Epistre au Dieu d'amour, 92, 145
Epistre d'Othea, 75–76, 96, 137, 146, 216–17, 218, 224
Fais d'armes et de chevalerie, 155, 159, 165n.28, 212, 223–24
L'Avision, 4, 42, 54, 80n.22, 210–11, 216, 215–16, 218–20, 222
Lamentacion sur les maux de la guerre civile, 145, 224
Lay de Dame, 12, 85, 146, 147, 179–80; as coda to the *Cent ballades d'Amant et de Dame*, 86–87, 95; diction, Christine's, in, 93; female complainte as coda to *Duc des vrais amans*, 146–48; looser form compared to ballade form, 97; manuscript evidence for division of, 87–88; mythological figures in, 88–89; relationship to *Cent ballades d'Amant et de Dame*, 85–86, 90
Livre de la paix, 163, 209, 226n.4
Le Livre des fais et bonnes meurs de Charles V, 119, 161, 165n.26, 209, 216, 224–25
Mutacion de Fortune, 13, 14, 89, 110, 114, 137, 143, 152n.21, 156, 158, 160–63, 208, 211, 216, 218–21; Jewish history in, 164n.4, 208, 225n.1
Trois Vertus, 92, 111, 119, 123, 226n.3
Cicero, 15, 136, 137, 157, 158
clergece (term for female *clerc*), 162, 213
clergie, 145–46
clerkliness, 135–52
coda: complainte in female voice as coda to *Duc des vrais amans*, 146–48; *Lay de Dame* as coda to *Cent ballades d'Amant et de Dame*, 86–87, 95; lyrical coda in *Duc des vrais amans*, 109
Code(s), linguistic operative in lyric. *See* Jakobson, Roman
Col, Pierre, 195, 201, 204n.14
Colby-Hall, Alice, 116
compilator, role of, 128n.14
complainte, 36; class, not gender, basis for complainte types, 140; combination with lai and lament, 94–95; by Christine in ballade form, 151n.18; examples of, in Machaut and Deschamps, 151n.13; form, compared to other lyric works by Christine, 94; formal freedom of, 139; as genre, 135; linear progression in, 100–101n.24; in Machaut, 151n.17; as nonnarrative genre, 139; as prototype for *Lay de Dame*, 93–94; relationship to ballade, 150n.8; relationship to complainte by Oton de Grandson, 151n.13; resemblance of lai to complainte, 151n.13; rules of versification in, 150n.8; similarity of Christine's second amorous complainte to Machaut, 151n.13; stanzaic form of, 138; thematic comparison with *Lay de Dame*, 94. *See also* Christine de Pizan, works, *Complaintes*
confinement, as theme in Christine's *Complaintes*, 141
conventions, courtly, 16, 107–10; in *Cent balades*, 168–82; connection of love and death, 179; in Froissart, 177; Ovidian, 115; for portrayal of women, 170, 172; of sincerity in Rutebeuf, 168; subversion of courtly code, 179. *See also* courtliness
courtliness, 135–52; Christine's dissatisfaction with artificiality of, 114; courtly world, in *Duc des vrais amans*, 110; critique of, 15, 16–17, 206; critique of, in *Lay de Dame*, 96; critique of, in letter of Sebille de la

courtliness—*Cont'd*
Tour, 111; as ideology, 17; relationship to self-referential paradoxes, 112; replacement of courtly conventional characters with historical ones, 168–69; repudiation of, in *Duc des vrais amans*, 112
Curtius, Ernst Robert, 136, 157, 213, 215

Daniel, Arnaut, 45n.18
Dante, 5, 7, 10, 19, 21n.14, 33, 109, 147, 159, 164n.8, 195, 197, 208, 215, 217, 218–20, 226n.6
Daudin, Jean, 165n.17
De Bruyne, Edgar, 3
de Lauretis, Teresa, 6
de Man, Paul, 103–4
De Rentiis, Dina, 202n.8
Delany, Sheila, 129n.27
Deschamps, Eustache, 4, 7, 9, 30, 34, 35, 55–56, 65, 68, 77, 83, 87, 98–99n.10, 109, 135, 137, 217; commentary on envoi in a ballade, 57
Deschaux, Robert, 87, 99n.11, 137
didacticism, in Christine de Pizan, 91
Diogina da Borgo San Sepulcro, 217
Doutrepont, Georges, 210, 223
Dragonetti, Roger, 45n.18
drama, lyrical, 105
Dronke, Peter, 8
Du Bellay, Jean 30
Duke's Manuscript. *See* Christine de Pizan, manuscripts, Duke's Manuscript
Dulac, Liliane, 111, 123, 139, 161, 226n.3

Eco, Umberto, 193, 200
Egidio Colonna (Gilles of Rome), 120, 124
Eleanor of Aquitaine, 17
Eliot, T. S., 105
Elwert, Theodor, 33–34
enjambment, 73, 83–84; as mirror of deceived woman's nervousness, 147
envoi: in ballade, as opposed to *chanson royale*, 57; change in, in the different redactions of the *Cent balades*, 53; changes of, in *Le Livre de Christine*, 65; commentary on, by Jacques Legrand, 55; in Deschamps, 101nn.25, 26; in Deschamps and contemporaries, 79n.10; form of, in *Cent balades*, 65–67, 70–71; relationship to *Lay de Dame*, 95–96; use in *chants royaux*, 95–96; varying forms in different manuscripts of Christine's works, 78n.2
Erlich, Victor, 211–12
ethics: ethical commentary in lyric, 38; moral message in *Les Cent balades*, 64; as theme, 47n.33
Étienne de Castel, 158
evolution: generic, 27–29, 33; literary, 46n.19; of lyric forms after Rutebeuf, 46n.22
exempla, in *Complaintes*, 141–43

fable, meaning of term in Christine, 76
fallacy, intentional, 103. *See also intentio auctoris*
Faral, Edmond, 128n.16
Farinelli, Arturo, 202n.8
Fenster, Thelma, 17, 86–87, 114, 119, 128n.17, 165n.27
fictio personarum, 114, 128n.16
figura personarum, 12. *See also* voice
fin'amors, 137, 146, 147, 151n.21. *See also* love, courtly
Finke, Laurie A., 6, 103, 181n.3
foot, metaphor of limping, 194–95
form(s), fixed (*formes fixes*), 27, 30–38, 41, 44–45n.11, 54, 83, 84, 87, 95, 145, 151n.13; alternate terminology, "arrested form" or "coiled form," 37–38, 54; invention of term, 31; role of refrain in, 37–38
form, inner, 8
formalism, Russian, 209, 211–13
formes fixes. *See* form(s), fixed
Fortune, as theme, 47n.33
Foscolo, Umberto, 8
Foucault, Michel, 6

Frappier, Jean, 2, 46n.22
Freccero, John, 202n.6
freedom, formal, in lyric composition, 2, 20–21n.2
Freeman, Michelle A., 164n.7
Froissart, Jean, 16, 80n.28, 169, 172–74, 177–78

Galataea, 141–43
Garencières, 84
Gaunt, Simon, 3, 21n.8
Gautier, Théophile, 31, 41
genre: list of, in Middle French, 44n.1; system in Middle French, 42; system of lyrical, 9
George, Stefan, 8
Godzich, Wlad, 213–14
Goethe, Johann Wolfgang, 8
Gottfried of Strasbourg, 109
Gower, John, 96
Gregory the Great, 194–95
grief: as subject of lyric, 38–41, 47n.33; as theme in *Cent balades*, 70
Guillaume de Lorris, 19
Guillaume IX, 14, 209
Guiraut Riquier, 47n.36

Habermas, Jürgen, 16
Hegel, Georg Wilhelm Friedrich, 108, 208
Heidegger, Martin, 214, 227n.18
Hero and Leander, in *Cent balades*, 67–68, 158
heterogeneity, formal: in *Lay de Dame*, 96–97; in *Duc des vrais amans*, 106–10
Hibernicus, Thomas, 2
Hicks, Eric, 202n.1
Hofmannsthal, Hugo von, 105
Hölderlin, 8
Horace, 3
Humboldt, Wilhelm von, 227n.18
humor, Christine's, 115
Huot, Sylvia, 129n.28
Husserl, Edmund, 226n.12

Imgarden, Roman, 226n.12

imitatio Christi, 156
ineffability topos, 106
intentio auctoris, 4, 18
Isabeau de Bavière, 4, 5, 17, 145
Isidore of Seville, 208, 221–22

Jakobson, Roman, 15, 178, 211–12; enunciating subject (*sujet de l'énonciation*), 170–72; functions of utterance (context, contact, code involving transmitter, message, and receiver), 173; model applied to Christine, 175; model applied to Froissart, 173; model of communication, 181nn.6–7; role of phatic function to create a dialogue, 17
Jameson, Fredric, 3
Jean de France, duke of Berry, 17, 61, 145, 164n.6
Jean de Meun, 13, 19, 140, 141, 194, 199
Jean de Montreuil, 136
Jean Gerson, 136, 159
Jean le Seneschal. See *Le Livre des cent balades*
Jerome, St., 2
jeux à vendre, 38, 41, 46n.27
John of Garland, 14, 208, 215
John the Fearless, Duke of Burgundy, 145, 161, 223
Jolles, André, 22n.15, 226–27n.13

Keats, John, 8
Kelly, Douglas, 35, 160
Kennedy, Angus, 1
Kent, Bonnie, 202n.4
Kerbat-Orecchioni, Catherine, 173, 181n.6
Kittay, Jeffrey, 213–14
Köhler, Erich, 9, 170
Krauss, Werner, 23n.28
Krueger, Roberta, 17–18, 103, 152n.29

lai, 30, 36, 137, 139; compared with complainte, 100–101n.24; generic interaction with ballade, 91; malleability and flexibility as genre, 91–92;

lai—Cont'd
 prescriptive rules and, 87; structural and thematic properties, 87, 99n.11
Laidlaw, James C., 10–12, 99n.13, 103–4, 106, 146, 149n.1, 151n.13, 168, 181n.4, 202n.2, 227n.16
Laird, Judith, 11, 12, 17
Leander and Hero, in *Cent balades*, 67–68
Le Livre des cent balades, 59–61; authorship, 60; comparison with *Lai de Dame*, 96–97; metric structure, 60–61; stanza form, 60–61
Legrand, Jacques, assessment of refrain in ballade, 55
Leontium, in *Cité des Dames*, 160
literariness, 209. *See also* formalism, Russian
literature, courtly, male orientation of, 137
Livre de Christine. *See* Christine de Pizan, manuscripts, *Le Livre de Christine*
locus amoenus, 14, 203n.10. *See also* biau lieu
Lote, George, 34
Louis d'Orléans, 17
love: Christine's judgment on, in *Cent balades*, 78; as consuming passion, theme in *Cent balades*, 72; destructive force of, as theme in *Lay de Dame*, 88–89; warning against temptations of, in *Cent ballades d'Amant et de Dame*, 90
love, courtly, 123–24; Christine's discovery of hidden meaning of (*encloeure*), 179; critique of, in the letter of Sebille de la Tour, 118–19. *See also* fin'amors
lyric, troubadour, implicit presence of gender and class in, 174

Machaut, Guillaume de, 7–9, 11, 30, 34, 42, 54, 57, 65–66, 77, 83, 100n.20, 109, 139, 141, 142, 203n.11; composition of lais, 87–88; influence on Christine's choice of meter in *Cent balades*, 66; influence of his use of ballade layée on Christine, 72–73; musical notations in collected manuscripts of, 79n.7
—works of: complaintes, Christine's inferiority of, compared to Machaut's, 150n.10; *Fontaine amoureuse*, Christine's reaction to, 147; *La Louange des Dames*, 55, 58–59, 80n.25 (comparison of rhythm in, with *Cent balades*, 66; music in, 79n.13); *Remède de Fortune*, 30, 35
MacKinnon, Catharine, 16, 22n.24, 226n.9
Macrobius, 157
Mallarmé, Stéphane, 8
Malpezzie-Price, Paola, 182n.9
manuscripts. *See* Christine de Pizan, manuscripts
Margolis, Nadia, 13, 14, 87, 92–93, 100n.17, 103–5, 163n.3, 225n.1
Marie de France, 170
Mary, Virgin, 4, 160, 170
Matthew of Vendôme, 9, 14, 15
McWebb, Christine, 13, 16
Meiss, Millard, 1
Minerva, 155, 160, 163n.1
Minnis, Alastair, 4
Molière, 20
Mombello, Gianni, 1
Mühlethaler, Jean-Claude, 137, 150–51n.12
Müller, Franz Walter, 22–23n.28
Murray, Alexander, 164n.8
music: and the *ars nova*, 56; in Deschamps, 80n.23; freedom from, 42; lyrical composition without, 56; in Machaut, 55, 79n.7; "natural," in lyric, 42, 56; role of, in composition of lyric, 42; split between lyric and music in late 14th c., 83

narrative: in lyric, 10–11; relationship to verse in *Duc des vrais amans*, 108
Nature, Dame, 161
Nelson, Hubbard, 181n.5

Nicolas de Clamanges, 165n.21
Nicole de Margival, 29–30; *Dit de la panthère*, 30, 35
nobility: rejection of inherited, 17; theme of, in *Cent balades*, Ballade 54, 71
Norden, Eduard, 215

Orléans, Duke of, 61; as theme, 164n.8
Ornato, Ezio, 159
Ouy, Gilbert, 165n.19
Ovid, 136, 158

Paden, William D., 9–10, 16, 54, 209
Paradis, François, 90–91
Patterson, Warner Forrest, 27, 44n.1
persons, attributes of, 15
Peter Lombard, 203n.11
Petrarch, 5, 156, 163, 164n.12, 165n.28; *Africa*, 157–58; pioneering of lyric poem sequence, 84; *Rime sparse*, poem 23, 159
Philip the Bold, duke of Burgundy, 223
Philip the Good, duke of Burgundy, 223
Pinet, Marie-Josèphe, 1
Plato, 157; Platonism, "literary," 197
poetic, meaning of term for Christine, 75–76
Poirion, Daniel, 1, 5, 45n.14, 62, 80n.23, 84, 91, 137, 139, 150n.12
præteritio, 119
prière, 139
prose, 19–20; curial, 214–15; deployed against lyric, 110; *dérimage*, 222; development of Christine's prose style, 129n.24; in *Duc des vrais amans*, 108; *mises en prose*, in 14th c., 209, 210, 212–13, 214; relation between poetry and, 210; relationship to lyric, 2; range of styles of, 208, 215–25
prosopopoeia, 12, 104, 111, 114, 119, 123, 128n.16. *See also* voice
Prospero, 13
Provençal lyric: influence on medieval French poets, 10, 14, 34; *trobairitz*, 169, 170
Pygmalion, 141–42, 163

Quarrel over the *Roman de la Rose*. *See* Rose, debate on
Queen's Manuscript. *See* Christine de Pizan, manuscripts, Queen's Manuscript (BL Harley 4431)

Raimon Vidal de Besalu, 35
Rasmussen, Jens, 227n.20
reception, reader: in Christine's texts, 188–89, 194–97; role of experience in, 196. *See also* Jakobson, Roman, model of communication
referentiality, 221; creation of dialogue, 178; dissolution of the referent, 3, 113; how works refer to experience outside of literary work, 169. *See also* Jakobson, Roman, self-referentiality
refrain: in Machaut, 55; use in ballade, 41
refrain: in *Cent balades*, 65; in Ballade 19, 70; in Ballade 50, 63; in Ballade 100, 63; in Machaut, 55; use in ballade, 41
Regalado, Nancy Freeman, 168
Règles de la seconde rhétorique, 30, 35
Reno, Christine, 149n.1, 228n.23
rhetoric: influence on Christine, 110–11; influence of tradition of *ars dictaminis* on Christine, 119; moral lessons of, 124
rhythm, subjective in Christine's lyrics, 84
Ribémont, Bernard, 149n.1, 213, 218, 226n.3
Richard of St. Victor, 201, 203n.13
Richards, Earl Jeffrey, 11, 12, 17, 19–20, 129n.24, 164n.12, 202n.8, 203n.10, 204n.14
Rilke, Rainer Maria, 8
Rimbaud, Arthur, 8
romance: artificialness of women's experience in courtly romance, 111; courtly, in prose, 109; conversation in, compared with *Duc des vrais amans*, 106; male romance heroics discredited in *Duc des vrais amans*, 122–23; relationship of Christine's lyric to, 104; "romance world," 124

Roman de la Rose, 13, 18, 109, 114, 115, 140, 187, 194, 195, 198, 211
rondeau, 29–30, 38, 54, 137, 139
Rose, debate on, 2, 151n.20, 159, 178, 187, 194–97, 214
Roy, Maurice, 36, 87, 93, 135, 146
Rutebeuf, 2, 21n.2, 46n.22, 109, 168

Saccaro, Alexander Peter, 165n.20
Said, Edward W., 207
Sapir-Whorf hypothesis, 214–15
Sasaki, Shigemi, 203n.12
Scaglione, Aldo, 17
Schillperoort, Johanna C., 150n.10
Schweickart, Patrocinio, 103
Scipio Africanus, 157
Scott, Clive, 45n.11
Sebille de Monthault, Dame de la Tour, 12, 92, 105, 109–10, 111, 151–52n.21; Letter of Sebille in *Duc des vrais amans*, 118–23
self-portrayal: Christine's 155–63; male, creation of trademark personality by male poets, 168. *See also* self-representation
self-referentiality, 3, 6, 12, 104, 112–17, 209. *See also* referentiality
self-representation, lyrical, 13. *See also* voice
Semple, Benjamin, 17–19
sentement: *balades sans sentement*, 216; as emotional resources of poetry in Christine, 189, 190, 196, 200
sequence, narrative: in *Cent balades*, 63; poetics of lyric, 85
Shakespeare, *The Tempest*, 13
Shelley, Percy Bysshe, 8
silence, masculine, as manipulative tool, 105
Sinnreich-Levi, Deborah, 22 n. 18
Sklodowska, Elzbieta, 46 n. 19
Socrates, 159
Solente, Suzanne, 1, 221
Solterer, Helen, 151 n. 20
speaker, male, 169–70; in Froissart's lyric, 172–74

speech, woman's: elimination of woman's status as speaker, 174; in Froissart, 174. *See also* voice
stanza, in *Cent balades*: form of, 65; length of, 65, 71
Stecopoulos, Eleni, 163n.1
Stendhal, 143, 152n.25
structures, parallel narrative, 106. *See also* symmetry
style clergial, 119, 135, 150n.6, 226nn.2, 4, 6
subgenres, lyrical, 28–30
subjectivity, 10; female, 168–80; of language, 176–77; male self-aggrandizement in lyric, 177
submission, women's linguistic, 170
suicide, rejection of, by Christine, 158
Switten, Margaret, 46 n. 18
symmetry, as organizational principle in *Cent balades*, 76–77

taille, as formal designation, 30, 44nn.6, 7
technique, privileging of, over content, 100n.23
Thomas Aquinas, *proprie dicta/figurate* 4, 12. *See also* voice
Tiresias, 165n.25; gender change of, 161
Tommaso di Benvenuto da Pizzano, 155, 161
translatio imperii, 160, 163n.1, 164n.7
translatio studii, 13, 14, 155–63
Tristan, 179
Tynjanov, Jurij, 46n.19

Uitti, Karl, 163n.1
utterance, site of (*scène de l'énonciation*), 169. *See also* Jakobson, Roman

Valerius Maximus, 217
Vance, Eugene, 3
Varty, Kenneth, 1, 35, 38, 47n.33, 67
Vegetius, 165n.28
Vergil, 220
Verlaine, Paul, 8
Vigny, Alfred, 8

virelai, 26–30, 36, 38, 47n.33, 54, 137, 139; as ordered fantasy, 45n.14; rhyme scheme in, 45n.14

voice, 10, 192; androgynous in *Epistre au Dieu d'amours*, 108; of author and lady in *Cent ballades d'Amant et de Dame*, 90–91; Christine's voice in the letter of Sebille de la Tour, 118–19; in *Duc des vrais amans*, 104–5, 111; female author's, in medieval works, 103; female complainte in coda to *Duc des vrais amans*, 146–48; first complaintes as experiments in writing the male voice, 147; as function of rhetoric not gender, 105; gendered in *Cité des Dames*, 106–7; mimicry of male courtly poetic voice, 141; polyphonic composition in *Duc des vrais amans*, 108; subordinate style as marker of Christine's voice, 120; writing in female voices, 16. See also *prosopopoeia*

Voltaire, 22n.28

Walters, Lori, 13, 14, 108, 149n.1, 164n.12
Wilkins, Nigel, 5, 34, 38
Willard, Charity Cannon, 1, 90, 149n.4, 165n.28, 226n.4
writing, gendered, 136

Zimmermann, Margarete, 228n.24
Zink, Michel, 33, 151n.13
Zumthor, Paul, 7, 15